MW00657162

THE

SEVEN LAST THINGS

7

THE

SEVEN LAST THINGS

An Exposition of Revelation 19–21

by
David J. MacLeod

Emmaus College Press

The Seven Last Things
copyright 2003 by ECS Ministries

Published by Emmaus College Press
ECS Ministries, Dubuque, IA 52001

Editing and design by Gregory C. Benoit Publishing
Old Mystic, CT 06372

www.gregwa.com

ISBN 1-59387-001-9

All rights reserved. No part of this book may be reproduced or transmitted in any form
or by any means, electronic or mechanical, including photocopying and recording, or
by any information storage and retrieval system, without the prior written permission
of the publisher, with the exception of brief quotations embodied in critical articles or
reviews.

All scripture quotations, unless otherwise indicated, are taken from the New American
Standard Bible (NASB), copyright the Lockman Foundation 1960, 1962, 1963, 1968, 1971,
1972, 1973, 1975, 1977. All rights reserved.

Scripture taken from THE HOLY BIBLE, NEW INTERNATIONAL VERSION®. Copyright ©
1973, 1978, 1984 by International Bible Society. Used by permission of Zondervan Publishing House. All rights reserved.

The "NIV" and "New International Version" trademarks are registered in the United
States Patent and Trademark Office by International Bible Society. Use of either trademark requires the permission of International Bible Society.

❦

For Two Mentors

Neil Dougal

1923–1998

Preacher of the Gospel

How beautiful are the feet of those who bring glad tidings of good things.
Romans 10:15

&

S. Lewis Johnson, Jr.

Preacher and Teacher of the Word

An eloquent man…mighty in the Scriptures.
Acts 18:24

❦

Contents

FOREWORD

The following chapters all began as expository sermons delivered to the congregation at Asbury Road Bible Chapel in Dubuque, Iowa. They were subsequently delivered at a number of Bible conferences in the United States and Canada. They first appeared in abridged form as articles in *Bibliotheca Sacra*, America's oldest theological quarterly. They now appear in book form through the kind permission of Dr. Roy B. Zuck, editor of *Bibliotheca Sacra*.

HEAVEN'S HALLELUJAH CHORUS:

AN INTRODUCTION TO THE "LAST THINGS"
REVELATION 19:1-10

In his play entitled *St. Joan*, George Bernard Shaw tells the story of Joan of Arc and how she left her home to inspire her fellow citizens in France to battle against the British conquerors. In Scene 2 the young heir to the throne—Prince Charles, aged 26—is whining and complaining because Joan, obedient to her heavenly vision, is rebuking him for his softness and cowardice. As she rebukes the prince he responds, "I want to be just what I am. Why can't you mind your own business and let me mind mine?" The peasant girl, filled with the urgency of the situation speaks. "Minding your own business is like minding your own body: it's the shortest way to make yourself sick. What is my business? Helping mother at home. What is thine? Petting lapdogs and sucking sugarsticks.... I tell thee it is God's business we are here to do: not our own. I have a message to thee from God; and thou must listen to it, though thy heart break with the terror of it."[1]

These words of Joan of Arc reflect, in a way, the urgency of apostolic Christianity. This urgency grew out of the apostles' belief in the return of the Lord. Belief in the Lord's return, they taught, produced purity in life (1 John

3:1–3), forbearance and patience toward our brethren (Rom. 14:10), comfort in sorrow (1 Thess. 4:13–18), urgency in service (1 Cor. 3:10–14; 2 Cor. 5:10), and vitality or vibrancy in worship (Rev. 19:1–5). It is my conviction that, as we examine the following passages, the Holy Spirit will restore some apostolic urgency to our lives.

Revelation 19–21 is the New Testament's *locus classicus* (classic passage) on the return of Christ, a passage that has sometimes been called "the last things."[2] In it the apostle John sets forth seven major motifs[3] of biblical eschatology.[4]

- ◇ The second coming of Christ, 19:11–16
- ◇ The defeat of Antichrist, 19:17–21
- ◇ The binding of Satan, 20:1–3
- ◇ The millennial kingdom of Christ, 20:4–6
- ◇ The loosing of Satan and his final defeat, 20:7–10
- ◇ The last judgment at the great white throne, 20:11–15
- ◇ The new heaven and the new earth, 21:1—22:5

The first ten verses of chapter 19 are an introduction to this great subject. It is a passage that not only introduces the last things, but draws the believer's heart to God in worship and awe and gives him cause as a Christian to look eagerly for the coming of our Lord. The "big idea"[5] of the text is that God is to be praised for both His judgments and His benefits. He is to be praised for His judgments upon this world because that judgment is both deserved and fair, and He is to be praised for His benefits because of the glorious destiny of the people of God.

"TE DEUM": GOD IS PRAISED FOR THE RIGHTEOUS JUDGMENT OF BABYLON (VERSES 1–5)

In chapters 17–18 John has described the destruction of Babylon. Babylon is the last great empire to dominate the earth before the coming of Christ. It is a vast commercial, political, and religious system centered in the Middle East that serves as the capital of Antichrist.[6] Like Babylon of old, it will be the source of collective rebellion against the Lord God upon the earth. It will be overthrown just before the return of the Lord and the whole earth will mourn over its loss. The world's business leaders will all lament, "'Woe, woe,' … and they were crying out as they saw the smoke of her burning" (Rev. 18:16–18).

THE VOICE OF THE MULTITUDE (VERSES 1–3)

The response of heaven is different from the merchant class of the earth: "Rejoice over her, o heaven, and you saints and apostles and prophets, because God has pronounced judgment for you against her" (18:20). And so, in chapter 19, the atmosphere is one of vibrant, exultant worship—not lamentation—over Babylon's fall. "Shadow yields to light," Kiddle has written, "above the smoke clouds from the ruined Babylon, a scene of ineffable

3

brightness opens out. The silence of the ruined city gives way to the shout and thunder of eager rejoicing."[7]

"After these things"—after the fall of Babylon—John's attention turns to heaven where he hears "the voice of a great multitude." Some understand this to be a throng of angels.[8] The same expression is used, however, in Revelation 7:9 to describe the martyred Gentiles of the tribulation, so it is more likely that the great multitude here is that group—that is, the martyrs.[9]

They shout, "Hallelujah!" This expression is a word taken from Hebrew which means "Praise *Yah*," "Praise the Lord." This term appears only here in the New Testament, and it occurs four times. It appears regularly in the Psalms to introduce them, but it never appears as *Hallelujah*—it is always translated "Praise the Lord!" (cf. Psalms 106, 111, 112, 113, 117, 135, 146, 147, 148, 149, 150)

There is a group of psalms (113–118) that are called the "Hallel psalms" or "the Hallel of Egypt" because of the reference in them (Ps. 114:1) to the Exodus. They were regularly sung by the Jews at Passover to celebrate the deliverance of Israel and the destruction of the wicked. It is most certain that Jesus and His disciples sang the Hallel after Passover on the night in which He was betrayed. Because of the close connection of the Hallel with Passover and the death of Jesus, the Lamb of God, the early church incorporated it in their Easter celebration of the triumph of Christ our Passover over sin, Satan, and death.[10] So in a yet future day the tribulation martyrs will sing the Hallel to God for His deliverance from the tyrant of Babylon, Antichrist, the Pharaoh of the last days.[11]

Because of its use here, this passage has been called "Heaven's Hallelujah Chorus."[12] It has also been called a "*Te Deum*" ("You God") by a number of commentators.[13] It is a hymn of worship to God. The great multitude worships God for His attributes and His actions. He is praised for His attributes: (1) "salvation"—He is a God who safeguards His people and delivers them into the kingdom. (2) "glory"—His moral excellence is seen in His judgment of sinful Babylon. (3) "power"—His might is seen in the overthrow of wicked civilization.[14] These things should awaken the believer's worship, also. His salvation should awaken our *gratitude*; His glory should awaken our *reverence*; His power should awaken our *trust.*[15]

He is praised for His actions. The word "because" in verse 2 introduces the reason for the great outburst of praise. God has executed a fitting ("true") and deserved ("righteous") judgment upon "the great harlot," Babylon. Babylon will be a literal city in the end times, yet in the Bible it also stands as a metaphor for the world and its opposition to the things of God. The world was corrupted by Babylon—by her secular and humanistic and hedonistic ideologies, her false religions that adulterate and oppose

God's Word, her pagan doctrines, and her deceitful practices that harm the human race.[16]

The gospel will be preached to all the nations during the tribulation, and men will have a clear choice between God and Satan. The sequel will be the universal worship of Antichrist, and the universal rejoicing over the death of the witnesses for Christ (CF. chapters 11, 13). Babylon, built on codes of fraud, will stand as an obstacle to the inauguration of the kingdom of God upon the earth,[17] but immorality and violence will be obliterated, and those in heaven will cry, "Praise the Lord!"[18]

A couple of observations should be made here. First, the reason for the praise in heaven should be noted. The multitude in heaven praises God for His destruction of wickedness. We like to think of the Hallelujah Chorus in the style of Handel, where the Hallelujah is the triumphant worship of the reigning king. John will have such a chorus in verse 6, but first there must be the equally triumphant rejoicing over the downfall of evil at the hand of God.[19] Many modern Christians do not want to hear of God's judgment and wrath; they only want to hear of His love and kindness. But the saints in this passage sing "Praise the Lord!" Babylon is judged. "Praise the Lord! Her smoke rises up forever," and she is totally destroyed. Heaven's estimate of things differs from this world's. The things that the world loves most fondly are the objects of God's most intense wrath.[20] All the worldly things that we believers too often love are going to be destroyed. May we aspire to heaven's attitude toward the things of Babylon.

One should also be struck by the reverence and awe of heaven. Many believers today are bored with the Christian faith. Eugene H. Peterson, well-known writer, pastor, and seminary professor, tells of the first church he pastored. They were a well-educated and financially successful group. Typical of the congregation was Jane, a gossip, and Bill, whose imagination was drugged by television. The Christians were all gossips, complainers, consumers, and fascinated with celebrities.[21] Significantly, Peterson found a message in the book of Revelation—a book, he says, that is a call to worship.

We have lost our sense of wonder, says Warren Wiersbe, and wonder is the basis of worship. "The world will never starve for want of wonders," says G.K. Chesterton, "but only for want of wonder." Wonder means amazement, surprise, astonishment, bewilderment, admiration, awe, and fascination.[22] May God give John's present day readers a heavenly perspective and a new sense of wonder as we contemplate the person and works of our God.

THE WORSHIP OF THE 24 ELDERS AND THE FOUR LIVING CREATURES (VERSE 4)

In verse 4 the 24 elders, the glorified church,[23] and the four living creatures (probably cherubs who serve as God's throne—4:6–7)[24] reappear. In chapter 5 (v. 6–10) they fall down and worship the Lamb and sing of His worthiness to break the seals of the scroll He has taken from the right hand of God. Here they perform the same act of worship, but this time honoring God for His righteous judgment. The 24 elders disappear from the Revelation at this point, only to reappear in verse 7 as the bride of the Lamb.[25]

THE EXHORTATION OF THE CHERUBS FROM THE THRONE (VERSE 5)

At this point (v. 5) John hears a voice from the throne, encouraging all to "give praise to our God." Some say it is Christ,[26] but it is very unlikely that Christ would say "our God." In John 20:17 Jesus says to Mary, "I ascend to My Father and your Father, and My God and your God." Our Lord is not ashamed to call us "brethren" (Heb. 2:11), yet He does make a distinction between His relationship to the Father and that of His people. It is more likely that the voice is that of the four living creatures, the cherubs who make up the throne of God (Rev 4:6).

A "Prothalamion": God Is Praised For The Marriage Of The Lamb (verses 6-8)

Verses 6–8 have been called a "Prothalamion,"[27] a wedding song. It is "the wedding march of the Church."[28] John hears the "great multitude" of martyrs again, and their praise turns from celebrating the judgment of Babylon to rejoicing over the marriage of the Lamb. This change of perspective suggests a new division in our outline.[29] The sound of the praises was in John's ears like the din of a vast, thunderous waterfall and the sharp cracks of thunder.

Praise For The Impending Kingdom (verse 6)

"Hallelujah [Praise the Lord]! For the Lord our God, the Almighty reigns." The martyrs in heaven know that the fall of Babylon means that the age-long prayer of God's people—"Thy kingdom come" (Matt. 6:10)—is about to be realized. The time of reward is about to begin. When our text says, "the Almighty reigns," it does not mean He is reigning at that very moment.[30] The verb is proleptic—that is, it is prophetic.[31] It views His future reign as certain.

The martyrs are not speaking of God's present sovereign control of the universe. Rather, they are looking ahead to the reign of Messiah upon the earth during the thousand-year kingdom (Rev. 20:4–6). At that time the existing governments of the earth will not be merely indoctrinated with Christian principles, nor will they be simply Christianized. Instead they will be totally displaced with God taking all dominion and authority out of their hands and placing it in the hands of Christ as the true and only king of the world.[32]

Domitian, the Caesar who ruled at the time Revelation was written (AD81–96), conferred upon himself the title "Our Lord and God" (*Dominus et deus noster*).[33] In this historical situation John was exercising great confidence in God. God, not Caesar, is "the Almighty," the One who holds all things in His control.[34]

JOY OVER THE LAMB'S WEDDING (VERSES 7-8)

No aspect of the Christian's hope is more radiant and reassuring than the disclosure made here by the apostle John concerning the marriage of the Lamb and the feast that follows.[35] In Ephesians 5 another apostle, Paul, gives counsel to husbands and wives about marriage. Having emphasized the oneness involved in marriage he concludes, "This mystery is great; but I am speaking with reference to Christ and the church" (v. 32). In just the same way our passage speaks of the relationship between Christ and His church as that of husband and wife.

Marriage, if you believe the encyclopedia, is a pretty drab and strange affair: "a legally and socially sanctioned union between one or more husbands and one or more wives that accords status to their offspring and is regulated by laws, rules, customs, beliefs, and attitudes that prescribe the rights and duties of the partners."[36]

For some it is a matter of humor. For example some New England Puritan gravestones were shown at a New York art exhibit. One read: "Here lies the body of Obadiah Wilkinson and Ruth, his wife. Their Warfare is Accomplished." One understanding husband wrote, "She lived with her husband for 50 years and died in confident hope of a better life."[37]

There was an Archbishop named Ryan who attended confirmation in a small parish. The local pastor was giving the preparatory questions to a rather frightened little girl. He asked her to define the state of matrimony. "It's a state of terrible torment which those who enter are compelled to undergo for a time to prepare them for a better world," she replied. "No, no," chided the rector, "that's not matrimony. That's the definition of Purgatory." "Leave her alone," said the Archbishop, "perhaps the child has been shown the light."[38]

Feminist "spokesperson" Gloria Steinem expressed the opinion of many modern women when she said, "A woman without a man is like a fish without a bicycle."[39] Zsa Zsa Gabor quipped, "A man in love is incomplete until he has married. Then he's finished."[40]

Far closer to the biblical perspective was Martin Luther (1483–1546) who wrote, "Marriage is…a gift of God: the sweetest, the dearest and the purest life above all celibacy and all singleness...."[41]

Marriage, the lawful union of one man and one woman, is a sphere of blessing. "I am my beloved's and my beloved is mine" (Song of Songs 6:3). It is a sphere of privilege with a man and a woman united in a relationship for companionship, fellowship, intimacy—the sharing of thoughts, purposes, and life itself. When the Bible pictures the relationship of Christ and His people as that of a husband and wife it is expressing the truth that there is a covenant or bond between them.[42] It means that there is to be an everlasting union between them.[43] As R.H. Charles puts it, the figure of marriage "denotes the intimate and indissoluble communion of Christ with the [believing] community, which He has purchased with His own blood."[44] It also contains the notions of love, joy, and fidelity.[45]

The Bridegroom: The bridegroom is identified as "the Lamb," our Lord Jesus Christ. It is significant, I believe, that the heavenly wedding is not called "the marriage of the Creator" (He is the Creator, Col. 1:16); it is not called "the marriage of the Lord" (He is the Lord, Phil. 2:11); it is not called "the marriage of the King" (He is the King, Rev. 20: 4–6). No, it is the "marriage of the Lamb."[46]

This title tells us more than any other that "Christ ... loved the church and gave Himself up for her" (Eph. 5:25).

He is Christ our Passover, celebrated by the singing of the Hallel psalms. Hallelujah! Praise the Lord for the Lamb!

The Bride: The bride,[47] as most commentators agree, is the church, the company of the redeemed.[48] Dispensational commentators have specifically identified her as all saints between Pentecost and the rapture of the church.[49] Our text actually says "wife" and not "bride."

In the New Testament the wife/bride metaphor is used of the church in two kinds of passages. In some (Rom. 7:1–4; 1 Cor. 6:17) the church is seen as an actual wife bound by marriage to Christ. In others (2 Cor. 11:2) she is seen as a virgin and the marriage is future.[50]

The Preparations: "His bride," John says, "has made herself ready" (v. 7). This is no reluctant bride. Her making herself ready suggests the repentance and faith that each person must exercise to become one of God's people.[51] He adds that "it was given to her to clothe herself in fine linen." Her wedding gown is described as "the righteous acts [*righteousnesses*] of the saints." That her wedding garment was given to her reminds us that all we have (faith, redemption, and holiness) is the gift of God.

There has been much debate over the expression "righteousnesses of the saints" (v. 8). Some say it refers to the doctrine of justification, whereby we are acquitted or declared righteous in God's courtroom.[52] It speaks, they say, of the church's holy state before God. This usage, however, would be very unusual.

Others say that John refers to two kinds of righteousness: justification and sanctification. Believers have more than one kind of righteousness. There is the righteousness we have the moment we exercise faith in the blood of Christ, and there is the righteousness we acquire as we respond in daily obedience to the heavenly bridegroom.[53] This view has been illustrated by the custom in the Roman world of wearing two robes. There was an inner garment called a tunic, and there was an outer, loose-fitting garment called a toga. "Both of these garments, the inner garment that Christ gives us, and the outer garment, the weaving of our own works, we shall wear in the beautiful, consummating day of our Lord.... There is a positional righteousness [and] a practical righteousness."[54]

Still others say that the "righteousnesses" should be viewed in the context of rewards. They would argue that the rapture of the church has taken place, and the judgment seat of Christ (2 Cor. 5:10) followed shortly thereafter. They see the bride clothed in her rewards or awards.[55]

Another group of expositors says the righteousnesses refer to the innumerable acts of faithful obedience that characterize the bride. In other words it speaks of the good works ("righteous deeds of the saints")[56] performed by her after salvation, good works enabled by the indwelling Spirit of God.[57] The fact that the same noun is used of God's righteous acts in Revelation 15:4 favors this fourth view. The bride receives the garment as a gift, but she must put it on.[58] A transformed life is the proper response to the call of the heavenly bridegroom.[59]

The Marriage: Jewish marriage customs in Bible times involved three major stages.[60] The first stage was the negotiation or betrothal stage. Parents would contract to marry their children, and a dowry would be paid to the father of the bride. The couple was then considered husband and wife (CF. Matt. 1:18–19), and only a divorce could sever the contract. Between the betrothal and the wedding there would be an interval or waiting period to demonstrate the chastity of the bride. The second stage involved a procession and the wedding. The groom would go to his bride's parents' home and take her to the home of his parents where the marriage would be consummated by physical union. There would be a procession from the bride's home to the groom's. The third stage was the wedding feast, the festivities of which could last up to seven days.

These three stages can be seen in Christ's relationship to the church. The first stage (negotiation or betrothal) answers to the Cross where the price—the dowry—was paid.

> From heaven He came and sought her
> To be His holy bride;
> With His own blood He bought her,
> And for her life He died."[61]

On another level it refers to the work of evangelism and the moment of faith when the individual sinner embraces Christ as Savior. While the believer's actual union with Christ is yet future (we live during the time of the interval between betrothal and wedding), it is his present hope (Eph. 2:6). This is the *already* but *not yet* of the New Testament doctrine of salvation.[62]

The second stage (procession and wedding) takes place at the rapture of the church. The Lamb comes to earth and takes His bride to His Father's home where she is united to Him forever. The apostle Paul wanted the church to be prepared for this event. He was concerned lest the bride be defiled on earth by false doctrine or immoral behavior (CF. Eph. 5:27).

Bible teachers differ widely[63] over the symbolism of the third stage (wedding feast, or "marriage supper of the Lamb"), but it is most likely that this takes place in the millennial kingdom upon the earth. It is the same feast of which the Savior speaks when He says, "I will not drink of this fruit of the vine from now on until that day when I drink it new with you in My Father's kingdom"

(Matt. 26:29). He also says of the Passover feast, "I shall never again eat it until it is fulfilled in the kingdom of God" (Luke 22:16). The Savior also speaks of the day when "many shall come from east and west, and recline at the table with Abraham, and Isaac, and Jacob, in the kingdom of heaven" (Matt. 8:11). That the feast takes place in the millennium is also suggested by Luke's parable of a wedding feast (12:35–37) in which the Lord serves supper when He returns *from* the wedding.[64]

A BLESSING: WE ARE ASSURED OF THE CERTAINTY OF THESE THINGS
(VERSES 9–10)

THE INVITATION TO THE WEDDING

In verse 9 an angel (probably the angel of Revelation 17:1) speaks to John and tells him to write of the blessedness of those who are invited to the marriage supper. Some commentators say that the term "wife" looks at the church collectively, while the individual invited guests describe the church as individuals.[65] "The guests and the Bride are one and the same."[66] Proponents of this view note the fluidity of metaphorical language. For example, in Revelation 7:17 the "Lamb" and the "shepherd" are one and the same.[67] Others distinguish between the bride and the invited guests. They argue that the guests are the saints converted during the tribulation and possibly Old Testament saints.[68]

In any case it is a blessed thing to be invited[69] to heaven to this wonderful meeting with Jesus Christ. The very word "invited" implies that we do not gain access to the wedding feast on our own merits. The initiative in salvation always lies with God (Matt. 22:3).[70]

The Basis Of Our Confidence

Is this invitation to come to Christ to participate in His glorious kingdom a delusion, a sweet hallucination? No, the angel assures John, "These are the true words of God." There is a Lamb who was slain in order that your sins may be forgiven. He is in heaven today preparing a place for His people. He is going to return one day for His people, and there is in store for them a banquet with Jesus Christ in the kingdom of heaven. There is no room for doubting. "These are the true words of God."[71]

The Dignity Of Our Message

John is so overawed by the message, the perfectly true message he hears from the angel, that he bows down to worship him (v. 10). John will do this again in chapter 22 (v. 8–9), and there the angel will rebuke Him and assert again that God alone must be worshipped. Why did John record this failing and a similar one in chapter 22? The lesson is twofold: He wanted to show his readers how idolatry can infiltrate into the life through innocent means. John was about to turn a messenger of the truth into an idol. We do not need the coercions of Antichrist and Satan to fall into idolatry. Idolatry is more than burning incense before a man-made statue; it is giving absolute worth and devotion to anything other than God, even a good cause.[72]

In chapter 19, however, the lesson is not so much that John was demeaning God's glory, but that he was demeaning his own prophetical office.[73] The "testimony to Jesus is the spirit of prophecy." The message about Jesus—His death, resurrection, and soon return—is at the heart of all prophecy.[74] The angel is not the object of the prophetic word. On the contrary, the angels, together with John and other prophets, bear witness to Jesus. They are no more than fellow servants with the saints in their relationship to Christ. "Go to God with your worship," the angel says. By bowing to the angels John was ignoring the fact that he had an office equal in dignity to that of any angel. He was a prophet who proclaimed the truth about Jesus.

Conclusion

There are a number of important lessons in Revelation 19:1–10 for the Christian who would be gripped by the urgency of apostolic Christianity. First, the passage teaches the inescapable consequences of sin. T.S. Kepler once said, "The moral law [of God] can no more be broken than the law of gravity; it can only be illustrated."[75] Do we honestly think that God is going to allow our world to persist in its unrighteousness? There is coming a day when God is going to right all the wrongs that have existed upon the earth. The punishment of Babylon and the punishment of all sinners is going to illustrate that God's commandments cannot be broken.

Also, God's judgment is true and righteous—His punishment will fit the crime. God is perfect in His judgment for three reasons:[76] first, He alone can see the inmost thoughts and desires of any person; second, He alone has that purity that can judge without prejudice; third, He alone has the wisdom to choose the appropriate judgment and the power to execute it.

Furthermore, it should be observed that there is a company of people who will escape the judgment of God. They will participate in the marriage supper of the Lamb. All are invited to come ("Blessed are those who are invited to the marriage supper of the Lamb," v. 9).

Finally, there are some important lessons about the nature of worship and its relevance to the Christian life:

THE NATURE OF WORSHIP

Heaven's worship has great dignity. There is no sense here of sitting around the campfire singing cozy songs. Furthermore, heaven's worship involves everyone—all who are around the throne are involved. Nobody says, "Well, I can't sing!" Most importantly, heaven's songs are theocentric. No one in heaven seems to be trying to entertain the other worshippers. All are offering praise for His satisfaction.[77]

THE RELEVANCE OF WORSHIP

A true worshipper accepts the will of God. In verse 4 the 24 elders say, "Amen," or "So be it, Lord," and in context they are applauding the judgment of God. Also a true worshipper is committed to the purposes of God. Those in heaven are delighted at the prospect of Christ's kingdom beginning ("the Lord, our God, the Almighty, reigns," v. 6). Furthermore, a true worshipper will discover joy in the fellowship of God ("Let us rejoice and be glad"). Believers are betrothed to Him now, and soon they will be united to Him at "the marriage of the Lamb" (v. 7). Finally, a true worshipper will rest in the assurance of the victory of God: He knows that His God is "the Almighty," the One who holds all things in His control.[78]

NOTES

[1]George Bernard Shaw, *Seven Plays by Bernard Shaw* (New York: Dodd-Mead, 1951), 829.

[2]CF. Austin Farrer, *The Revelation of St. John the Divine* (London: Oxford University Press, 1964), 196.

[3]CF. Alan F. Johnson, "Revelation," in *The Expositor's Bible Commentary*, 12 vols., ed. Frank E. Gaebelein (Grand Rapids: Zondervan, 1981), 12:573.

[4]The five last things of traditional Roman Catholic eschatology are: death, judgment, heaven, hell, and purgatory. CF. Joseph Pohle, *Eschatology or The Catholic Doctrine of the Last Things* (Herder: St. Louis, 1917; reprint ed., Westport, Connecticut: Greenwood, 1971); Regis Martin, *The Last Things* (San Francisco: Ignatius, 1998).

[5]For a defense of the view that an expository sermon should be the explanation, interpretation, or application of a single dominant idea, see Haddon W. Robinson, *Biblical Preaching: The Development and Delivery of Expository Messages* (Grand Rapids: Baker, 1980), 31–48.

[6]Among evangelical students of the Revelation there have been at least five interpretations of the identity of Babylon (pagan Rome, papal Rome, eschatological Rome, apostate Jerusalem, eschatological Babylon). For a defense of the view adopted here, CF. Harry Goehring, "The Fall of Babylon—Historical or Future?" *Grace Journal* 2 (Winter, 1961): 23–34; Kenneth W. Allen, "The Rebuilding and Destruction of Babylon," *Bibliotheca Sacra* 133 (1976):19–27; Charles H. Dyer, "The Identity of Babylon in Revelation 17–18, part 2," *Bibliotheca Sacra* 144 (1987): 433–49.

[7]Martin Kiddle, *The Revelation of St. John*, Moffatt New Testament Commentary (New York: Harper, 1940), 375.

[8]E.G., Henry Barclay Swete, *The Apocalypse of St. John* (London: Macmillan, 1906), 238; R. H. Charles, *The Revelation of St. John*, International Critical Commentary, 2 vols. (Edinburgh: T. & T. Clark, 1920), 2:118; Leon Morris, *The Revelation of St. John*, Tyndale New Testament Commentaries (Grand Rapids: Eerdmans, 1969), 224; George Eldon Ladd, *A Commentary on the Revelation of John* (Grand Rapids: Eerdmans, 1972), 244; Robert L. Thomas, *Revelation 8–22: An Exegetical Commentary* (Chicago: Moody, 1995), 355–56. It is argued that they must be angels in that most earlier songs of thanks in Revelation involve angels (4:8, 11; 5:12–14) and human believers are called to add their hallelujah in v. 5.

[9]CF. G.B. Caird, *The Revelation of St. John the Divine*, Harper New Testament Commentary (New York: Harper, 1966), 232; John F. Walvoord, *The Revelation of Jesus Christ* (Chicago: Moody, 1966), 268; Robert H. Mounce, *The Book of Revelation*, New International Commentary on the New Testament (rev. ed., Grand Rapids: Eerdmans, 1998), 341.

[10]Johnson, "Revelation," 12:570.

[11]G.R. Beasley-Murray, *The Book of Revelation*, New Century Bible (London: Oliphants, 1974), 271.

[12]Ford C. Ottman, *The Unfolding of the Ages* (New York: Baker & Taylor, 1905), 402.

[13]This title is taken from Arethas' description of the passage in his commentary on Revelation. Arethas was bishop of Caesarea in Cappadocia (C AD900). Cf. Swete, *The Apocalypse of St. John*, CXCV, 238.

[14]Cf. William Barclay, *The Revelation of John*, 2 vols. (rev. ed., Philadelphia: Westminster Press, 1976), 2:169; Walter Scott, *Exposition of the Revelation of Jesus Christ* (4TH. ed., London: Pickering & Inglis, n.d.), 375.

[15]Barclay, *The Revelation of John*, 2:169.

[16]Cf. Thomas F. Torrance, *The Apocalypse Today* (London: James Clarke, 1960), 154.

[17]Kiddle, *The Revelation of St. John*, 377.

[18]Significantly, the first occurrence of *Hallelujah* in the Bible is in Ps. 104:35 where the context is also judgment. See E. W. Bullinger, *The Apocalypse* (3RD. ed., London: Eyre and Spotiswoode, 1935; reprint ed., Grand Rapids: Kregel, 1984), 584.

[19]J. P. Love, *1 John—Revelation*, Layman's Bible Commentary (Atlanta: John Knox, 1960), 104.

[20]Joseph Seiss, *Lectures on the Apocalypse*, 3 vols. (9TH ed., New York: Charles C. Cook, 1906), 3:199.

[21]Eugene H. Peterson, "Learning to Worship from Saint John's Revelation," *Christianity Today* (Oct. 28, 1991), 23–25.

[22]Warren W. Wiersbe, *Real Worship* (rev. ed., Nashville: Oliver Nelson, 1990), 43–44.

[23]The identity of the 24 elders is one of the great interpretive problems of the book of Revelation. Most modern commentators identify them as either an exalted angelic order or as a redeemed company of people. For a helpful summary of seven solutions as to the identity of the 24 elders, see David Aune, *Revelation 1–5*, Word Biblical Commentary (Dallas: Word, 1997), 288–92.

[24]C.R.G. Hall, "Living Creatures in the Midst of the Throne: Another Look at Revelation 4:6," *New Testament Studies* 36 (1990): 609–13.

[25]"This may seem to some a little difficult, but it is of no use to evade difficulties" (William Kelly, *The Revelation Expounded* (reprint ed., Oak Park: Bible Truth Publishers, 1970), 221–23. The fact that the church can be both the 24 elders and the bride is due to the free and flexible nature of apocalyptic literature. Kelly's view is somewhat different from mine in that he includes both the Old Testament saints and the bride in the 24 elders (CF. P. 84).

[26]E.G., G.H. Lang, *The Revelation of Jesus Christ* (London: Paternoster, 1948), 312.

[27]Kiddle, *The Revelation of St. John*, 375.

[28]Torrance, *The Apocalypse Today*, 153. The term *prothalamion* was coined by Edmund Spenser (1552–99), the English poet who called one of his famous poems a "spousall verse." It was written in anticipation of the double marriage of the Ladies Elizabeth and Catherine Somerset. Cf. A. Skevington Wood, *Prophecy in the Space Age* (Grand Rapids: Zondervan, 1963), 96.

[29]Cf. Mounce, *The Book of Revelation*, 346.

[30]Unlike most interpreters Lenski takes the aorist as historical and causative. He says that it looks back over all past history and in all of it sees the Lord God reigning. Cf. R.C.H. Lenski, *The Interpretation of St. John's Revelation* (Minneapolis: Augsburg, 1943), 540.

[31]Cf. James Hope Moulton, *A Grammar of New Testament Greek*, 4 vols., vol. 3: *Syntax* by Nigel Turner (Edinburgh: T. &. T. Clark, 1963), 71–72, 74.

[32]Seiss, *Lectures on the Apocalypse*, 3:205.

[33]Seutonius, *The Lives of the Caesars*, Book 8: *Domitian* 13, in *Suetonius*, 2 vols., trans. J. C. Rolfe, The Loeb Classical Library (New York: Macmillan, 1914), 2: 367.

[34]Mounce, *The Book of Revelation*, 346.

[35]A.S. Wood, *Prophecy in the Space Age*, 95.

[36]*The New Encyclopedia Britannica, Micropedia*, see "Marriage," 7 (1988), 871.

[37]James C. Hefley, *A Dictionary of Illustrations* (Grand Rapids: Zondervan, 1971), 185.

[38]Edmund Fuller, ed. 2500 *Anecdotes for All Occasions* (New York: Crown, 1970; reprint ed., New York: Avenel, 1978), 152.

[39]Quoted by Elaine Partnow, ed., *The New Quotable Woman* (New York: Meridian, 1993), 451.

[40]Quoted by Laurence J. Peter, *Peter's Quotations* (New York: Bantam, 1979), 326.

[41]Quoted by William Neil, *Concise Dictionary of Religious Quotations* (Grand Rapids: Eerdmans, 1974), 116.

[42]Beasley-Murray, *The Book of Revelation*, 273.

[43]Kiddle, *The Revelation of St. John*, 379.

[44]Charles, *The Revelation of St. John*, 2:126.

[45]Barclay, *The Revelation of John*, 2:173.

[46]Robert T. Ketcham, "The Marriage Supper of the Lamb," in *Understanding the Times*, eds. W. Culbertson and H. B. Centz (Grand Rapids: Zondervan, 1956), 171–79.

[47]In the Old Testament Israel is viewed as the unfaithful wife of Yahweh who was put away (Hos. 2:2) yet will one day be reunited to Him (Hos. 2:19–20; CF. Isa. 62:1–5).

[48]Not all agree. There are other interpretations: (1) Those who hold to a partial pretribulational rapture say that the bride is made up of a select group of believers whose lives have been characterized by dedicated discipleship and watchful preparedness (CF. Luke 17:33–37; 21:34–36). CF. Robert Govett, *The Apocalypse: Expounded by Scripture*, 4 vols. (London, 1861; reprint ed., Miami Springs: Conley & Schoettle, 1981), 4:167; Seiss, *Lectures on the Apocalypse*, 3: 213–19; Lang, *The Revelation of Jesus Christ*, 315–16. (2) Ultradispensational writers argue that the wife of Rev. 19 is Israel and the bride of Rev. 21 is the church. CF. Bullinger, *The Apocalypse*, 589–91.

[49]Scott, *Exposition of the Revelation of Jesus Christ*, 380.

[50]The choice of term (I.E., "wife" instead of "bride") is probably not all that significant. CF. Morris, *The Revelation of St. John*, 227.

[51]Beasley-Murray, *The Book of Revelation*, 274.

[52]E.G., Henry Alford, *The Greek Testament*, 4 vols., vol. 4: *Hebrews–Revelation* (reprint ed., Chicago: Moody, 1958), 725. Alford says the plural is distributive, implying not many righteousnesses for each believer, but one state of righteousness for each of the saints.

[53]Seiss, *Lectures on the Apocalypse*, 3:223–24; CF. Beasley-Murray, *The Book of Revelation*, 274.

[54]W. A. Criswell, *Expository Sermons on Revelation*, 5 vols. (Grand Rapids: Zondervan, 1969), 5:29.

[55]CF. Bullinger, *The Apocalypse*, 593.

[56]*Theological Dictionary of the New Testament*, see "δικαίωμα," by G. Schrenk, 2 (1964), 222; Walvoord, *The Revelation of Jesus Christ*, 272; Thomas, *Revelation 8–22*, 370–71.

[57]Mounce, *The Book of Revelation*, 348.

[58]Robert Wall, *Revelation*, New International Bible Commentary (Peabody: Hendrickson, 1991), 222–23.

[59]Mounce, *The Book of Revelation*, 348.

[60]On Jewish marriage customs, CF. *The Universal Jewish Encyclopedia*, see "Marriage," by Marcus Cohn, 7:372; *Encyclopaedia Judaica*, see "Marriage," by Raphael Posner, 11:1032–34; *Theological Dictionary of the New Testament*, see "νύμφη," by J. Jeremias, 4 (1967), 1099–1101; Ralph Gower, *The New Manners and Customs of Bible Times* (Chicago: Moody, 1987), 64–69; William Hendriksen, *More Than Conquerors* (Grand Rapids: Baker, 1939), 215–17; Walvoord, *The Revelation of Jesus Christ*, 271.

[61]Samuel J. Stone, "The Church's One Foundation," in *Hymns of Truth and Praise* (Fort Dodge: Gospel Perpetuating Publishers, 1971), 226.

[62]Beasley-Murray, *The Book of Revelation*, 273.

[63]There are at least three views: (1) The marriage supper is millennial (CF. Seiss, *Lectures on the Apocalypse*, 3:230–31; Beasley-Murray, *The Book of Revelation*, 275). (2) The marriage supper takes place after the millennium in the eternal state (CF. Charles, *The Revelation of St. John*, 2:126–29; Mounce, *The Book of Revelation*, 348). (3) The marriage supper takes place in heaven before the return of the Lord to the earth (Renald E. Showers, "The Marriage and Marriage Supper of the Lamb," *Israel My Glory* (June, 1991), 9–12). Texts like Isa. 25:6–8 and Luke 12:36–37 would seem to support the first view.

[64]The word "feast" does not appear in the Greek text of Luke 12:36.

[65]Caird, *The Revelation of St. John the Divine*, 234.

[66]Charles, *The Revelation of St. John*, 2:129.

[67]Caird, *The Revelation of St. John the Divine*, 234; Ladd, *A Commentary on the Revelation of John*, 250.

[68]CF. William Kelly, *Lectures on the Book of Revelation* (London: G. Morrish, 1874), 392–98; Walvoord, *The Revelation of Jesus Christ*, 273. Proponents make the following observations: (1) Psalm 45:13–14 and the parable of the virgins

(Matt. 25:1–13) distinguish between the Bride and her companions. (2) In Hebrews 12:23 the church is distinguished from "the spirits of righteous men made perfect;" I.E., the Old Testament saints in the eschatological city to come. (3) In Rev. 21:24 the nations are distinguished from the bride. CF. also Seiss, *Apocalypse*, 3:232.

Classic dispensationalists make a sharp distinction between Israel and the church. They argue, for example, that the Bible distinguishes between two husbands (Father and Son) and two wives (Israel and the church). The double marriage idea is felt to solve the dilemma of two distinct peoples both being married to the Lord. "The company that constitutes the bride of the one marriage would constitute the guests at the other. When [God] shall take Israel into eternal union with Himself, the Church shall be there as 'the called.' When Christ shall take the Church into a like eternal union, Israel shall be there as 'the guests'" (Ottman, *The Unfolding of the Ages*, 411; Donald Grey Barnhouse, *Revelation: An Expository Commentary* [Grand Rapids: Zondervan, 1971], 353; CF. Showers, "The Marriage," 11).

A modified dispensationalism recognizes more continuity than discontinuity between the people of God in each age and concludes that the new covenant people of God as a whole (including both redeemed Israel in the millennium and the church) is the bride of Christ. The marriage supper in the millennium will celebrate the union between Christ and His people—that is, the church and Israel. CF. Robert L. Saucy, *The Case for Progressive Dispensationalism* (Grand Rapids: Zondervan, 1993), 184–85. Also see: Ladd, *Revelation*, 248–49, for a similar perspective.

[69]The verb καλέω (here = perf. pass. ptc. κεκλημένοι) is also used of the effectual call to salvation, I.E., election (E.G., Rom. 8:30; 2 Thess. 2:14). Here, however, it seems to have the idea of "invited" without any connotation of election. In the parable of the wedding feast (Matt. 22:14) it is clearly used of a general call or invitation. CF. A.F. Johnson, "Revelation," 572.

[70]Ladd, *A Commentary on the Revelation of John*, 250.

[71]Seiss, *Lectures on the Apocalypse*, 3:234–35.

[72]Caird, *The Revelation of St. John the Divine*, 237.

[73]David Chilton, *The Days of Vengeance* (Ft. Worth: Dominion Press, 1987), 480; cf. Charles, *The Revelation of St. John*, 2:130.

[74]Morris, *The Revelation of St. John*, 228. "A situation, then, in which…opponents of Christianity are trying to make its adherents deny that Jesus is the Messiah, curse Christ, say that Caesar is Lord, and swear by the tuvch [Fortune] of Caesar…, is the setting for the angel's assurance that it is the prophetic Spirit which inspires every confession of Jesus, and, conversely that the form which inspired prophecy takes in this struggle is testimony to Jesus" (G.W.H. Lampe, "The Testimony of Jesus is the Spirit of Prophecy [Rev. 19:10]," in *The New Testament Age*, 2 vols., ed. William C. Weinrich [Macon, GA: Mercer University Press, 1984], 1:257–58).

[75]Barclay, *The Revelation of John*, 2:169.

[76]Barclay, *The Revelation of John*, 2:169.

[77]Bill Wymond, "The Music of Heaven's Worship," *Table Talk* (Dec., 1991), 10–11.

[78]James Stewart, *The Wind of the Spirit* (Nashville: Abingdon, 1968), 47–55.

The Seven Last Things

꿏

THE FIRST LAST THING:

THE SECOND COMING OF CHRIST
REVELATION 19:11-16

꿏

In the city of Milan, Italy there stands a magnificent cathedral, the chief glory of the city and one of the most beautiful religious buildings in the world. The 52 marble columns which hold up its lofty dome, and the 4,440 turrets, pinnacles, and statues of angels and saints produce an incomparable combination of grace and grandeur, beauty and vastness. Behind the high altar is one of the largest stained-glass windows in existence. Its subject matter is arresting. It depicts no scene from the Old Testament—not the creation, the fall, or the flood; no person—not Abraham, Moses, David, or the prophets; nor scenes from the Gospels such as the birth of Christ, His temptation, His transfiguration, His crucifixion, or His resurrection; nor scenes from the Acts of the Apostles or the early spread of the gospel. No, the artist's subject is the tremendous imagery of the book of the Revelation: the sounding trumpets, the outpoured bowls, Michael and his angels in battle with the dragon and his angels, the woman with the sun and moon under her feet, Satan bound with a chain and cast into the abyss, and—most impressive of all—the rider on the white horse going forth to war with the armies of heaven following behind.[1]

The artist of this great masterpiece was undoubtedly convinced that his subject—the second coming of Christ—was of great importance, and it is. Yet it is a subject that is puzzling to many people, Christians as well as non-Christians. They think that it is perhaps something they ought to understand, but they find it hard to grasp or swallow. Perhaps the only people they know who have any interest in the subject are cultists or religious cranks—such as the Jehovah's Witnesses who predicted the Lord's return in 1975, the radio preacher who predicted the return of Christ in 1988, and the radio preacher who predicted the year of His coming to be 1994.[2] As a result, this great subject has fallen into disrepute in some quarters, and it has been long neglected in others. It is safe to say that in the major communions and denominations of the Christian church this fundamental doctrine of the Christian faith is only lightly touched upon, if it is mentioned at all.[3]

Dr. Andrew Bonar (1810–92), the great Scottish minister, tells of a man in his parish whom he often used to visit. He was a simple and poor man, but he had found Christ and had great joy in the thought that He would one day return to earth. On one occasion he went to Edinburgh and heard some of the famous preachers of the day. But he came home much dissatisfied on one vital issue. When

Dr. Bonar asked him why he felt that their ministry was deficient, he replied, "Oh, they all flee wi' ae wing!" (That is, "they all fly with one wing.") He meant they were like lame birds, since they spoke of Christ's first but not His Second Coming.[4]

Dr. Bonar's friend was right. Too often Christians have conceived of the Incarnation, the first coming, as the sole center of God's dealings with the world, when in reality there are two focal points: the first coming and the Second Coming of our Lord. "In His cross and resurrection," says George Ladd, "Christ won a great victory over the powers of evil; by His Second Coming, He will execute that victory. Apart from His return to purge His creation of evil, redemption remains forever incomplete."[5] As a German commentator has written, "Those who believe in the reality of the resurrection of Jesus Christ must also look for His return."[6] The Second Coming, then, like the first coming, is "an absolutely essential theme" in New Testament teaching.[7]

A fact often forgotten is that the Second Coming of Christ is not just the aberrant fascination of "end–time junkies" and apocalyptic doomsdayers. It is the historic faith of the Christian church. If one reads the writings of the early church Fathers, the men who wrote soon after the time of Christ's apostles, one finds that they believed in the Second Coming. For example,[8] *The Epistle of Barn-*

abas, probably written in Alexandria between AD70 and 100, says this: "When His Son comes He will destroy…the wicked one, and will judge the godless, and will change the sun and the moon and the stars, and then He will truly rest…."[9] Likewise, Clement of Rome, writing about AD96, says, "Therefore we must be prompt in well doing: for all things are from Him. For He warns us, 'Behold the Lord cometh, and His reward is before His face, to pay to each according to His work.'"[10] A later Church Father, Justin Martyr (C. AD100–C. 165), writing to the emperor in the second century (C. AD155) says, "Hear, too, how He was to ascend into heaven according to prophecy…. And how also He should come again out of heaven with glory…."[11] And then Irenaeus (C. AD130–C. 200), considered by many to be the first great Catholic theologian,[12] writes in a famous work on heresy: "But when this Antichrist shall have devastated all things in this world, he will reign for three years and six months, and sit in the temple at Jerusalem; and then the Lord will come from heaven in the clouds, in the glory of the Father, sending this man and those who follow him into the lake of fire."[13] The African church father, Tertullian, who lived in the second and third centuries (C. AD160–C. 225), alludes to 1 Thessalonians 4:17 when he says, "For we shall, according to the apostle, be caught up into the clouds to meet the Lord (even the Son of man who shall come in the clouds [I.E., in glory]."[14]

In similar fashion the great Reformers eagerly anticipated the return of Christ. Martin Luther (1483–1546) says, "The prophets spoke and preached of the second coming of Christ as we do now."[15] In another place he says, "It is my firm belief that the angels are getting ready, putting on their armor and girding their swords about them, for the last day is already breaking, and the angels are preparing for battle...."[16] One of his students, Erasmus Alber, writes,

> Your dear children are waiting all:
> For the world apart to fall,
> The devil's power to pass away,
> And he be damned to hell alway.

Another student, Nikolaus Herman, puts it this way:

> For your coming, Lord, we're waiting all,
> And listening for the trumpet's call.
> Lord Jesus, come—do not delay
> And help your church—we are afraid.[17]

John Calvin (1509–64) writes, "For he will come down from heaven in the same visible form in which he was seen to ascend [Acts 1:11; Matt. 24:30]. And he will appear to all with the ineffable majesty of his kingdom, with the glow of immortality, with the boundless power of divinity, with a guard of angels.

From thence we are commanded to await him as our Redeemer on that day when he will separate the lambs from the goats.... No one—living or dead—shall escape his judgment."[18]

In the same way the great creeds and confessions all express the conviction of Christians that Jesus Christ will one day bodily and visibly return to this earth. The so-called *Apostles' Creed*, not written by the apostles but a popular summary of apostolic teaching, says, "I believe in God the Father Almighty, and in Jesus Christ, his only Son, our Lord; Who was conceived by the Holy Ghost, born of the Virgin Mary; suffered under Pontius Pilate, was crucified, dead, and buried. He descended into Hades; the third day he rose from the dead; He ascended into heaven; and sitteth on the right hand of God the Father Almighty; from thence he shall come to judge the quick and the dead."[19] In similar fashion, the *Nicene Creed*, highly honored in the Greek Orthodox Church, says, "And he shall come again, with glory, to judge the quick and the dead."[20] The *Augsburg Confession* (AD1530) of the Lutheran Churches says, "[The churches] teach that, in the consummation of the world [at the last day], Christ shall appear to judge, and shall raise up the dead, and shall give unto the godly and elect eternal life and everlasting joys."[21] The *Belgic Confession* (AD1561) of the Flemish and Dutch Reformation churches says, "We believe, according to the Word of God... that our Lord Jesus Christ will come from heaven, corporally [I.E., bodily] and visibly, as he ascended with great glory and majesty, to declare himself Judge of the quick and the dead, burning this old world with fire and flame to cleanse it."[22]

The Westminster Confession (AD1647) of the Presbyterian churches, says, "[The Lord Jesus] shall return to judge men and angels at the end of the world."[23] The "Thirty Nine Articles" (AD1571) of the Church of England or Anglican Church (Episcopal Church in North America) says, "he ascended into Heaven, and there sitteth, until he return to judge all Men at the last day."[24] The confession of the Congregational Union of England and Wales (AD1833) has these words: "They believe that Christ will finally come to judge the whole human race according to their works."[25] Finally, the *New Hampshire Confession* (AD1833) of the Baptist Churches affirms, "We believe that the end of the world is approaching; that at the last day Christ will descend from heaven, and raise the dead from the grave to final retribution; that a solemn separation will then take place; that the wicked will be adjudged to endless punishment, and the righteous to endless joy."[26]

The reason the fathers, the reformers, the creeds and confessions are so firm, of course, is that they reflect the teaching of the Scriptures. The second coming of Christ is the historic faith of the church because it is deeply embedded in the pages of the infallible Word of God. It is the teaching of the prophets of the Old Testament, and it is the teaching of the apostles in the New Testament. Most important, it is part of the basic teaching of the Lord Jesus Christ Himself. "And then the sign of the Son of Man will appear in the sky, and then all the tribes of the earth will mourn, and they will see the Son of Man coming on the clouds of the sky with power and great glory" (Matt. 24:30). "And when the Son of Man comes in His glory, and all the angels with Him, then He will sit on His glorious throne" (Matt. 25:31). "And if I go and prepare a place for you, I will come again, and receive you to Myself; that where I am, there you may be also" (Jn. 14:3). If belief in, and proclamation of, the second coming is the mark of a "crank" or a "kook," then our Lord Himself was the greatest "crank" and "kook" of all.[27]

In light of the united testimony of the prophets, apostles, our Lord, and the greatest teachers of the church, evangelical ministers of the Word dare not be part of the conspiracy of silence that surrounds the doctrine of the second coming in the churches of today. The creeds and confessions suggest a number of reasons why the Lord Jesus is going to return: First, He is going to come to rescue His people from this earth, raising from the dead those who have died before His coming. Second, He is coming to judge His people, evaluating their faithfulness and watchfulness during the time of His absence (2 Cor. 5:10; Mark 8:38). Those who say, "Come, Lord Jesus" (Rev. 22:20), should live in such a way that they will not be ashamed at His coming. Third, He is coming in great glory. At His first coming He lived in obscurity and weakness. At His second coming there will be an open manifestation of the character and splendor of the Lord Jesus Christ. Fourth, He is coming in order that He might transform the universe and bring about a new heaven and a new earth (Rev. 21:1). Finally, He is coming that He might conquer all that is evil, whether it be human or demonic in form.[28]

It is this fifth reason that is the subject (the "big idea") of the passage under consideration, the *locus classicus* of the New Testament doctrine of the second coming of Christ.[29] The One who today sits on the throne of Almighty God in heaven is going to return to earth wielding great power and authority to extirpate, to root up and destroy totally, evil from this world.

It should be noted that John's subject in verses 11–16 is the revelation of Jesus Christ and not the rapture or translation of the church. In the rapture God's people meet Christ in the clouds (1 Thess. 4:16–17); in the revelation they come with Him to the earth. At the rapture Christ returns with His saints to heaven; at the revelation He comes with them to earth and establishes His kingdom. At the rapture the saints put on immortality and incorruptibility (1 Cor. 15:53); at the revelation they are displayed in glory (Rom. 8:21–23). In the book of the Revelation John does not describe the rapture as such, and there has been much debate among evangelicals over its timing. Several theories have been advanced, but three are common: (1) Some argue that the rapture takes place at the same time as the revelation, and they are popularly known as post-tribulationists.[30] (2) Others argue that the rapture takes place at the middle of the tribulation period,[31] and they are popularly known as mid-tribulationists.[32] (3) A third group of scholars places the rapture prior to the tribulation, that is, prior to Revelation 4:1, and they are popularly known as pre-tribulationalists.[33] I would argue for the pretribulational view due to the following observations on the text of the Revelation: (1) the promise of 3:10, (2) the absence of any mention of the church on earth in chapters 6–18, and (3) the presence of the church (24 elders, the bride) in heaven during the tribulation and prior to the revelation.

JESUS CHRIST WILL RETURN AS A RIGHTEOUS AND VICTORIOUS WARRIOR KING (VERSE 11)

HIS ORIGIN

At verse 11 we come to one of the most dramatic moments in the Revelation.[34] Babylon, the commercial and political capital of the earth at the end of the age, has been defeated. Earlier in the book (4:1) a door in heaven was opened and John was called up to the throne room of God in heaven.

Now the heavens themselves open to disclose a rider on a white horse. There is no doubt about His identity. "The sublime hero" of the scene is none other than our Lord Jesus Christ,[35] and He is portrayed as a man of war on horseback.[36]

There are two settings for horses—the farm and the race track—that have colored my own thinking about these beautiful animals. When I was a boy on Cape Breton Island in northern Nova Scotia, there was a special time each summer that I can still vividly remember. I would be invited to spend a week on the farm of Donald Phillips and his family, friends of my parents. Every year Mr. Phillips would buy or rent an old horse (one on the way to the "glue factory") for the hay-making season. After the hay was cut with a horse–pulled mower, I would be allowed to ride the rake in back of the horse to rake up the hay. Later, with other children, I would ride the hay wagon as the men tossed the hay to them with pitch forks. At other times during the summer I would visit the stables of a nearby race track where my Uncle Malcolm kept his beautiful brown mare, "June Bee." I tend always to think of horses as farm animals or as graceful, racing animals.

But this is not the way people in the ancient world thought of horses. They thought of them as military machines, used primarily in war. The prophets picture the horse in battle as swift, sure-footed, and determined (Jer. 12:5; 8:6; Isa. 63:13).[37]

41

This picture is in sharp contrast to that of Christ's first coming.[38] You will remember the account in the Gospels of Jesus' procession into Jerusalem on Palm Sunday. He rode on a donkey, a lowly beast of burden (Matt. 21:5; cf. Zech. 9:9).[39]

> They were all looking for a king
> To slay their foes and lift them high:
> Thou cam'st a little baby thing
> That made a woman cry.[40]

At His second coming Jesus will arrive, not as a babe, but as a warrior to destroy His enemies. The little domestic animal, the donkey, will be exchanged for the military steed.

The scene before us is in marked contrast to that in chapter 6 where there was another rider on a white horse. That rider was Antichrist who brought new levels of evil to the earth. The rider in chapter 19 will remove that evil. Also, we should note that He rides a white horse. White in Revelation is a symbol of judgment (20:11) and victory.[41] The white stallion was a favorite of Roman generals as they rode in victory processions.[42]

His Reputation[43]

John tells his readers that the rider is called and known to be[44] "Faithful and True." The word "faithful" has the idea of trustworthiness; God is faithful to His promises and will fulfill them all. Christ will come and fulfill all the covenant promises of the Old Testament.[45] All those who place their confidence in Him will be vindicated.[46] The word "true" can have an almost synonymous sense of "trustworthy" or "truthful." It can also have the sense of true or genuine in contrast to the falseness of idols.[47] Thus the Messiah is in sharp contrast to the Dragon who is a deceiver, the Beast who is a false Christ, the second Beast who is a false prophet, and the worshippers of the tribulation who worship the false gods of this age.

His Character

The warrior king from heaven judges and wages war "in righteousness," says John. Clarence Macartney says, "There are times when the heart grows dull and heavy with the deadly monotony of evil in the world."[48] Evil in the hearts of men and in human institutions is constantly reemerging, he says. It is seen today in unending warfare, terrorism and death squads, the shameful dishonesty of businessmen, media moguls and lawmakers, the perversion of the arts and culture, and the injustice against the poor and weak. Is God not omnipotent? Is He not good? The answer this text gives is that God is going to destroy and overthrow evil at the second coming of Christ. Righteousness is "that phase of God's holiness … whereby He gives to everyone what is due him."[49]

Gregory Fisher was a teacher in a West African Bible College. One of his students asked him to comment on 1 Thessalonians 4:16, "the Lord Himself will descend from heaven with a shout." "What will He say when He shouts?" asked the student. Fisher thought of the senseless terrorism he had seen in that part of the world, of the hopeless looks of starving beggars. "Enough!" Fisher answered. He will shout "Enough!" when He returns. "Enough starvation, enough suffering, enough terror, enough death, enough indignity, enough hopelessness, enough sickness and disease." Enough corruption, enough dishonesty, enough perversion, enough violence, enough infidelity in marriage, enough disobedience to parents, enough abuse of children, enough cheating, enough blasphemy and irreverence toward God. Enough![50]

Thus He will come and make war against all that is evil. Righteously He will give to all men exactly what they deserve.

HIS RETURN WILL BE MARKED BY DISCERNMENT, AUTHORITY, AND MYSTERY (VERSE 12)

HIS DIVINE DISCERNMENT

In verse 12 John writes, "His eyes are a flame of fire." This speaks of the Lord's ability to see through all pretense. Nothing can be hidden from the penetrating gaze of the Messiah.[51] He is omniscient, all-knowing (Rev. 1:14; 2:18). There are many things in human experience that are mysteries and unsolved riddles to most of us. The eyes of Christ search and understand all things.[52] There are sins in the lives of people that no one else can see, yet He sees them all. There are many sins and crimes in the lives of people that they rationalize and refuse to censure as evil. Christ sees into the innermost heart and evaluates everything by the perfect standard of the holiness of God.[53]

HIS SUPREME AUTHORITY

Upon the warrior's head John sees "many diadems." The diadem is a royal crown. At His crucifixion our Lord was crowned with a crown of thorns (Matt. 27:29; Mark 15:17; John 19:2, 5). To the soldiers it was an attempt to mock royalty. To His followers, however, it constituted testimony to His true kingship, and it anticipated His victory over death and His return to rule the world.[54]

Earlier in the book the Dragon, Satan, wears seven diadems (12:3). The Beast or Antichrist wears ten of them (13: 1; 17:12)—one for each of the ten kings who are subservient to him in the tribulation.

The accumulated crowns on the rider's head speak of accumulated victories and dominions—the greatest of all, by far, being His victorious Passion.[55] It says He is the winner of many mighty battles and the holder of many sovereignties.

King David conquered the Ammonites, and he put the crown of the vanquished king on his own head, in addition to the crown he already owned (2 Sam. 12:30). In similar fashion, when Ptolemy entered Antioch, he set two crowns upon his head, the crown of Asia and the crown of Egypt (1 Macc. 11:13).[56] Not just Ammon, Egypt and Asia belong to Christ, but all the provinces of God's universe.[57]

His Transcendent Mystery

John adds that "He has a name written upon Him which no one knows except Himself." In the ancient world and in the thinking of those who wrote the Bible a name often revealed the nature of an individual. In Revelation 13:1 the Antichrist has many names, but they are "blasphemous names." What does it mean that Christ has a name that no one knows? There have been many attempts to explain this.[58]

Some say it is the tetragrammaton, often pronounced *Jehovah* or *Yahweh*. Others say it is the name *Lord*, and they argue that this is the name that is above every name (CF. Phil. 2:9–11). Another view is that it is the name in verse 13, "The Word of God."[59] Others say that it is a name that the Lord will reveal to His own only when they are finally united to Him.[60] Others see a reference to the magical and occultic practices of the first century. Such people believed that to know the name of a god or demon gave one power over him. John may have meant that no one has power over this warrior king—He is supreme.[61]

I am inclined to adopt yet another view. John meant that the human mind cannot grasp the depth of Christ's being. There is a lesson here in *humility*. In spite of all the help given to us by the theologians of the church, there are unrevealed and unknowable wonders to His person that we can never fathom. Of course, by "no one" John means no created being. In Matthew 11:27 we read, "No one knows the Son, except the Father."[62] There is also a lesson here in *reverence*. We live in a day when people feel free to be familiar with the person of Christ. He's the "man upstairs," just one of the boys. This name is purposefully left in obscurity that we might remember that it is God the Son of whom we are speaking.

His Garments Will Be Covered With The Marks Of Battle (verse 13)

The Blood Of His Foes

John writes, "He is clothed with a robe dipped in blood." Some have suggested that this refers to the blood of Christ shed at the Cross.[63] However, the context, especially verse 15, shows that the Old Testament background to John's thought is Isaiah 63, and the imagery there is of the blood of Messiah's foes.[64] Others have argued that this cannot be the blood of His enemies because the battle has not yet begun.[65] They suggest that His garment bears the traces of the blood of the martyrs He will now avenge. This misunderstands the fluidity and symbolic nature of prophetic language.[66]

The Targums are translations or paraphrases of the Hebrew Bible, the Old Testament, into Aramaic (completed 5TH century AD). Some are literal, and some are interspersed with illustrative material. The Palestinian *Targum* on Genesis 49:11 reads in part, "How Beauteous is the King Messiah! Binding His loins and going forth to war against them that hate Him, He will slay kings with princes, and make the rivers red with the blood of their slain.... His garments will be dipped in blood and He Himself like the juice of the winepress."[67]

It is most likely that the blood-stained garment points in two directions: first, it points ahead in anticipation to the victory in the coming battle of Armageddon; but second, it also points back over many enemies already vanquished. Christ comes to this final great war not as a raw recruit, but as a veteran in battle. He is the One who fought for Israel in days of long ago (Isa. 51:9). He fought the kings of Canaan at Taanach (Judg. 5:19–20). He won a great victory over Satan and his host at the Cross (CF. Col. 2:15). He is the one who brought down the great powers mentioned earlier in the book (Rev. 17:10; CF. Dan. 2:21). So He comes in the same garment worn and stained on many battlefields, and He comes in the same invincible power.[68]

The Means Of His Victory

John then mentions the third name of the warrior in this same passage. "His name is called The Word of God." Here John clearly identifies the victorious and returning Christ with Jesus of Nazareth who, in John chapter 1, is called "the Word." In that passage John tells his readers (v. 1, 14) that the Word is God the Son and that He became flesh, that He took human nature. Thus, as "the Word," Christ expresses God in His being.[69]

Words reveal what is on our minds. Thus, Christ reveals the mind of God in His life and teaching (CF. John 1:18). And He is the agent of the divine will in creation (John 1:3) and, as here, in judgment.[70]

The Hebrew idea of a word is very interesting. A word is not lifeless sound but an active agent; it does things. It achieves the intention of the one who speaks. For example, when Isaac gives Esau's blessing to Jacob, he cannot take the blessing back (Gen. 27).[71] Now if a human word is charged with power, how much more a word from God! When God spoke, the universe was created (Gen. 1). Christ is the Word through whom God made the universe (John 1:3), and, in this passage, Messiah is the Word through whom God will bring judgment.

In one of the books of the Apocrypha (Wisdom of Solomon 18:15, 1ST century BC) there is a similar description. It says, "Thy all-powerful word leaped from heaven, from the royal throne, into the midst of the land that was doomed, a stern warrior carrying the sharp sword of thy authentic command."

HE WILL BE ACCOMPANIED BY A CELESTIAL ARMY OF THE SAINTS
(VERSE 14)

THE IDENTITY OF THE ARMY

The royal commander, says Swete, is "followed by a dazzling retinue."[72] Who are the "armies which are in heaven" that follow Christ? Most,[73] perhaps, say that this is the angelic host. It is certainly true that other New Testament passages say that the angels wait upon Christ at His coming (CF. Matt. 25:31; Mark 13:27; 2 Thess. 1:7–8). The apostle Paul, for example, says that "the Lord Jesus shall be revealed from heaven with His mighty angels in flaming fire." There is no doubt that angels will accompany Christ at His coming.

However, in this passage it is clear that the armies are the glorified church[74] for two reasons: In Revelation 17:14 the Lamb goes to war with an army identified as "the called and chosen and faithful."[75] Furthermore, just a few verses above our text (in v. 8) the bride is dressed in "fine linen bright and clean"—in the same clothing as this army. Those who have been Christ's companions in His rejection now accompany Him at the judgment.[76]

THE DESCRIPTION OF THE ARMY

In the description of the cavalry that accompanies the warrior king we should note that their clothing is "white and clean." Their garments are not "dipped in blood" (CF. v. 13). They do not wear armor, nor do they carry weapons; they are still wearing the apparel of festivity; they are on their way to a wedding feast![77] On their way they are going to watch their commander single-handedly engage in mortal combat. The victory against evil will be won by Him alone.[78]

His Mission Will Be The Extirpation Of All Evil (verse 15)

The Quotation Of Isaiah 49:2[79]

The judgment of Christ is now depicted by four figures all drawn from Old Testament Messianic passages. First, John alludes to Isaiah 49:2, "And He has made my mouth like a sharp sword."[80] In its Old Testament setting the prophet speaks of the Messiah as the true or ideal Israel.[81] Israel's task was to be the means by which the nations could come to God, but she had become a blind, deaf, and rebellious nation unable to show anyone else the way. God did not destroy Israel, but He devised another way whereby Israel's servanthood could be worked out—through Jesus Christ who would effectively do what the nation had failed to do.[82] In the present context it is obvious that part of Messiah's role is to wage war against God's enemies and bring them physical harm and death.[83]

The Quotation Of Isaiah 11:4

Then there is the echo of Isaiah 11:4. The prophet writes, "And He will strike the earth with the rod of His mouth." In the Old Testament context Isaiah speaks of Messiah who will "usher in a reign of safety and security to which the weary exiles may come streaming in return."[84] In Revelation 19:15 we are told that Isaiah looked to the future return of Christ when God's enemies would be defeated.

This should alert us to the fact that the final battle will not be a prolonged affair with Christ using military weapons against the forces of Antichrist. That Antichrist and the nations will have military weapons cannot be doubted. But Messiah need only speak, and they will be destroyed.

When Jesus is confronted by Judas and the Roman cohort at Gethsemane, He asks them, "Whom do you seek?" They reply, "Jesus the Nazarene." He responds, "I am He," and they fall to the ground (John 18:4–5). If such a mild utterance had that effect, what will it be like when Christ arms Himself for the "war of the great day of God, the Almighty" (Rev. 16:14)?[85]

THE QUOTATION OF PSALM 2:9

This is followed by a citation from Psalm 2:9. The psalmist writes, "Thou shalt break them with a rod of iron."[86] The picture is of a shepherd who guards His flock by destroying the predators that would harm it. The psalmist is speaking of the great warrior-Messiah who would destroy the rebellious nations at His coming. God "has appointed the dominion of the world to His Son.... This authority...is most terrible for the rebellious ones.... For these His scepter of dominion (Ps. 110:2) becomes a rod of iron, which will shatter them into a thousand pieces like a brittle image of clay (Jer. 19:11)."[87]

The Quotation Of Isaiah 63:3

Finally, John alludes to Isaiah 63:3, "I have trodden the wine trough alone…. I also trod them in my anger, and trampled them in My wrath." The figure of speech combines both the biblical imagery of battle and the region from which the warrior comes, a region famous for its viticulture.[88] The picture is adopted by John and is powerful and graphic. Christ is the vintner, the winemaker, and His enemies are the grapes that are crushed in His fury.[89] Any view of God which eliminates His judgment and hatred of sin emasculates the witness of the Bible.[90]

The man of the world has many answers to the problems confronting society. For some the answer is progress, growth and development. All that man needs is time and solutions will come, for he has the tools of education, science, and democracy. For others the answer is found in various religious systems and the development of spiritual forces. The Bible repudiates all human answers. The solution to the problem of evil in the world is not through some sort of improvement or development of the present order. The solution is the complete rooting up and throwing over of the present order.

When the army of Julian the Apostate (AD332–63) was on the march to Persia, some of his soldiers were tormenting and torturing a Christian believer. Tiring of their brutal games, they looked down on their victim and asked him with unconcealed scorn, "Where now is your Carpenter-God?" The man looked up at them through his bloodied eyes and answered, "He is making a coffin for your emperor."[91]

Yes, for every God-defying person and power and ideologue, for all that exalts itself against God and His word, the coffin is now being prepared. When Christ comes as conqueror, He shall pronounce the divine doom upon our wicked civilization and all forms of cruelty and lust, and upon all enemies of God and righteousness.

He Will Come Back To Earth In Great Majesty (verse 16)

The Display Of His Name

The paragraph closes with one final glimpse of the Divine Warrior and His heavenly horsemen as they sweep downward from heaven and onward against the armies of the Beast. As they thunder along their garments stream behind them and on the leader John sees the name displayed KING OF KINGS, AND LORD OF LORDS. The name appears to be embroidered on His robe and inscribed on his thigh.[92] In antiquity the titles and signs of kingship were often inscribed on a monarch's limbs. Christ bears on His garment and on His person the sign of universal sovereignty.[93]

THE SIGNIFICANCE OF HIS NAME

When Jesus Christ returns it will be with the authority and right to punish rebels and evildoers. For centuries the government of this world has been in other hands. Daniel the prophet (chapter 7) affirms that Beasts have held the sword and reigned. At the end they will confederate with hell to oppose Christ. Dreadful miscalculation! The Lion of the tribe of Judah comes to meet them, and He is armed to enforce His rights as sole king of the earth.

Many years ago (1927) at the annual exhibition of the Royal Academy in London, Charles E. Butler unveiled his now famous painting, "King of Kings." It pictures the Lord Jesus Christ standing at the foot of His cross and receiving the homage of the crowned heads of the world. Some 158 portraits are included on the canvas. Louis the Ninth of France offers His crown. Constantine the Roman emperor kneels before Him. Julius Caesar, Richard the Lion Hearted, and Napoleon Bonaparte are all in the worshipping throng.[94] If painting such a scene today we would include the portraits of Hitler, Stalin, and Mao Tse Tung. We would add Winston Churchill, Franklin D. Roosevelt, John F. Kennedy, Richard M. Nixon, Ronald Reagan, Bill Clinton, and George W. Bush.

This painting will be fulfilled in the future at the return of Christ when every knee shall bow to Him (CF. Phil. 2:9–11). The picture is not true in one sense. Not all kings will bow to Christ in glad belief. All will bow the knee—some in glad surrender, but some because they are forced to do so against their hardened wills.

Conclusion

The doctrine of the Second Coming is the historic faith of the Christian church. We must not join the conspiracy of silence in the churches and neglect this doctrine. Yes, there is too much sensationalism on the subject of Biblical prophecy in some quarters. As Reinhold Niebuhr wrote, "It is unwise for Christians to claim any knowledge of either the furniture of heaven or the temperature of hell; or to be too certain of any details of the Kingdom of God in which history is consummated."[95] That is a valid warning. But there is much in the Revelation that is clear and about that we must clearly speak out.

There is a day coming when Jesus Christ is going to return to earth to root out and destroy all evil. This should fill every heart with the fear and reverence of God. There is one group of people who do not need to fear that judgment—that is the group of people who are portrayed here in white garments. They are the church, the bride of Christ, those who have confessed their sins to Him and embraced Him as Savior, accepting the forgiveness that He offers to all.

For Christians, then, there are three brief lessons:

THE NEED TO BE FAITHFUL

After the fall of Atlanta in July 1864, General John B. Hood, the commander of the Confederate army, marched westward to attack the communications of General Sherman with Chattanooga and Nashville. He hoped to draw Sherman's army from Georgia. One of the posts he attacked was Allatoona Pass, commanded by the brave and capable General Corse. Sherman himself went back with part of his army as far as Kenesaw Mountain. From the summit of the mountain he signaled to the beleaguered garrison at Elation Pass, "Hold the fort! I am coming!"

In Sherman's army at the time was a Major Whittle, who was an evangelical Christian. He related this incident to the hymn writer P.P. Bliss, who was inspired to write,

> Hold the fort, for I am coming,
> Jesus signals still;
> Wave the answer back to heaven,
> By Thy grace we will.[96]

THE NEED TO BE WATCHFUL

Canon J. E. Fison once remarked that the second coming of Christ is "a moral stimulant, not a moral narcotic." In similar fashion English Bible teacher A. Skevington Wood said that the study of the events surrounding the second coming of Christ should change the believer's life. "Our enthusiasm for the prospect of Christ's appearing is proved spurious unless it issues in purity of character."[97] Believers should be able to reverently say with John, "Come, Lord Jesus" (Rev. 22:20). They need to heed His admonition, "Be on the alert, for you do not know which day your Lord is coming" (Matt. 24:42).

THE NEED TO BE WORSHIPFUL

In this passage four names are applied to our Lord: First, He is "Faithful and True" (v. 11). He can be trusted to fulfill all His promises; He is a true object of worship in contrast to all the false gods of our time. Second, He has "a Name … which no one knows," (v. 12). This is a reminder of the fathomless wonders of His person. Third, He is called, "the Word of God," (v. 13). He is the One who created the universe; He is the One who will judge it. Finally, He is called KING OF KINGS, AND LORD OF LORDS (v. 16). He is the One who will rule over the kingdom of God during the millennial age.

One day He will reign as "King of kings and Lord of lords." Believers should make Him that today in their own hearts.

Jack Hayford and his wife Anna were vacationing in Britain during the 25TH anniversary of the coronation of Elizabeth II. While there, they saw constant reminders of royalty. Hayford began to think of what it would be like to live in such regal settings and asked his wife to write down these words, "Majesty, worship His majesty. Unto Jesus be all glory, power, and praise." How should Christian believers respond? Jack Hayford's song suggests that we are to "exalt, lift up on high the name of Jesus." Each day and in all that we do we are to "glorify Christ Jesus the King."[98]

NOTES

[1]For this description I am indebted to Clarence E. Macartney, "Behold, A White Horse," in *Classic Sermons on the Second Coming*, ed. Warren W. Wiersbe (Grand Rapids: Kregel, 1992), 73–74.

[2]Charles R. Taylor, *Watch 1988! The Year of Climax* (Huntington Beach: Today in Bible Prophecy, 1988); cf. Rodney Clapp, "Overdosing on the Apocalypse," *Christianity Today* (Oct. 28, 1991), 26. Cf. also Harold Camping, *1994?* as reported in "End–time Prediction Draws Strong Following," *Christianity Today* (June 20, 1994), 46–47.

[3]The silence of many pulpits on the subject of the second coming of Christ is often due to the intellectual apostasy of much modern scholarship. Marcus Borg, a self-styled "mainline" biblical scholar, argues that the New Testament does not speak about the second coming "in our time or at *any* future time." See "Thinking About the Second Coming," *Bible Review* 10 (August, 1994), 16, 55.

[4]For this account and much of my introduction I am indebted to A. Skevington Wood, *Prophecy in the Space Age* (Grand Rapids: Zondervan, 1963), 27–31.

[5]George Eldon Ladd, *A Commentary on the Revelation* (Grand Rapids: Eerdmans, 1972), 252–53.

[6]Hanns Lilje, *The Last Book of the Bible*, trans. Olive Wyon (Philadelphia: Muhlenberg, 1957), 244.

[7]Ladd, *A Commentary on the Revelation of John*, 252.

[8]For a number of the following examples I am indebted to Wood, *Prophecy in the Space Age*, 28–29 and William F. Kerr, "The Lord's Return in Patristic Literature," in *Understanding the Times*, eds. W. Culbertson and H. B. Centz (Grand Rapids: Zondervan, 1956), 90–91.

[9]*The Epistle of Barnabas* 15.5, in *The Apostolic Fathers*, 2 vols., trans. Kirsopp Lake, The Loeb Classical Library (Cambridge: Harvard University Press, 1912), 1:395.

[10]*1 Clement* 34.2–3, in *The Apostolic Fathers*, 1:65.

[11]Justin Martyr, *The First Apology* 51, in *The Ante-Nicene Fathers*, vol. 1, eds. Alexander Roberts and James Donaldson, trans. A. Cleveland Coxe (1885; reprint ed., Grand Rapids: Eerdmans, 1967), 180.

[12]*Oxford Dictionary of the Christian Church*, see "Irenaeus," 713.

[13]Irenaeus, *Against Heresies* 5.30.4, in *The Ante-Nicene Fathers*, 1:560.

[14]Tertullian, *Against Marcion* 3.25, in *The Ante-Nicene Fathers*, 3:343.

[15]Martin Luther, *Table Talk*, quoted by Hugh T. Kerr, ed., *A Compend of Luther's Theology* (2ND. ed., Philadelphia: Westminster, 1966), 244.

[16]*Conversations with Luther*, quoted by Kerr, *Compend of Luther's Theology*, 244.

[17]Alber and Herman quoted by Paul Althaus, *The Theology of Martin Luther*, trans. Robert C. Schultz (Philadelphia: Fortress, 1966), 422.

[18]John Calvin, *Institutes of the Christian Religion* 2.16.17, 2 vols., trans. Ford Lewis Battles (Philadelphia: Westminster, 1960), 1:525.

[19] *The Apostles' Creed*, in *The Creeds of Christendom*, 3 vols., ed. Philip Schaff (4th ed., New York: Harper, 1884; reprint ed., Grand Rapids: Baker, 1977), 1: 21. The present text of the *Apostles' Creed* is not earlier than the 5TH or 6TH centuries, but the kernel of its teaching goes back to the apostolic church (Schaff, 1:19–20).

[20] *The Nicene Creed*, in *The Creeds of Christendom*, 1:28. The original *Nicene Creed*, containing the words quoted above, dates from the Council of Nicea in AD325.

[21] *The Augsburg Confession*, Article 17, in *The Creeds of Christendom*, 3:17.

[22] *The Belgic Confession*, Article 37, in *The Creeds of Christendom*, 3:433–34. During a visit to Scotland in the summer of 1993, I was crossing a busy street and the light at the cross walk changed when I was half way across. An oncoming bus had the light timed perfectly, and the driver did not seem to care that pedestrians were still crossing. He almost ran some of them down. My guide, Jim Bertram, said, "Watch it lad, in Glasgow there are only two kinds of pedestrians: the quick and the dead!"

[23] *The Westminster Confession* , Chapter 8.4, in *The Creeds of Christendom*, 3: 620–21. Cf. also Chapter 33.3, p. 672–73.

[24] *The Thirty Nine Articles of the Church of England*, Article 4, in *The Creeds of Christendom*, 3:489. The above quotation is from the American revision of 1801.

[25] *The Declaration of the Congregational Union of England and Wales*, Principle 19, in *The Creeds of Christendom*, 3:733.

[26] *The New Hampshire Baptist Confession*, Article 18, in *The Creeds of Christendom*, 3:748.

[27] Wood, *Prophecy in the Space Age*, 29.

[28] Stephen Travis, *I Believe in the Second Coming of Jesus* (Grand Rapids: Eerdmans, 1982), 106–9.

[29]Remarkably, this is denied in the exposition by David Chilton, *The Days of Vengeance* (Ft. Worth: Dominion Press, 1987), 485–86. Following Swete, he argues that the passage describes the expansion of Christianity and conversion of the Western nations subsequent to the Fall of Jerusalem in AD70. Cf. Henry Barclay Swete, *The Apocalypse of St. John* (London: Macmillan, 1906), 250–51.

[30]For example, Alexander Reese, *The Approaching Advent of Christ* (London: Marshall, Morgan & Scott, 1937); George E. Ladd, *The Blessed Hope* (Grand Rapids: Eerdmans, 1956); Robert H. Gundry, *The Church and the Tribulation* (Grand Rapids: Zondervan, 1973).

[31]Citing, for example, Rev. 11:12–19 or 14:14.

[32]For example, Norman B. Harrison, *The End: Rethinking the Revelation* (Minneapolis: Harrison, 1941), 109–18, 231–33; J. Oliver Buswell, *A Systematic Theology of the Christian Religion*, 2 vols. (Grand Rapids: Zondervan, 1962), 2: 397; Gleason L. Archer, Jr., "The Case for the Mid–Seventieth Week Rapture Position," in *The Rapture*, by G. L. Archer, P. D. Feinberg, D. J. Moo, and R. R. Reiter (Grand Rapids: Zondervan, 1984), 115–45].

[33]For example, J. Dwight Pentecost, *Things to Come* (Grand Rapids: Dunham, 1958), 193–218; John A. Sproule, *In Defense of Pre-Tribulationism* (Winona Lake: BMH, 1980); Paul D. Feinberg, "The Case for the Pretribulation Rapture Position," in *The Rapture*, 45–86. For a survey of the main positions, see *The Rapture*, written by members of the Trinity Evangelical School faculty.

[34]William Barclay, *The Revelation of John*, 2 vols. (rev. ed., Philadelphia: Westminster Press, 1976), 2:177.

[35]Joseph Seiss, *Lectures on the Apocalypse*, 3 vols. (9TH ed., New York: Charles C. Cook, 1906), 3:288.

[36]R. H. Charles, *The Revelation of St. John*, 2 vols., International Critical Commentary (Edinburgh: T. & T. Clark, 1920), 2:131.

[37]*International Standard Bible Encyclopedia*, see "Horse," by D. F. Morgan, 2 (1982), 759–60.

[38]Kelly writes, "None, I trust, would be so foolish as to imagine that, when this blessed scene really comes, it will be a question of horses literally. It is the symbol that passed before the eye of the prophet." As Beasley-Murray has it, "There is no cavalry kept in heaven." Johnson points out that although the horse is not one that might be entered in the Kentucky Derby, the apostle is, nevertheless, describing a literal, historical event. See William Kelly, *Lectures on the Book of the Revelation* (rev. ed., London: G. Morrish, 1874), 399; G. R. Beasley-Murray, *The Book of Revelation* (London: Oliphants, 1974), 278; S. Lewis Johnson, Jr. *The Old Testament in the New* (Grand Rapids: Zondervan, 1980), 13. Incidentally, Seiss (3:249–50) does argue for literal horses in this paragraph (v. 11, 14), as does Thomas. See Robert L. Thomas, *Revelation 8–22: An Exegetical Commentary* (Chicago: Moody, 1995), 387–88. Writes Thomas, "These are real armies and horses....The origin of the horses need not create a problem as they conceivably are a special creation of 'the Word of God' for the purposes of this occasion. A literal understanding of them is in order just as a literal meaning for the other features in this sequence."

[39]Cf. *International Standard Bible Encyclopedia*, see "Ass," by R. K. Harrison, 1 (1979), 330.

[40]George MacDonald, "That Holy Thing," in *The Gifts of the Christ Child*, 2 vols., ed. Glenn Edward Sadler (Grand Rapids: Eerdmans, 1973), 2:261.

[41]Cf. Swete, *The Apocalypse of St. John*, 247.

[42]Barclay, *The Revelation of John*, 2:178. Tenney writes, "The symbolism follows the pattern of a Roman triumphal procession. When a general returned from a successful campaign, he and his legions were granted the right to parade up the Via Sacra, the main street of Rome that led from the Forum to the Temple of Jupiter on the Capitoline Hill. Mounted on a white horse, the general rode at the head of his troops, followed by the wagonloads of booty that he had taken from the conquered nations, and by the chained captives that were to be executed or sold in the slave markets of the city. The chief captives or rebels were remanded to the Mamertine prison, where they were usually executed, while sacrifices of thanksgiving were offered in the temple." See Merrill C. Tenney, *The Book of Revelation*, Proclaiming the New Testament (Grand Rapids: Baker, 1963), 94.

[43]Swete, *The Apocalypse of St. John*, 248.

[44]Swete, *The Apocalypse of St. John*, 247.

[45]Ladd, *A Commentary on the Revelation of John*, 253.

[46]Robert H. Mounce, *The Book of Revelation*, New International Commentary on the New Testament (rev. ed., Grand Rapids: Eerdmans, 1998), 352.

[47]*Theological Dictionary of the New Testament*, see "ἀληθινός," by R. Bultmann, 1 (1964), 249.

[48]Macartney, "Behold, a White Horse," 76.

[49]William G. T. Shedd, *Dogmatic Theology*, 3 vols. (Edinburgh: T. & T. Clark, 1889; reprint ed., Grand Rapids: Zondervan, N.D.), 1:365.

[50]Gregory L. Fisher, "To Illustrate," *Leadership* 12 (Fall, 1991), 45. Careful students will note that Fisher's text (1 Thess. 4:13–18) deals with the rapture and not the Second Advent to the earth. In light of the context in 1 Thessalonians 4 (rapture, resurrection), it is more likely that our Lord will shout, "Come up here"(Rev. 4:1), or "Come forth" (John 11:43). Yet with regard to the passage at hand (Rev. 19:11–16), Fisher's point is well taken. Christ will return to the earth to judge all that is evil.

[51]Beasley-Murray, *The Book of Revelation*, 279; Mounce, *The Book of Revelation*, 353.

[52]Ladd, *A Commentary on the Revelation of John* , 254.

[53]Martin Kiddle, *The Revelation of St. John*, Moffatt New Testament Commentary (New York: Harper, 1940), 384.

[54]*New International Dictionary of New Testament Theology*, see "Crown," by C. J. Hemer, 1:405–6. The στέφανος (wreath, often worked in gold) played its part in many ancient customs, and bore diverse connotations of victory, festivity, worship, kingship, and royal visitation. The view that στέφανος could never be used of kingship is overstated.

[55]Swete, *The Apocalypse of St. John*, 248.

[56]Seiss, *Lectures on the Apocalypse*, 3:243.

[57]Swete, *The Apocalypse of St. John*, 248.

[58]Cf. the discussions in Charles, *The Revelation of St. John*, 2:132–33 and Barclay, *The Revelation of John*, 2:179–80.

[59]E.G., Albert Barnes, *Notes on the New Testament: Revelation* (1851; reprint ed., Grand Rapids: Baker, 1972), 412–13.

[60]E.G., Henry Alford, *The Greek Testament*, 4 vols., vol. 4: *Hebrews–Revelation* (reprint ed., Chicago: Moody, 1958), 727; CF. A. R. Fausset, "1 Corinthians–Revelation," in *A Commentary Critical, Experimental and Practical on the Old and New Testaments*, eds. R. Jamieson, A.R. Fausset, and D. Brown (reprint ed., Grand Rapids: Eerdmans, 1967), 6:719.

[61]Leon Morris, *The Revelation of St. John*, Tyndale New Testament Commentaries (Grand Rapids: Eerdmans, 1969), 230; cf. Isbon T. Beckwith, *The Apocalypse of John* (New York: Macmillan, 1919; reprint ed., Grand Rapids: Baker, 1979), 463, 732–33; Charles, *The Revelation of St. John*, 2:132–33. As Mounce (*The Book of Revelation*, 353) observes, however, it is highly unlikely that this returning warrior king would fear any power, human or demonic.

[62]Swete, *The Apocalypse of St. John*, 248; CF. Beasley-Murray, *The Book of Revelation*, 280.

[63]E.G., Swete, *The Apocalypse of St. John*, 249; Morris, *The Revelation of St. John*, 230. For a view even further removed from the context, see J. Massyngberde Ford, *Revelation*, Anchor Bible (New York: Doubleday, 1975), 313, 320–21. She sees the rider as the priestly Messiah with blood upon His garments from the sacrifice He offers.

[64]Beasley-Murray, *The Book of Revelation*, 280. Walvoord writes, "Christ as the slain lamb in Revelation [5:6] speaks of redemption by blood; here blood represents divine judgment upon wicked men." See also John F. Walvoord, *The Revelation of Jesus Christ* (Chicago: Moody, 1966), 277.

[65]E.G., G. B. Caird, *The Revelation of St. John the Divine*, Harper New Testament Commentary (New York: Harper, 1966), 242–44.

[66]Ladd, *A Commentary on the Revelation of John*, 255; Mounce, *The Book of Revelation,* 354.

[67]Quoted by Mounce, *The Book of Revelation*, 354.

[68]Seiss, *Lectures on the Apocalypse*, 3:245.

[69]Walter Scott, *Exposition of the Revelation of Jesus Christ* (4TH ed., London: Pickering & Inglis, N.D.), 387.

[70]Philip Edgcumbe Hughes, *The Book of the Revelation* (Grand Rapids: Eerdmans, 1990), 204. Tenney (*The Book of Revelation*, 97) writes, "Because He embodies the revelation of God to men, He must express God's severity as well as His goodness."

[71]Mounce, *The Book of Revelation*, 354; CF. Barclay, *The Revelation of John*, 2: 181.

[72]Swete, *The Apocalypse of St. John*, 246.

[73]E.G., Swete, *The Apocalypse of St. John*, 250; Morris, *The Revelation of St. John*, 231; Beasley-Murray, *The Book of Revelation*, 281; Ladd, *A Commentary on the Revelation of John*, 255.

[74]Some would argue that the army includes both the angels and the church. CF. Walvoord, *The Revelation of Jesus Christ*, 277.

[75]CF. Caird, *The Revelation of St. John the Divine*, 244.

[76]Part of the difficulty for some commentators is that they believe that the church is still on earth awaiting Christ's coming at this point. There is no problem, however, if we see that the church has been translated and in heaven since chapter 4. CF. Kelly, *Lectures on the Book of Revelation*, 403.

[77]Beasley-Murray, *The Book of Revelation*, 281.

[78]Morris, *The Revelation of St. John*, 231. "They wear no armor because, being immortal, they are immune to injury. They are noncombatant supporters

of the Messiah as He wages war single-handedly" (Thomas, *Revelation 8–22*, 387).

[79]John's citations of these Old Testament texts demonstrates His own conviction as well as the prophets' conviction that God is sovereign and omniscient. Curiously this has been denied by Clark Pinnock, a professing evangelical Christian. He asserts that predictive prophecy does not prove that God knows everything about the future. A high percentage of predictive prophecy, he suggests, can be accounted for by one of three factors: (1) The announcement ahead of time of what God intends to do, (2) conditional prophecies which leave the outcome open, and (3) predictions based on God's exhaustive knowledge of the past and the present. In response I would argue that Pinnock's statements are merely assertions. Classical theism, which Pinnock would reject, has always affirmed that: (1) God is sovereign and will fulfill His promises and judgments (Eph. 1:11). If He tells man what He intends to do, will it not be done? The precise fulfillment of prophecies relating to Christ's first advent suggest that God will do that which He announces He intends to do! (2) Pinnock gives no examples of conditional prophecies, and if he could give such they would not be prophecies. If the outcome is left open, then the outcome has not been prophesied. (3) Does not God's exhaustive knowledge of the past and present suggest that His knowledge of the future is also exhaustive? One must ask how Pinnock can be sure that God will eventually win over evil? How can it be more than a hope, or even a wish? If God is not all-powerful, all-loving, and all-knowing, then there is no such guarantee. See Clark Pinnock, "God Limits His Knowledge," in *Predestination & Free Will*, eds. David and Randall Basinger (Downers Grove: Inter Varsity Press, 1986), 157–58. See also the responses of John Feinberg and Norman Geisler to Pinnock in the same volume (p. 163–73). For another defense of classical theism, cf. Robert A. Morey, *Battle of the Gods* (Southbridge, Massachusetts: Crown Publications, 1989), 9–15 and *passim*.

[80]"All of these passages point to the sad consclusion that in the day of judgment it is too late for men to expect the mercy of God" (Walvoord, *The Revelation of Jesus Christ*, 278).

[81] William Kelly, *An Exposition of the Book of Isaiah* (Fourth ed., London: Hammond, 1947), 324.

[82] John N. Oswalt, *The Book of Isaiah, Chapters 40–66*, New International Commentary on the Old Testament (Grand Rapids: Eerdmans, 1998), 290–91.

[83] Robert L. Thomas, *Revelation 8–22: An Exegetical Commentary* (Chicago: Moody, 1995), 389.

[84] John N. Oswalt, *The Book of Isaiah, Chapters 1–39*, New International Commentary on the Old Testament (Grand Rapids: Eerdmans, 1986), 277. Oswalt (289), following other commentators, notes that the phrase "from the body of my mother" argues strongly against identifying the servant as the collective nation.

[85] Seiss, *Lectures on the Apocalypse*, 3:246.

[86] The NASB and NIV have "rule" reflecting the Greek ποιμανεῖ ("shepherd," NASB mg.). The Masoretic text has תְּרֹעַ ("break") while the LXX read the verb as תִּרְעֵ ("you shall shepherd"), the only difference being in the vowels. It is evident that both the LXX and John understand the verb in the sense of shepherding by guarding the flock from its enemies. CF. Johnson, *The Old Testament in the New*, 15–19.

[87] Franz Delitzsch, *Biblical Commentary on the Psalms*, 3 vols., trans. Francis Bolton (Edinburgh: T. & T. Clark, 1871), 1:96.

[88] Oswalt, *The Book of Isaiah, Chapters 40–66*, 597. As Oswalt notes, Messiah's answer to the question in Isa. 63:2 stresses four things: (1) the imagery of the wine press, v. 3, 6; (2) the motive of anger, v. 3, 6; (3) the fact that the work was done without assistance, v. 3, 5; and (4) the purpose of redemption.

[89] Kiddle, *The Revelation of St. John*, 384. John evidently changes his metaphor from 14:10 where the followers of the Beast are not crushed like grapes but are made to drink "the wine of the wrath of God." In 19:15 the two ideas of the winepress and the cup are combined. CF. Charles, *The Revelation of St. John*, 2:137.

[90] CF. Mounce, *The Book of Revelation*, 356.

[91] Macartney, "Behold, a White Horse," 80.

[92] CF. Charles, *The Revelation of St. John*, 2:137; Beasley-Murray, *The Book of Revelation*, 281–82; Morris, *The Revelation of St. John*, 231–32. Commentators differ in their interpretation of the inscription. Some have suggested that the

name is inscribed on the rider's belt. Others have it displayed on his robe where it falls over the thigh. Another view is that it is inscribed on the hilt of his sword where He wore it at His side. Greek and Roman authors mention statues inscribed on the thigh with the name of the person represented.

[93]Beasley-Murray, *The Book of Revelation*, 282.

[94]Wood, *Prophecy in the Space Age*, 147–48.

[95]Reinhold Niebuhr, *The Nature and Destiny of Man*, 2 vols. (New York: Scribner's, 1943), 2:294.

[96]As told by Macartney, "Behold, a White Horse," 81. In the Fall of 1993 I watched Paul Crouch of the Trinity Broadcasting Network interview John F. Walvoord, David Breese, and others on the subject of the kingdom and eschatology. Crouch professes to be a premillennialist, but he evidently finds the triumphal "optimism" of postmillennialism attractive. He quoted the words of Bliss' hymn with disdain. Bliss' hymn, however, more accurately than postmillennialism, portrays the New Testament church as a band of pilgrims in hostile territory looking to Christ for protection and to His coming for victory.

[97] The quotations from Fison and Wood are found in A. Skevington Wood, *Prophecy in the Space Age* (Grand Rapids: Zondervan, 1963), 152–53.

[98]J.D.B., "Worship His Majesty," in *Our Daily Bread*.

◈

THE SECOND LAST THING:

THE DEFEAT OF ANTICHRIST
REVELATION 19:17–21

◈

On September 2, 1945, aboard the Battleship Missouri, the Japanese government formally surrendered to the Allied forces. After all the representatives had signed the instrument of surrender, General Douglas MacArthur (1880–1964), the Supreme Commander of the Allied Forces in the Pacific, announced, "Let us pray that peace be now restored to the world and that God will preserve it always." He then broadcast a speech to the American people. Remarkably, on that cool day in Japan, MacArthur could say, "the entire world is quietly at peace." There would be very few days thereafter in which that could be said. Today, over fifty years later, at any given time as many as forty nations are at war with one another. The general went on, "Men since the beginning of time have sought peace, [but all their attempts to secure it have only led them back to war]." He added this, "We have had our last chance. If we do not now devise some greater and more equitable system, Armageddon will be at our door."

It is General MacArthur's diagnosis of the problem, however, that is most significant. "The problem is basically theological…[and the solution] involves a spiritual… im-

◈

provement of human character."[1] From the vantage point of Scripture MacArthur was absolutely correct, although we might argue that what is needed is a radical transformation of human character. Yet the problem is a spiritual one—man is a sinner. Since the days of Cain and Abel his war-like heart has led him to war against his fellow man. Each new discovery—knives, clubs, swords, gunpowder, ships, tanks, airplanes, missiles, nuclear weapons—has been used to make war, to force one nation's designs on another or to seize their possessions. One of the earliest of all historical records, a Sumerian bas-relief from Babylon (c. 3000 BC), shows soldiers fighting in close quarter, wearing helmets and carrying shields. Wars fill the history—in fact, they are often the great defining moments—of every culture, ancient and modern—Babylon, Syria, Assyria, Egypt, Greece, Rome, Turkey, Germany, England, Russia, and America.[2]

There is a sense of hopelessness about it all in the hearts of many people. President Franklin D. Roosevelt spoke of World War II as "the war to end all wars." More recently, newspaper columnist Ellen Goodman has spoken of the future war "to end all life." Even in the relatively peaceful days of the 1950s former English Prime Minister Winston Churchill (1874–1965) asked evangelist Billy Graham, "Young man, can you give me any hope?" The late theologian and medical missionary, Dr. Albert Schweitzer

(1875–1965) lamented, "Man has lost the capacity to foresee and to forestall. He will end by destroying the earth." Pop singer and actress Barbra Streisand is reported by *Esquire* to have said, "I do believe the world is coming to an end. I just feel that science, technology, and the mind have surpassed the soul—the heart. There is no balance in terms of feeling and love for fellowman."

Harvard University Professor B.F. Skinner shocked the American Psychological Association Convention a number of years ago (1982) when he asked in anger and anguish, "Why are we not acting to save the world? Is there to be much more history at all?" After his speech, the 78 year old behaviorist was asked, "Has the observer of social conditioning lost his optimism?" He replied, "I have…. When I wrote *Beyond Freedom and Dignity*, I was optimistic about the future. A decade ago there was hope, but today the world is fatally ill…. It is a depressing way to end one's life…. The argument that we have always solved our problems in the past and shall, therefore, solve this one is like reassuring a dying man by pointing out that he has always recovered from [earlier illnesses]."[3]

How can such pessimistic remarks be biblically evaluated? First, it can be agreed that General MacArthur's diagnosis is correct: the problem is theological. Man is estranged from God. His alienation from God has led to his alienation from his fellow man. Second, the Bible reinforces, in the short term, the pessimism of people about the future. Mankind is not going to turn over a new leaf. The world as we now know it is going to continue to be sinful and violent up to the very last day.

But third, there is every reason to be optimistic in the long term for two reasons. First, God has provided a cure for the hearts of men. The apostle Peter (1 Pet. 3:18) writes, "For Christ also died for sins once for all, the just for the unjust, in order that He might bring us to God." The apostle Paul adds that, "God was in Christ reconciling the world to Himself, not counting their trespasses against them" (2 Cor. 5:19). Jesus died on the cross and bore the penalty due our sins so that God might forgive us and receive us back into fellowship with Him. Second, Jesus Christ is returning to judge all evil and establish His kingdom of peace upon the earth. The return of Jesus Christ is a source of great assurance for the Christian.

Rabbi Seymour N. Siegel, formerly Professor of Ethics and Theology at the Jewish Theological Seminary of America, has commented, "The central problem of Christianity is: If the Messiah has come, why is the world so evil? For Judaism, the problem is: If the world is so evil, why does the Messiah not come?" The passage assures us that the Messiah is coming to solve both dilemmas.

The late historian Arnold Toynbee of Cambridge University foresaw that "only a world government can save mankind from annihilation by nuclear weapons." He was right, and Jesus Christ will be the king over all the earth when He returns. Jonathan Schell, author of the book *The Fate of the Earth*, envisions a day when "existing institutions must give way to some sort of transcendent sovereignty and security, presumably by a government that embraces all mankind," in fact "world government."[4] That will happen when Christ returns.[5]

Revelation 19:17–21 describes the last and most terrible battle of human history, the battle between Christ and Antichrist. It is a battle that has already been described earlier in the Book of Revelation (14:14, 18–20; 16:13–16).[6] It is also described in the Old Testament prophecies of Isaiah (63:1–2), Ezekiel (39:17–20), Daniel (2:34, 45; 7:11; 9:27; 11: 40–45), Joel (3), and Zechariah (14:1–5).

Revelation chapters 6–19, which describe a yet future time of tribulation (CF. 7:14) upon the earth, provide the background of the events described in the passage under consideration. During that time of tribulation a notable, charismatic political figure will appear on the world stage for a brief time and shall gain world-wide influence and dominion (CF. 13: 7). He will provide the one-world government that many crave today. Revelation 13 clearly states that this man will be inspired by and empowered by Satan himself. He is called the "Beast...out of the sea" (13:1) or the "Antichrist" (CF. 1 John 4:3). Although he himself is probably an atheist (CF. Dan. 11:37), his government, aided by another figure—the "Beast...out of the earth" (Rev. 13:11) or the "false prophet" (19:20)—will follow the example of all previous world dictatorships and deify the world dictator.

The reign of Antichrist will prove to be a reign of terror against both messianic Judaism and gentile Christianity. He will impose a seven-year peace treaty on the Middle East, and for a short period of three and one-half years Israel will enjoy a false sense of security. After three and one-half years, however, he will break the treaty and persecute the nation (CF. Dan. 9:27). His reign will last seven years, a time of great bloodshed and natural calamities.

Just before the events described in this passage the Antichrist has been crushing the last pockets of rebellion in North Africa and Babylon. His armies, numbering in the millions, have gathered at a great staging area called Armageddon. From there they head south to Jerusalem. The final battle against Israel comes as the nations gather at the Valley of Jehoshaphat, today called the Kidron Valley, that runs on the east side of Jerusalem.[7]

The "big idea" of our text here is that the return of Christ constitutes the conclusion of all warfare against Messiah and His people by Antichrist and the antichristian world.[8]

THE INVITATION TO THE FEAST: THE VULTURES ARE SUMMONED TO THE GREAT SUPPER OF GOD (VERSES 17–18)

THE SUMMONS BY THE ANGEL (VERSE 17)

In verse 11 the heavens opened to reveal Jesus Christ, the warrior king, and His armies about to engage in battle. Now John sees "an angel standing in the sun." The thought is twofold. First, he is standing in the highest point in the sky where all the birds can see and hear him.[9] Second, he stands in the place of splendor to herald a great victory.[10] He is about to announce the dawn of a new day, the day of God.[11] The *civitas diaboli*, the city of the devil, is about to fall. The *civitas Dei*, the city of God, is about to be established. With a loud voice the angel summons "all the birds which fly in midheaven" to assemble for a feast. Most assume that it is carrion eaters such as vultures that are invited since they are summoned to eat corpses on the ground.

Modern readers are inclined to view vultures as unpleasant because they are associated with death. To ancient man, however, they had a noble function. With incredible swiftness a vulture would discover and make its way to its prey.[12] There was no need for a sanitary inspector in the desert to make provision for the disposal of corpses; that could safely be left to the vultures.[13]

The vultures are invited to "the great supper of God." This supper is "a terrible counterpart to the marriage supper of the Lamb"[14] in verse 9. Jesus tells a parable of a big dinner to which all were invited (Luke 14:16–24), and that dinner is a picture of the kingdom of heaven. For two thousand years men and women have been invited to come; many have accepted the invitation, but many have refused. That feast and the wedding supper of Revelation 19 picture the same thing, a supper of joy. The supper in verse 17, however, is not a supper of joy but a supper of judgment.

THE NIGHTMARE FEAST OF GOD (VERSE 18)

Verse 18 provides the menu of this "nightmare feast"[15] of God. One writer calls it a "gory supper,"[16] and another calls it a "revolting scene."[17] One of the older commentators puts it quaintly, "At ordinary banquets men eat the flesh of birds; here, the birds are to eat the flesh of men."[18] John sees a great battlefield strewn with the corpses of a great army that included many nations. His description is borrowed from the prophecy of Ezekiel 39:17–20. Every kind of person, every rank of human being, is represented on the field: the politically powerful and the politically powerless, the important and the unimportant. The field is piled high with the dead, "a great repast spread by the hand of God."[19] The text implies that all the armies that followed the Beast will be destroyed.[20] At the end there seems to be a complete division of the human race into two groups, namely those who have embraced Christ and those who fight for Antichrist. The unbelievers who are in his army will be destroyed by the returning Christ.[21]

The well known liberal commentator, William Barclay, says, "This bloodthirsty picture is…far more in line with Old Testament apocalyptic expectations than with the gospel of Jesus Christ."[22] It is a terrible misunderstanding on Professor Barclay's part to try and sever the Old Testament from the New. Many people have the false notion that Jesus Christ is completely different from the God of the Old Testament. They think that when Jesus appeared God changed His mind and decided to be a gentleman and forgot all His thoughts of judgment. It is a terrible folly to be misled by such ideas. Yes, there is good news: one need not bear the punishment for his own sins—another, the Lord Jesus Christ, has paid the price in our behalf. But there is bad news for those who reject Christ, and it is described in our text. When He comes again to this earth it will be to judge His enemies.[23]

In any case, the corpses lie unburied on the field. It was considered a great dishonor by the ancients to leave an enemy unburied on the field.[24] Some three and one-half years earlier, in the middle of the tribulation, two bold witnesses for Christ will have been assassinated by the Beast.

Their bodies will have been allowed to lie in the streets of Jerusalem (Rev. 11:8–10) where they are vilified. Now the Beast's own followers lie in defeat and disgrace, a meal for vultures.

THE PRELUDE TO THE FEAST: THE MESSIAH IS VICTORIOUS AT THE GREAT BATTLE OF ARMAGEDDON (VERSES 19–21)

THE ASSEMBLING OF THE ARMIES (VERSE 19)

At this point John's attention is drawn to the events that immediately precede this terrible supper of God. He sees the Beast and the kings of the earth gathered to make war on Christ and His army. He says they are "assembled" to make war against the rider on the white horse. It might be asked, "How could such an army be assembled to make war on Christ?" How could rational men join together as one to attempt anything so absurd? There are two valid explanations, one demonic and one divine.

The first answer is demonic. In Revelation 16:13–16 John speaks of "spirits of demons, performing signs, which go out to the kings of the whole world to gather them together for the war of the great day of God, the Almighty." No Caesar, Napoleon, Hitler or U.S. President could bring about such a vast combination for such a purpose. It is clearly stated that Satan is behind the movement.[25]

The second explanation is divine. In 2 Thessalonians 2: 8–12 the apostle Paul speaks of a "deluding influence" sent by God to blind the followers of Antichrist.[26] Modern autonomous man does not believe in a sovereign God who controls world affairs, nor does he believe in a God who judges sin and rebellion in His creatures. The inspired authors of the New Testament do not share that unbelief. In the end, the sovereign Judge of the universe uses demonic delusion and human folly to inflict His judgment on the world. "God cannot remain passive toward active evil. Sin must be punished in a moral universe."[27]

Can it be that our modern civilized world will really follow Antichrist against the Lord? H.B. Swete, the noted biblical commentator, once said, "Those who take note of the tendencies of modern civilization will not find it impossible to conceive that a time may come when throughout Christendom the spirit of Antichrist will, with the support of the State, make a final stand against a Christianity which is loyal to the person and teaching of Christ."[28]

Whenever great nations go to war their rulers and generals evaluate the "chances of war."[29] No one starts a war thinking he will lose. He knows there are risks, yet he thinks the odds are in his favor. In the 1880s, when England was still an empire and Lord Salisbury was prime minister, a sultan somewhere in Africa committed an unspeakable offense against the British crown. Lord Salisbury summoned Captain Hornsby of the Royal Navy, instructing him to sail up the river and deliver to the sultan a stern remonstrance. Either the sultan ceased and desisted or Her Majesty's government would take important action.

The captain asked what he was to do if the sultan refused to accede to the ultimatum. Lord Salisbury considered the question, and then, mumbling in the approved diplomatic manner, said, "Well, yes, of course…well, you'll have to steam away, won't you?" The captain took his gunboat to Africa and proceeded upriver to the sultan's compound. Knowing that if the sultan resorted to a test of arms he had no hope of victory, the captain made a show of noisily running out his guns. He went ashore with as much pomp as he could muster, attended by flags, drums, and smartly dressed marines.

The sultan listened politely to the sermon from London. "And what happens, Captain," he said, "if I reject this singularly insolent communication?" The captain bowed and calmly placed his hand on the hilt of his sword. "Although I assure Your Highness that I would do so with profound regret, I would have no choice but to carry out the second part of my instructions." The sultan immediately panicked and promptly capitulated to the British demand. Upon his return to England, Captain Hornsby was promoted to Admiral.[30]

Unlike the English Captain, the Lord Jesus will not return trembling about the "chances of war." His promise of victory is not the empty threat of a human power. There is no possibility at all that He might fail.

There is an awe-inspiring passage in Psalm 2 describing this scene.[31] "The nations take counsel together against the Lord and against His Messiah" (2)—and then we read these words: "He who sits in the heavens laughs, the Lord scoffs at them" (4). How dreadful is this laughter of God. From the depth of His being He loved the world (John 3:16); no gift was too precious, and no sacrifice too great, to be made for our redemption. His prophets came and were often rejected; His Son came and He was put to death. For two thousand years His servants have invited men and women to the great marriage feast in the kingdom of heaven. But now, at the end, He laughs. He scoffs: the mystery of judgment! It is as if His love has failed, His grace has been exhausted, the sea of His mercy has been emptied, and His patience has run out.[32]

The rebels are confident. Their leader, the Beast, has never failed. Never has there been such a ruler. They despise and blaspheme both the names and the sword of Him who rides on the white horse. There is an illustration of this in Jonathan Swift's great tale, *Gulliver's Travels*. Lemuel Gulliver, a ship's surgeon, leaves England for the South Sea on a ship named *Antelope* that sinks in a violent storm, killing all but Mr. Gulliver. He wakes up to find himself tied to the ground on an island called *Lilliput* whose inhabitants are little people about six inches in height. Gulliver pulls one arm free and they shoot at him with tiny arrows. He realizes that he would be more than a match for the greatest armies they could bring against him, and he says that at one point he is tempted to grab about forty or fifty of them and dash them on the ground.[33] How puny they are. How puny Messiah's enemies are! How rebellious and sinful! People comfort themselves in their selfishness and sin by thinking that God is too good and merciful to carry out His threats. But God is not Gulliver: one day He is going to laugh His terrible laugh and smash all who have rebelled against Him.

Joseph Seiss (1823–1904), the great Lutheran commentator on the Revelation, captures some of the powerful images from the prophets describing the victorious Messiah in the following words:

> The great Conqueror bows the heavens and comes down. He rides upon the cherub horse and flies upon the wings of the wind [2 Sam. 22:10–11]. Smoke goes up from his nostrils, and devouring fire out of his mouth [2 Sam. 22:9]. He moves amid storms and darkness, from which the lightnings hurl their bolts, and hailstones mingle with the fire [Isa. 30:30; Ezek. 38:22]. He roars out of Zion, and utters his voice from Jerusalem, till the heavens and the earth shake [Joel 3:16; Amos 1:2]. He dashes forth in the fury of his incensed greatness amid clouds, and fire, and pillars of smoke [CF. Isa. 63:3,5; Nah. 1:4–6]. The sun frowns.

2: Defeat of Antichrist

The day is neither light nor dark [Rev. 6:12]. The mountains melt and cleave asunder at his presence [Mic. 1:4; Nah. 1:5; Zech. 14:4]. The hills bound from their seats and skip like lambs [Ps. 114:4,6]. The waters are dislodged from their channels [Rev. 12:16]. The sea rolls back with howling trepidation. The sky is rent [Rev. 6:14] and folds upon itself like a collapsed tent. It is a day for executing an armed world—a world in covenant with Hell to overthrow the authority and throne of God.[34]

THE DESTINY OF THE BEASTS (VERSE 20)

The armies of Antichrist with great military pomp deploy for battle. His air forces come like a storm to cover the land. His mechanized divisions swing into place. His navies lie at anchor in the Red Sea, the Persian Gulf, and the Mediterranean. Amazing new weapons from the arms merchants are in the hands of the troops.[35] Surely this will be the most prolonged, complex battle in the history of warfare! But it is not! The Antichrist and his lackey, the false prophet, are summarily seized and cast alive into the "lake of fire."

Dr. Northcote Deck was an outstanding missionary pioneer to the Solomon Islands, and the people to whom he ministered spoke a kind of "pidgin English." They had an expression for the Lord God: "Big Fella, Master Too Much, Who Boss both Heaven and Ground." It is a magnificent title.[36] That is the God who is going to exercise judgment one day, and that is what is portrayed in this scene.

In this demon-obsessed world people often forget who it is that men are to fear. As Stephen Travis once said, "In the New Testament it is not believers who tremble at the power of Satan, but demons who tremble at the power of God."[37] There is a savor of the truth of Messiah's power in Martin Luther's great hymn, "A Mighty Fortress is Our God:" "One little word shall fell him."[38] And Antichrist will be felled—just as we fell a tree for firewood.[39]

John mentions the "false prophet," the priest of the last form of emperor worship before the end, and then repeats his great crimes of performing magic and sorcery in order to deceive men into receiving the mark of the Beast and following him. He does this for a couple of reasons: First, he wants to warn us again of the seductive powers of false religionists. The world is full of false cults, occultic activity, witchcraft, and religious systems that blind people to the truth of Christ. And, second, he wants to point out how empty all of his magic and occultic powers really are. None of his miraculous power can save him now. All of the armies of the world cannot rescue him.[40]

Both the Beast and the false prophet are taken and cast alive into the lake of fire. The present participle "alive" is placed in an emphatic position in the original text to add horror to the picture: "Alive the two were cast...."

The fate of the Beast and the false prophet contrasts dramatically and miserably with the fate of two great Old

2: Defeat of Antichrist

Testament heroes. Both Enoch (Gen. 5:24) and Elijah (2 Kings 2:11) were taken to heaven without dying. The Beast and his lackey are cast into hell without physically dying first. As God interposed and showed mercy to Enoch and Elijah in bringing them alive to heaven, so He now interposes in judgment and severity in casting these two evil ones into hell.[41]

Their destination is described as "the lake of fire which burns with brimstone." This description of hell occurs only in the Book of Revelation. Brimstone is combustible sulfur known to most Near Eastern peoples. The inhabitants of Palestine had, no doubt, experienced the terrors of burning sulfur. Once a sulfur deposit took fire it would melt and run in burning streams down the ravines spreading everywhere its suffocating fumes.[42] A lake of burning sulfur would be very hot and offensive in smell. It is a terrible picture of the destiny of all that is sinful and wicked in the world.[43]

Jesus uses the expression "Gehenna" (Matt. 5:22; Mark 9:43). Gehenna was the valley lying to the south and west of Jerusalem. In Old Testament times it had been the site of a cultic shrine where human sacrifices were offered (2 Kings 16:3; 23:10). Because of prophetic denunciation (Jer. 7:32; 19:6), it came to be viewed as a place of terrible wickedness. The Jews began to use it as a picture of the hell of final judgment. It is the abode of the wicked dead,[44] and the Beast and the false prophet are its first inhabitants.

Hell is not in fashion today. "Hell disappeared," says University of Chicago church historian Martin Marty, "and no one noticed." University of Virginia sociologist James Hunter says that even evangelical Christians "have a difficult time conceiving of people, especially virtuous nonbelievers, going to hell." Within liberal religious circles hell has slipped from polite conversation. "There's not much hell and not much heaven either," says United Church of Christ theologian Max Stackhouse. "The prevailing opinion," he says, "is that when you die you're dead but God still cares." The fact is that many mainline Protestant clergy do not believe in the afterlife. The pulpits are filled with men and women who do not believe the Scriptures.[45] Our Lord Jesus Christ and His apostles believed in heaven and hell. They were compassionate, yet they warned men and women of hell.

THE FATE OF THEIR FOLLOWERS (VERSE 21)

With the two leaders gone, short work is made of their followers.[46] Just as the Lord spoke and created the world, so He now speaks a word of divine retribution, and His opponents are slain. Their physical lives are destroyed by the sword—by the Word of God. Their souls are consigned to Hades to await the final judgment.[47] Contrary to those who teach Universalism, the doctrine that all mankind will eventually be saved, this passage shows that there are masses of men who remain unrepentant in heart up to the very end, and they can expect nothing but the wrath of the returning Christ.[48]

Many today hate the doctrine of judgment. They accept the simpering remarks of their liberal ministers who say, "Surely the bitterness of all this talk about hell is a thing of the past. God is a God of love, and everything will turn out all right." The story of King Agag in the Old Testament (1 Samuel 15: 1–3, 32–33) carries a warning for such misguided teachers. Saul had been ordered to kill all of the Amalekites, yet he spared Agag, their king. Samuel, the prophet of God, rebuked Saul for his sin of disobedience. Then he demanded that they bring him King Agag who came up cheerfully and said, "Surely the bitterness of death is past." The next verse gives us real insight into the holy character of God. Samuel said, "As your sword has made women childless, so shall your mother be childless among women." He then "hewed [chopped] Agag to pieces before the Lord at Gilgal."[49]

Some scholars interpret verse 21 in light of such texts as Hebrews 4:12 and Ephesians 2:16 and argue that Christ defeats His enemies by converting them and reconciling them.[50] This is an impossible view. The context is one of judgment, not conversion of the rebellious. This is made clear by the summons of the vultures to feed not on the flesh of the Beast and the false prophet but on the flesh of their followers. In short, the very people Swete and Chilton say are converted are, in fact, destroyed and eaten by the vultures. To say the least, this would be a unique metaphor for conversion and reconciliation![51]

Dr. Vernon Grounds, retired President of Denver Seminary, tells a story of some seminary students. Since the school had no gymnasium, some of the students would play basketball in a nearby public school. The elderly janitor would wait patiently until the seminarians finished playing. Invariably he sat there reading his Bible. One day one of the students asked him what he was reading. The man answered, "The book of Revelation." Surprised, the young man asked if he understood it. "Oh, yes," the man assured him. "I understand it." "What does it mean?" Very quietly the janitor answered, "It means that Jesus is gonna win."[52] That is the best summary I have ever read of this passage. That's the primary lesson: Jesus is "gonna win" over Antichrist. To again quote Luther's great hymn, "And He must win the battle."

The second lesson has to do with the power of deceit and delusion in the world. The spirit of Antichrist is already at work in the world (1 John 4:3). It is often at work, not in what appears outwardly bad, but in what may seem religious and innocuous.[53] It is seen, for example, in the modern philosophy of pluralism wherein Jesus is not (yet, at least) openly attacked but is demoted to the position of being just one of many doorways to God.

The third lesson is the unifying power of evil. We live in a world where it is almost impossible to get people to cooperate on anything. At the end, the entire world finally unites—to fight the King of kings.[54]

The fourth important contribution of this passage is to a proper understanding of the afterlife and divine judgment. The Bible teaches the reality of hell. It warns people, furthermore, that rebellion against God is death—that no weapon raised against Almighty God can prosper, that those who will not have Christ to rule over them must perish![55]

Finally, it should be remembered that the rider on the white horse is also known as the Lamb of God who takes away the sin of the world. The good news of the Christian gospel is that no one needs to fear facing Christ in judgment or being cast into the lake of fire. Christ has paid the price for the sins of all who believe in Him as Savior. Unbelievers need to be warned not refuse the forgiveness He freely offers them today.[56]

❦

NOTES

[1]Douglas MacArthur, *Reminiscences* (New York: MacGraw-Hill, 1964), 272–76.

[2]James Montgomery Boice, *The Last and Future World* (Grand Rapids: Zondervan, 1974), 98–99.

[3]Quoted in the *Philadelphia Inquirer* (Sept. 25, 1982). For the quotes from Franklin Roosevelt, Ellen Goodman, Winston Churchill, Albert Schweitzer, Barbra Streisand and B.F. Skinner, the writer is indebted to Billy Graham, *Approaching Hoofbeats: The Four Horsemen of the Apocalypse* (Waco: Word, 1983), 222–24.

[4]Quoted in *Time* (April, 1982).

[5]For the quotations by Seymour Siegel, Arnold Toynbee, and Jonathan Schell the writer is indebted to Billy Graham, *Approaching Hoofbeats*, 226–27.

[6]As Charles notes, these passages are proleptic accounts of the destruction of the kings. Cf. R. H. Charles, *The Revelation of St. John*, International Critical Commentary, 2 vols. (Edinburgh: T. & T. Clark, 1920), 2:131.

[7]For a satisfying reconstruction of the events leading up to Antichrist's fall, cf. Charles H. Dyer, *World News and Bible Prophecy* (Wheaton: Tyndale House, 1993), 227–39.

[8]Cf. Martin Kiddle, *The Revelation of St. John*, Moffatt New Testament Commentary (New York: Harper, 1940), 388.

[9]Cf. G.R. Beasley-Murray, *The Book of Revelation*, New Century Bible (London: Oliphants, 1974), 282.

[10]Robert H. Mounce, *The Book of Revelation*, New International Commentary on the New Testament (rev. ed., Grand Rapids: Eerdmans, 1998), 357.

[11]Robert Wallace Orr, *Victory Pageant: A Commentary on the Book of Revelation* (London: Pickering & Inglis, 1972), 150.

[12]Cf. T.W. Manson, *The Sayings of Jesus* (London: SCM, 1949), 147.

[13]G.B. Caird, *The Revelation of St. John the Divine*, Harper New Testament Commentary (New York: Harper & Row, 1966), 247.

[14]Beasley-Murray, *Revelation*, 282. The same word (δεῖπνον) is used for both suppers. Cf. John F. Walvoord, *The Revelation of Jesus Christ* (Chicago: Moody, 1966), 279.

[15]Beasley-Murray, *The Book of Revelation*, 282.

[16]Gerhard A. Krodel, *Revelation*, Augsburg Commentary on the New Testament (Minneapolis: Augsburg, 1989), 324.

[17]John Sweet, *Revelation*, Trinity Press International New Testament Commentaries (London: SCM, 1990), 285.

[18]Robert Govett, *The Apocalypse: Expounded by Scripture*, 4 vols. (London, 1861; reprint ed., Miami Springs: Conley & Schoettle, 1981), 4:190.

[19]Henry Barclay Swete, *The Apocalypse of St. John* (London: Macmillan, 1906), 252.

[20]Cf. Mathias Rissi, *The Future of the World* (Naperville: Alec R. Allenson, 1966), 33. Rissi concludes that all unbelievers die at Christ's coming. Others reject this notion, pointing to 20:1 which refers to the nations that survive Armageddon (cf. Beasley-Murray, *The Book of Revelation*, 282–83). Three observations are in order: (1) It is unlikely that John conceived of any unregenerate people entering the millennium (cf. John 3:5). Therefore, the nations of 20:1 cannot include the unregenerate. (2) Jesus described a judgment that was to take place prior to the millennium in which the nations are gathered before Messiah the judge (Matt. 25:31–46). Only believers (sheep) are admitted into the kingdom; the goats are excluded. (3) Revelation 20:5 clearly suggests that the unsaved dead will not be raised at the beginning of the millennium. This, coupled with Matthew 25, would seem to imply that there are unbelievers who physically survive the coming of Christ only to face Him at the judgment of Matt. 25:41 and be cast into Hell.

[21]At the present time the relationship between Christians and non-Christians is governed by God's common grace. God in His mercy allows the non-Christian to enjoy life and many of its benefits. However, at the consummation, a new relationship will ensue—the era of common grace will, at least for a time, come to an end. The non-Christians will be judged by the Lord. Cf. Tremper Long-

man III, "The Divine Warrior: The New Testament Use of an Old Testament Motif," *Westminster Theological Journal* 44 (1982):306.

[22]William Barclay, *The Revelation of John*, 2 vols. (rev. ed., Philadelphia: Westminster, 1976), 2:184.

[23]Cf. Mounce, *The Book of Revelation*, 357. Tenney writes, "The book of Revelation was not given to the church to terrorize it nor to inculcate hatred and brutality. It does, however, expose the nature of human sinfulness and rebellion against deity. A revolt deliberately organized for the purpose of banishing God and Christ from the world would have seemed almost unthinkable a century ago, but through the rising secularism of our age it is fast becoming a live option even in America. Faithful witnessing and a keen understanding of God's plans for the consummation of the age are imperative in this situation." Cf. Merrill C. Tenney, *The Book of Revelation*, Proclaiming the New Testament (Grand Rapids: Baker, 1963), 96.

[24]Cf. Kiddle, *The Revelation of St. John*, 388; Mounce, *The Book of Revelation*, 358.

[25]Walter Scott, *Exposition of the Revelation of Jesus Christ* (Fourth ed., London: Pickering & Inglis, N.D.), 392.

[26]Joseph Seiss, *Lectures on the Apocalypse*, 3 vols. (New York: Charles C. Cook, 1906), 3:253.

[27] D. Edmond Hiebert, *The Thessalonian Epistles: A Call to Readiness* (Chicago: Moody, 1971), 318.

[28]Swete, *The Apocalypse of St. John*, 253.

[29]Cf. Govett, *The Apocalypse: Expounded by Scripture*, 4:189.

[30]As told by Lewis H. Lapham, "Comic Opera in Hemisphere," *The Dallas Morning News* (April 12, 1982), 11A.

[31]Psalm 2:1–2 finds partial fulfillment at the cross and ascension of our Lord, as well as at His second advent.

[32]Cf. Seiss, *Lectures on the Apocalypse*, 3:256.

[33]Jonathan Swift, *Gulliver's Travels: An Annotated Text With Critical Essays*, ed. Robert A. Greenberg (New York: W.W. Norton, 1961), 6–8.

[34]Seiss, *Lectures on the Apocalypse*, 3:257–58.

[35]Cf. Donald Grey Barnhouse, *Revelation: An Expository Commentary* (Grand Rapids: Zondervan, 1971), 362; John Phillips, *Exploring Revelation* (Chicago: Moody, 1974), 249.

[36]For this account I am indebted to S. Lewis Johnson, Jr., "The Great Supper and the Binding of Satan" (cassette tape, Dallas: Believers Chapel, 1990). For the complete story of Northcote Deck and the South Sea Evangelical Mission, cf. Alison Griffiths, *Fire in the Islands!* (Wheaton: Harold Shaw Publishers, 1977).

[37]Quoted by John Blanchard, *More Gathered Gold* (Welwyn: Evangelical Press, 1986), 117.

[38]Martin Luther, "A Mighty Fortress is Our God," trans. Frederick H. Hedge, in *Hymns of Truth and Praise* (Ft. Dodge: Gospel Perpetuating Publishers, 1971), 588.

[39]Cf. Ray C. Stedman, *God's Final Word: Understanding Revelation* (Grand Rapids: Discovery House, 1991), 316.

[40]Cf. Seiss, *Lectures on the Apocalypse*, 3:259.

[41]William Kelly, *Lectures on the Book of Revelation* (London: G. Morrish, 1874), 405–6. Cf. Govett, *The Apocalypse: Expounded by Scripture*, 4:195; Scott, *Exposition of the Revelation of Jesus Christ*, 394.

[42]*International Standard Bible Encyclopedia*, see "Brimstone," by J. A. Patch, 1 (1979), 547.

[43]Mounce, *The Book of Revelation*, 359.

[44]The Lake of Fire and Gehenna refer to the same place. Both terms describe hell and are to be distinguished from *Hades* (ᾅδης, CF. Luke 16:23), although the AV does not make this distinction clear. Hades is the intermediate state between death and the resurrection (Matt. 16:18; Luke 16:23; Acts 2:27) and is sometimes used synonymously with the grave (Rev. 1:18; 6:8; 20:13). CF. George Eldon Ladd, *A Commentary on the Revelation of John* (Grand Rapids: Eerdmans, 1972), 258.

[45]For the quotations from Martin Marty, James Hunter and Max Stackhouse I am indebted to Kenneth L. Woodward, "Heaven," *Newsweek* (March 27, 1989), 52, 54.

[46]Seiss, *Lectures on the Apocalypse*, 3:259.

[47]Charles, *The Revelation of St. John*, 2:140.

[48]CF. Ladd, *A Commentary on the Revelation of John*, 258.

[49]I am indebted to Dr. S. Lewis Johnson, Jr. for suggesting this illustration.

[50]CF. Swete, *The Apocalypse of St. John*, 255; David Chilton, *The Days of Vengeance* (Ft. Worth: Dominion Press, 1987), 491–92.

[51]CF. Beasley-Murray, *The Book of Revelation*, 284.

[52]Vernon C. Grounds, "Getting Into Shape Spiritually," *Christianity Today* (Feb. 2, 1979), 27.

[53]Kelly, *Lectures on the Book of Revelation*, 407.

[54]CF. Swete, *The Apocalypse of St. John*, 254.

[55]Seiss, *Lectures on the Apocalypse*, 3:261.

[56]CF. Mounce, *The Book of Revelation*, 357.

༺ ༻

THE THIRD LAST THING:

The Binding Of Satan

Revelation 20:1-3

༺ ༻

In the nineteenth century, Christian theologians began
to openly question the existence of Satan.[1] Friedrich Schleiermacher (1768–1834), the father of modern liberalism,
declared, "The idea of the devil as developed among us is
so unstable that we cannot expect anyone to be convinced
of its truth."[2] He preferred that Satan be seen as a po-
etic device, a metaphor for evil. In the midst of the titanic
struggle of World War II, with evidences of demonic evil
all about him, Rudolf Bultmann (1884–1976), the most
distinguished New Testament scholar of his time, made his
celebrated plea that we should demythologize the New Testament. It is impossible, he argued, to live in the modern
world of electricity, radio, and scientific medicine and still
believe in the New Testament world of miracles, angels,
and the devil.[3] In the highly respected *Encyclopedia of Philosophy* there is but one reference to the devil in the entire
eight volumes. Belief in the devil's existence, the author asserts, is rejected by agnostics, atheists, and most believers in
God.[4] In the author's opinion, "Billy Graham is one of the
few Protestant ministers who still believe in the devil."[5]

The reasons for this modern attitude are many, three of which may be mentioned.[6] First, there is the modern secular world view that has no room for the supernatural. Second, there are the popular conceptions of the devil as half man, half beast with horns, cloven hooves, tail, and trident which have turned him into a figure of fun for many. Third, there is the devil's own lie. As the French critic and poet Baudelaire (1821–67) wrote, "The devil's cleverest wile is to convince us that he does not exist."[7]

But the Lord Jesus Christ and His apostles assured their hearers that the devil does exist. As the popular Bible teacher and evangelist, Hal Lindsey, has said, "Satan is alive and well on planet earth."[8] The foolish and unbelieving denial of Satan's existence is illustrated by the story of a boxer who was being badly beaten in a match. Between rounds, battered and bruised, he pled with his trainer, "Throw in the towel! This guy is killing me!" The trainer replied, "Oh, no, he isn't. He's not even hurting you. He hasn't laid a glove on you!" At that point the boxer wiped the blood away from his eye and said, "Well, then, keep your eye on the referee. Somebody in that ring is hitting me!"[9]

The Bible tells us that Satan is from a high order of angelic beings, and was created good (Ezek. 28:12, 15). He is, says J.I. Packer, the supreme illustration of good gone wrong.[10] He heads an army of rebel angels or demons whose moral nature is like that of their king (Rev. 9:11). Jesus called him a "murderer" (John 8:44) because of his fierce, sustained and pitiless hatred of humanity. He is called "the evil one" (1 John 5:19) because he embodies all that is evil. He is called a "roaring lion" (1 Pet. 5:8–9) because of his strength and destructiveness. He is called the "accuser of the brethren" (Rev. 12:10) because he is always calling upon God to banish Christians because of their sins. We learn in Revelation 12:9 that he deceives the nations. The apostle Paul says (2 Cor. 4:3–4) that he blinds the eyes of people. He snatches away God's Word before it takes root in their understanding (Matt. 13:4, 19). He lays moral snares for people (2 Tim. 2:25–26), he mixes truth with error (Matt. 13:25–28), and he seeks to corrupt human society (2 Tim. 3:1–5). He is the father of confusion and lies (John 8:44).

This last description ("father of lies") underscores the importance of knowing what the Bible says about him. Only the pure spring of the Word of God will tell us the truth about this great enemy of mankind. "Satan's regular way of working is to deceive and get people to err without any suspicion that what they are thinking and doing is not right. He plays on their pride, willfulness, unrealism, addictions, stupidities, and temperamental flaws to induce all forms of mental and moral folly—fantasies, cults, idolatries, unbelief, misbelief, dishonesty, infidelity, cruelty, exploitation, and everything else that degrades and dehumanizes God's image bearers. Love, wisdom, humility, and pure-heartedness—four basic components of Christ-likeness—are special objects of his attack."[11]

That is why Revelation 20:1–3 should be of real encouragement to all who love the Lord Jesus Christ. The "big idea" of the passage is simply this: there is a time coming during the millennial age when Satan's activities in our world will cease.

As the passage is read its setting should be borne in mind: Babylon, the world commercial and political capital of the end time, has fallen. John then begins to describe the "last things" of history as we know it. The first "last thing" is Christ's return from heaven with His saints. Second, the armies of the Antichrist will be defeated, and the Beast and the false prophet will be cast into the lake of fire. At this point John sets forth the third "last thing," which has been traditionally called "the binding of Satan."

THE INSTRUMENT OF THE DIVINE WILL: AN ANGEL EQUIPPED FOR HIS TASK (VERSE 1)

THE ANGELIC JAILER

The Beast has been cast into hell. "From the Beast John now turns to the Beast's master."[12] Behind the kings and armies that have been destroyed in the battle in chapter 19 is a sinister, cunning personality that has led them to the winepress of God's wrath and judgment. God has singled him out for a special judgment.[13] John saw "an angel coming down from heaven." That he has come from heaven indicates that he has come as an agent of Almighty God.

It is striking that God sends "an angel." Some people think of Satan as God's equal. Surely, they think, God will send Christ Himself to wrestle with the dragon. But, no, He sends an angel. He does not send a cherub, a seraph, the archangel, or one of the principalities and powers. It is simply "a nameless angel."[14] He comes with the authority of heaven, and that is enough.

When does this take place? The text is very clear on this point. First, it takes place after the second advent of Christ and after the destruction of Antichrist and his armies. The reader should carefully note the expression at the beginning of the verse, "And I saw." This phrase occurs several times (E.G. Revelation 19:11, 17, 19; 20:1, 4, 12; 21:1). It appears to establish a sequence of visions[15] which describes a sequence of events beginning with the return of Christ, followed by the terrible supper and slaughter of the battle, followed by the binding of Satan, followed by the thousand-year kingdom, followed by the last judgment, followed by the new heaven and new earth.[16]

This seems obvious to many, but it is not obvious to others.[17] There are some students of Revelation who find in the prophecy the principle of recapitulation. They see the whole book as a series of several visions—usually seven—each going over the same ground, each vision beginning with the first coming and extending to the second.[18] Thus, at Revelation 20:1 they argue that John goes back to the first coming, and the binding of Satan refers to what Jesus accomplished at the cross. The repeated phrase, "And I saw," is, I believe, a strong argument against that view.[19] The binding of Satan comes after the second coming of Christ.

Second, the binding of Satan comes before the thousand-year reign of Christ. Again, this may seem obvious, but there are other interpreters who argue that the thousand-year reign of Christ described in verses 4–6 is a symbolic description of the present age.[20] They argue that Satan is gradually being bound during the present age, symbolized by the thousand years. Again, the verses before us clearly refute that view. Satan is bound before, not during, the thousand years.

His Authoritative Equipment

The angel in verse 1 is obviously involved in a spiritual police action, and he is equipped with the tools of his office. In his hand he carries "the key of the abyss," which suggests that absolute authority and control over the abyss has been delegated to him. Many readers of the Scriptures hold confused and inadequate ideas about the unseen world. It might be helpful at this point to define a few terms.[21]

The Hebrew term *Sheol* and the Greek word *Hades* both refer to the place where the soul or spirit of man goes at death. It is the "realm of the dead,"[22] the conscious state of existence before the resurrection and judgment (Luke 16: 19–31). For the unsaved it is a place of torment, but for the saved it is a place of bliss—that is, paradise (Luke 23:43).

Many commentators believe that before the resurrection of Christ there were two compartments in sheol or hades,[23] one compartment for the lost and one for the saved, and at His resurrection Jesus emptied the one compartment of all believers (Eph. 4:8–9).[24] It is certainly the teaching of the apostle that all believers who die today go directly to heaven to be with the Lord (2 Cor. 5:6–8).[25] Today hades is the place where departed souls go who are not saved.

The second place of which the Bible speaks is hell or "the lake of fire" (Rev. 19:20). This is the place of final torment after the last judgment. In the Old Testament it is called "topheth" (literally, "place of burning;" CF. Isa. 30:33; Jer. 7:31–32);[26] Jesus calls it "gehenna" (Mark 9:43). Gehenna was a wadi or valley (Valley of Hinnom) in South Jerusalem that acquired a bad reputation because child sacrifices to Moloch were offered in it during the days of Ahaz and Manasseh (2 Kings 16:3; 21:6). Because of the threats of judgment by the prophets against this sinister place (Jer. 7:32; 19:6), it came to be equated with the hell or lake of fire of the last judgment.

Hell and hades are not the same place in Biblical think-ing.[27] Hades receives the unsaved for the intervening period between death and the resurrection; hell or gehenna is the place of punishment after the judgment of the nations (Matt. 25:31–41) and the last judgment (Rev. 20:11–15).[28] Just before the millennium the Beast and his followers and the false prophet (but not the devil) are cast into the lake of fire (Rev. 19:20).

The third place of which Scripture speaks is "the Abyss," the place mentioned in our present passage. It was original-ly an adjective that meant "bottomless" or "unfathomably deep."[29] This is the place of imprisonment for disobedient angels or demons (Luke 8:31).[30] The picture is of a vast sub-terranean cavern where the fallen angels await the day of judgment.[31] Antichrist is said to be animated by a demon from the Abyss (Rev. 11:7; 17:8). In chapter 9 (v. 3–11) de-monic "scorpion centaurs"[32] are released from the Abyss to terrorize the earth during the tribulation. The Abyss is not hell or the lake of fire.

Satan is going to dwell in the Abyss during the thou-sand-year reign of Christ. It is not hell or the lake of fire; he will only be cast into hell at the end of the thousand-year reign (CF. 20:10). The Abyss is a kind of "fore-hell." It is the prison in which the fallen spirits are detained prior to their final judgment. It is much like the county jail in which prisoners are kept prior to their sentencing, prior to being

3: Binding of Satan

sent to the federal prison. The Abyss is the county jail, and hell is the federal penitentiary.[33]

In any case the angel carries a key with which he unlocks the shaft that leads down to the Abyss, Satan's millennial home. Looped over the angel's arm[34] is a "great chain" with which to take his prisoner. The term used here was sometimes (CF. Mark 5:4) used in the sense of manacles or handcuffs.[35] Here it may refer to something to bind the hands or it may refer to a chain with which the whole body is tied up.[36]

By this time you have probably gathered that I am somewhat of a literalist in my understanding of the book of Revelation. I say this because those who disagree with this approach are always warning their readers that the book of Revelation is written in highly symbolical apocalyptic language.[37] I should point out that I do not know anyone who denies that the Revelation is symbolic;[38] however, those who stress the symbolic nature of this passage often do so to avoid its clear teaching. If students of Scripture were to neglect all symbolical passages in the Bible they would be ignoring large sections of Scripture—from Genesis to Revelation—containing symbols and figures of speech. But the believer who reads in faith with the help of the Holy Spirit will find a way to understand his God.

A helpful illustration may be found in the book of Genesis, in many ways a simple book, yet a book containing profound truths often couched in bold and figurative language. In Genesis 3:15 the Lord God pronounces judgment upon the serpent and intimates that one day the "seed" of the woman—that is, a Redeemer—would come and "bruise [the serpent's] head." Believers have generally understood that symbol to mean that one day Christ and His people would win a great victory over Satan (CF. Rom. 16:20; Gal. 3:16; 4:4).

My point is this: Even when God uses symbols and figures of speech the general thought (even if not all of the particulars) is sufficiently plain to the believing heart. Josephus, the unbelieving Jewish historian, lacking the New Testament and the teaching ministry of the Holy Spirit, says that Genesis 3:15 means only that men should strike snakes on the head because that is where their poisonous fangs are.[39] He misses the symbolism altogether. The believer, however, has no question about the general sense. Do not let talk of symbolic language, therefore, keep you from this great book and its lessons.

We must remember that the book is called a "revelation," an unveiling (1:1). It was not intended by our Lord to be obscure. In fact, special blessing is promised to those who read and give heed to its pages (1:3). It is only the influence of prejudice against the book that causes so many people to have difficulty with it. Tragically, there are Christian communions and churches where the book of Revelation is scarcely looked at.[40]

While John uses symbolic language, his symbols mean something. All symbols have referents, or else language is meaningless. Someone might ask, "Do you literalists actually expect Satan to be tied down by an ordinary iron or steel chain?"[41] I would answer that our text says nothing about an iron or steel chain; it says "a great chain." Literalists understand that the passage does not speak of a literal iron or steel chain; it is a "spirit-chain," the kind that can bind up spirits and strap down angels.[42]

What this passage is teaching us is that God has complete control over evil.[43] He is completely sovereign, even over the Satanic realm.[44] Yet it is teaching something more specific than just that. It is teaching us that one day an angel is going to actually come to imprison Satan in a place that is called the Abyss. Furthermore, he will be chained, completely immobilized.

One of the great evangelical commentators on Revelation suggests that the chapter before us may contain a clue as to why many churches ignore most of this book. There is no book, he opines, that Satan fears more. Why? "It announces first his sure humiliation by angelic power, and then his destruction afterwards."[45] The devil hates this book and its prophecy of his doom, and he hates to have us read it.

THE VERDICT (OR MANDATE) OF THE DIVINE WILL: THE DEVIL
APPREHENDED FOR HIS IMPRISONMENT (VERSES 2–3A)

THE ARREST OF THE EVILDOER

The angel first lays hold of Satan. The verb "laid hold"
(NASB; NIV has "seized") literally means "to exercise power."
It is used in Matthew 26:50 of the arrest of the Lord Jesus
Christ: they "took Him into custody." That is precisely
how it is used here.[46]

THE NAMES OF THE EVILDOER

In verse 2 all four titles by which Satan is designated in
Revelation are brought together.[47] First, he is called "the
dragon."[48] He is the horrible monster who sought the life of
the Christ child in chapter 12 (v. 4). As the Dragon, Satan
gave his authority to Antichrist in chapter 13 (v. 4), and this
title links him to the political powers of the earth that he
seeks to influence (CF. Dan. 7).

Next, he is called "the serpent of old." Serpents were
known for their subtlety and poison. They were viewed
as dangerous and malevolent, and they were also associated with idolatry in Israel (2 Kings 18:4) and with heathen
gods and demons.[49] That he is called the serpent "of old"
reminds us that he was the one who in Eden deceived Eve
and brought ruin upon the race.[50] As the serpent Satan
deceives souls, beguiles them with false doctrine and false

moral values. The title refers to his subtle temptation of the good.

Third, he is called "the devil." The word "devil" is from a verb that has the sense of "separating"—that is, to set in opposition to someone. In some contexts it has the sense of "accuser;" in others, the thought is of a "slanderer."[51] The dominant idea seems to be "adversary." The work of the adversary is to attempt to separate God and man.[52] He is a malignant liar, and this has been one of his chief characteristics from the beginning (John 8:44). The essential character of Satan is that he is a murderous liar. He is the author of slander and malignant untruth. He reminds God perpetually of the guilt of the human race that he has perverted.[53] He is the one who is behind the Beast's blasphemies against God and Christ.

Finally, he is called "Satan." There is no material difference between this name and "devil;"[54] it means literally "the adversary."[55] Satan is the malignant adversary of God. He disputes God's right to rule and seeks to defeat Christ's becoming King of the earth.

THE INCARCERATION OF THE EVILDOER

The description of Satan's imprisonment should be read with care. He is taken into custody, thrown down the shaft of the abyss, and locked inside the shut cell door. John actually says that the shaft of the abyss is "sealed," which parallels Matthew 27:66 where the evangelist says that Jesus' tomb was sealed—that is, some kind of mark or object was used to prevent its being opened. Here we see the comparative power of Satan and God. Satan had his minions seal the tomb of our Lord to keep His body in the grave, but their effort was futile. Now an angel seals the prison of Satan, and he is powerless and totally without influence for a thousand years.[56]

The elaborate measures taken with this prisoner clearly imply the complete cessation of his influence during the thousand years.[57] It is hard to imagine how John could have expressed more emphatically the complete inability of Satan during the thousand years to deceive the human race.[58] This should be noted because there are interpreters who argue that Satan was bound during Christ's first advent (CF. Matt. 12:29; Luke 19:17–18; John 12:31; Col. 2:15) and is today chained in the abyss.[59] It is true that Jesus did curtail demonic activity during His earthly ministry and did demonstrate His authority over Satan, but that is not what is described here. Here we have the complete cessation of Satanic influence upon the earth.[60]

The New Testament elsewhere flatly states that "your adversary, the devil, prowls about like a roaring lion, seeking someone to devour" (1 Pet. 5:8).[61] When amillennial students of Revelation are confronted with a text like this and asked how they can say that Satan is today bound, they answer, "Well, he has a long chain."[62] Language is meaningless if such a view is true.

If the amillennialist is asked to explain the meaning of Satan's imprisonment, he answers that it means that Satan is not allowed to prevent the extension of the church among the nations by its missionary program.[63] This is contradicted by a comparison of Revelation 19:20 and 20:3. Satan, the Beast, and the false prophet form an evil triad of deception. The deception described in verse 3 is not one that ended at the cross; it is one that is yet to be interrupted at the future battle of Armageddon. At that point the Beast and the false prophet are cast into the lake of fire and their deceptions end, and Satan is cast into the Abyss, ending his deceptions.[64]

By God's grace people are being converted to Christ every day, yet Satan is not bound in the sense that he does not fight it. Listen to the words of the apostle Paul: "Our gospel is veiled…to those who are perishing, in whose case the god of this world has blinded the minds of the unbelieving" (2 Cor. 4:3–4). History simply does not permit the amillennial interpretation that says that Satan is bound today and unable to prevent the spread of the gospel.

It is true that the story of the expansion of the Christian faith is an amazing testimony to the power of the Holy Spirit, yet it is no less a testimony to the failures and limitations attending the spread of the gospel. The Jews as a nation were not won to the gospel. Every city east of Greece and in North Africa that is mentioned in the New Testament or that was gained for Christ in the eastern Roman empire during the first six centuries is now under Muslim control. Over the centuries large segments of the human population have remained impervious to the gospel. Most of teeming Asia, for example, is still Islamic, Buddhist, or Hindu. The 20TH century saw large geographical areas go under Communist ideological and political control. In the early part of the 21ST century we have seen a resurgence of superstition, sorcery, pseudo-religion, and overt demonism that is baffling and frightening. Within professing Christendom itself there has arisen a secularist spirit that is undermining belief in the supernatural. Far from being limited and fettered, Satan is free and rampant, and none suffer more from his attacks and frustrations than the church of God.[65]

What, then, of our Lord's earthly ministry and death? The apostle John tells us that He came "that He might destroy the works of the devil" (1 John 3:8). He delivered His people from "the fear of death," the devil's great weapon (Heb. 2:14–15). At the cross He made a public spectacle of the demonic host and exposed them to disgrace, Paul tells the Colossians (2:5). The cross, says Kurt Koch, is "the end of demons" and, we might add, "the end of Satan."[66] Since Easter morning, he adds, "the power of Satan is an empty

3: Binding of Satan

display." No longer can he bring any accusations against God's elect (Rom. 8:33–34), so we preach the gospel—the "good news." The word *gospel* originated in the language of war and combat and is a technical term for the announcement of victory.[67]

Yet the devil is still on the loose, within the bounds determined by the sovereign plan of God. At the cross our God delivered the verdict against Satan. He is like a criminal who has been sentenced but is not yet in custody. It makes no difference; his fate has been determined.

In June of 1967, war broke out between Israel and her Arab neighbors. I was a college student at the time, working with a land-surveying company in New Hampshire. Every evening I came back to my motel room and watched the news with great interest. For several days news reports from Cairo reported on how many Israeli planes and tanks were lost and how Egypt was penetrating Israel. In seven days, however, the war was over and Israel was the victor. It was then revealed that, by destroying the air forces and air fields of the surrounding Arab states, Israel had won the war two hours after hostilities had begun. The Arabs fought on for a week, even though they were defeated. So today the defeated Satan continues his warfare against God and His people.[68]

The two advents of Christ have been compared to D-DAY (June 6, 1944) and V-E DAY (May 8, 1945) during World

War II.[69] The decisive action was the Allied invasion of Europe (D-DAY), but the final victory did not come until almost one year later (V-E DAY). So it is with Satan: the decisive battle has been won, yet the war continues. V-E DAY will come when a nameless angel throws the old serpent into the Abyss.[70]

Ray Bakke tells of an old Glasgow professor named MacDonald who, along with a Scottish chaplain, had bailed out of an airplane behind German lines. They were put in a prison camp where a high wire fence separated the Americans from the British, and the Germans made it next to impossible for the two sides to communicate. MacDonald was put in the American barracks and the chaplain was housed with the British.

Every day the two men would meet at the fence and exchange a greeting. Unknown to the guards, the Americans had a little homemade radio and were able to get news from the outside, something more precious than food in a prison camp. Every day, MacDonald would take a headline or two to the fence and share it with the chaplain in their ancient Gaelic language, indecipherable to the Germans.

One day, news came over the little radio that the German High Command had surrendered, and the war was over. MacDonald took the news to his friend, then stood and watched him disappear into the British barracks. A moment later, a roar of celebration came from the barracks.

Life in that camp was transformed. Men walked around singing and shouting, waving at the guards, even laughing at the dogs. When the German guards finally heard the news three nights later, they fled into the dark, leaving the gates unlocked. The next morning British and American prisoners walked out as free men. Yet they had truly been set free three days earlier by the news that the war was over. While Satan still prowls this earth, and Christ's kingdom has not been manifested upon the earth, the decisive battle at the cross has sealed Satan's ultimate doom. We know the final outcome, and we rejoice in anticipation of it. God has His purposes for prolonging history, and one of those purposes is that He might save people before the end (2 Pet. 3:9).[71]

THE PURPOSE OF THE DIVINE WILL: THE NATIONS PROTECTED FROM DIABOLIC DECEPTION (VERSE 3B–C)

THE OBJECTS OF HIS DECEPTION

According to verse 3 Satan's imprisonment during the thousand years is not so much a punishment as it is a precaution against his deceiving the nations.[72] Who are "the nations" in verse 3? Were not the nations all killed with the sword at Christ's coming?[73] Some argue that there were outlying nations that had not joined Antichrist in his campaign.[74] It is more likely, however, that this term refers to the redeemed[75] from all nations who were converted during the tribulation and who were left to populate the millennial kingdom.[76] Earlier in the book (5:9–10) John speaks of those redeemed from every "nation" who would "reign upon the earth."

THE NECESSITY OF HIS RELEASE

After his thousand-year imprisonment Satan is to be released. John says that he "must" be released. This expression implies logical necessity. For some reason, grounded in the Divine will, Satan will be released after the thousand years and will deceive the nations again. It is apparent that his long imprisonment will not change either his own plans or the character of man. Further elaboration of why it is necessary for Satan to be released we must put off until we come to verses 7–10.

CONCLUSION

CHRISTIANS SHOULD BE THE MOST REALISTIC OF PEOPLE

Believers have an explanation for the terrible condition of the world in which they live. They know sin when they see it.[77] They know that there is a great malevolent being in our world who actively promotes the love of wrongdoing and the hatred of all that is good. They know that evil is personal,[78] not just the accidental, impersonal results of nature.[79]

They know that the devil is on the loose in our world. In his kingdom are enthroned error, falsehood, deception, lies, and moral rottenness. Reverence for God is scarce, truthfulness is nothing, falsities and treacheries confront us at every point. People "speak falsehoods, print falsehoods, and believe falsehoods.... They eat them, and drink them, and wear them, and act them, and live them, and make them [the central essence] of their being." At least half of all that "the eye can see, or the ear hear, or the hands can touch, or the tongue taste, is bogus, counterfeit... shoddy, [or some kind of] untruth."[80]

In business, politics, social life, the professions, and especially in religion, untruthfulness reigns in our day so that we scarcely know whom we can trust. The devil's supporters attack the church, the church that Christ loves. They call the Lord's Supper and baptism absurd. They speak of prayer as a delusion and of the Bible as a dull record of superstitious beliefs. It is laughable to them to think that all will one day render an account of their moral lives at a future judgment. Heterosexuality and monogamous marriage are outdated, optional conventions. The immortal soul is a fiction. Life itself is a mere freak of Mother Nature. If there is a god, we are all that god.

The devil is not bound, he is loose; and his lies are being spread every day by thousands of his emissaries. He has his nests in every city, town, and village in the world.[81] He is a liar and a murderer.

CHRISTIANS HAVE REASON TO BE THE MOST HOPEFUL OF PEOPLE

Evil is not going to be prevalent forever, however. The powers of evil are ultimately doomed.[82] In his great novel, *Robinson Crusoe*, Daniel Defoe (1659–1731) tells of an Englishman who is involved in a shipwreck off the coast of America. In the original version Robinson Crusoe realizes he is a sinner and accepts Christ as his Savior. After several years on an uninhabited island he finds a footprint and eventually meets a native, whom he names "Friday." He speaks to Friday about the devil and God, and one day Friday asks, "Well, you say God is so strong, so great, is He not much strong, much might as the devil?"

"Yes, yes," says Robinson Crusoe. "Friday, God is stronger than the devil; God is above the devil; and therefore we pray to God to tread him under our feet, and enable us to resist his temptations, and quench his fiery darts."

"But," Friday says, "if God much strong, much might, as the devil, why God not kill the devil, so make him no more wicked?"

Crusoe ponders this for a while. Then he answers, "God will at last punish him severely; he is reserved for the judgment, and is to be cast into the bottomless pit to dwell with everlasting fire."[83]

In Revelation 20:1–3 John writes of one phase of that final stage of Satan's history; another stage of that history shall be considered in a later chapter.

CHRISTIANS HAVE EVERY REASON TO BE THE MOST OPTIMISTIC OF PEOPLE

As believers, we know that future history has terrible
chapters to endure—yet we should have the expectation of
victory. There was a Christian in the 8TH century (680–754)
named Boniface, later called the "apostle of Germany."[84]
When he came upon the sacred oak tree of the pagan god
Thor he had no thought of peaceful coexistence with the
heathen world. He chopped it down and built a chapel
with the wood. Thousands of Thor worshippers, seeing
that their god had failed to strike Boniface with lightning,
converted to Christianity on the spot. Boniface knew that
he was on the winning side. The terrorizing deities of paganism meant nothing to him. He worshipped the one true
God to whom alone ultimate victory belonged.[85]

Evangelist Billy Graham was asked by a reporter if he
was an optimist or a pessimist. "Oh," he said, "I'm an optimist!" "How can you be an optimist," asked the reporter,
"when your sermons are so full of warnings about God's
judgment and the sins, immorality, and perversions of
mankind?" "I'm optimistic," said Mr. Graham, "because
I've read the end of the Book—I've read the biblical prophecies of Christ's return and Satan's defeat."[86]

CHRISTIANS HAVE EVERY REASON TO LIVE TRUTHFULLY AND WITH INTEGRITY

We know the enemy and his character, and we should
live lives that honor the holiness, goodness, and truthful-

ness of our Savior. "I hate the devil!" yelled undergraduate and future missionary to India, Paget Wilkes (1871–1934), across an Oxford street to a friend walking on the opposite side. "So do I!" his friend roared back. Passersby were struck by the exchange, and perhaps it did them good (says J.I. Packer, in his inimitable way), for their sentiment was right. Those who have learned to hate the devil as Christians should, rejoice and praise God that he has been defeated at the Cross and that one day he will be imprisoned.[87]

❦

NOTES

[1]Ken Dyers, "Not Giving the Devil His Due," *Tabletalk* 17 (July, 1993), 60–61. Doubts about Satan's existence actually arose earlier. Richardson wrote, "Until the age of Enlightenment [1650–1780] belief in an objectivized personal Devil and his minions was all but universal among theologians. Today, however, it is generally recognized that belief in Satan, the leader of the fallen angels, etc. is not a satisfactory answer to the problem of evil." See *The Westminster Dictionary of Christian Theology*, see "Satan," by Alan Richardson, 522.

[2]Friedrich Schleiermacher, *The Christian Faith*, eds. H. R. Mackintosh and J.S. Stewart (Edinburgh: T. & T. Clark, N.D.), 161, 169–70.

[3]Rudolf Bultmann, "New Testament and Mythology," in *Kerygma and Myth*, ed. Hans Werner Bartsch (New York: Harper Torchbook, 1961), 4–5.

[4]Rejection of belief in Satan's existence is not universal, of course. Russell writes, "The horrors of twentieth-century genocide and war have revived serious philosophical concern with radical evil, and the Devil is once again a serious issue for modern theology." See Jeffrey Burton Russell, *Mephistopheles: The Devil in the Modern World* (Ithaca: Cornell University Press, 1986), 12.

[5]*The Encyclopedia of Philosophy*, see "Atheism," by Paul Edwards, 1 (1967), 182.

[6]Russell suggests that there are seven major objections to belief in the devil's existence today: (1) The general disbelief in theology and metaphysics; I.E., the belief that only scientific knowledge is true knowledge. (2) The objection that belief in the devil is not progressive or up-to-date, an objection that arises from hunches and fads rather than careful or coherent thought. (3) The objection that arises from theological traditions (E.G., rabbinical Judaism or Buddhism) that deal with the problem of evil without recourse to the Devil. (4) The manifestly and untrue objection that belief in the devil is inconsistent with the main lines of the Christian Tradition. (5) The argument—based on the violent wrenching of the text away from the meaning intended by the authors—that belief in the devil is inconsistent with the Scriptures, specifically with the New Testament. (6) The objection—grounded in a dogmatically materialistic world view—that belief in the devil is inconsistent with experience. (7) The objection that diabology is inconsistent with the doctrine of a sovereign and good God. Jeffrey Burton Russell, *Satan: The Early Christian Tradition* (Ithaca: Cornell University Press, 1981), 220–22.

[7]Pierre Charles Baudelaire, *Short Prose Poems*, quoted by Denis De Rougemont, *The Devil's Share* (New York: Meridian, 1956), 17.

[8]Hal Lindsey, *Satan is Alive and Well on Planet Earth* (Grand Rapids: Zondervan, 1972).

[9]Michael P. Green, ed., *Illustrations for Biblical Preaching* (Grand Rapids: Baker, 1989), 322–23.

[10]J.I. Packer, "The Devil's Dossier," *Christianity Today* (June 21, 1993), 24.

[11]Packer, "The Devil's Dossier," 24.

[12]Leon Morris, *The Revelation of St. John*, Tyndale New Testament Commentaries (Grand Rapids: Eerdmans, 1969), 233.

[13]W.A. Criswell, *Expository Sermons on Revelation*, 5 vols. (Grand Rapids: Zondervan, 1969), 5:49–50.

[14]G.R. Beasley-Murray, *The Book of Revelation*, New Century Bible (London: Oliphants, 1974), 284.

[15]Swete denies that καὶ εἶδον is used here to describe sequential chronological events, but he gives no reason for this assertion. See Henry Barclay Swete, *The Apocalypse of St. John* (London: Macmillan, 1906), 256.

[16]Robert H. Mounce, *The Book of Revelation*, New International Commentary on the New Testament (rev. ed., Grand Rapids: Eerdmans, 1998), 361. This, says Pieters, an amillennialist, is "a very good feature" of premillennialism. See Albertus Pieters, *Studies in The Revelation of St. John* (Grand Rapids: Eerdmans, 1954), 294.

[17]Against the evidence Garlington asserts that John shows "very little concern...for a precise chronological program." Cf. Donald Garlington, "Reigning With Christ: Revelation 20:1–6 and the Question of the Millennium," *Reformation and Revival Journal 6* (Spring, 1997), 80.

[18]Cf. R.C.H. Lenski, *The Interpretation of St. John's Revelation* (Minneapolis: Augsburg, 1943), 564; William Hendriksen, *More Than Conquerors: An Interpretation of the Book of Revelation* (Grand Rapids: Baker, 1939), 221; Anthony A. Hoekema, *The Bible and the Future* (Grand Rapids: Eerdmans, 1979), 223–26; Garlington, "Reigning With Christ," 68–72.

[19]White, a proponent of the recapitulation view, argues that the presence of καὶ εἶδον in 20:1 is irrelevant. The only relevant point is the content of the visions. White himself acknowledges that the repeated καὶ εἶδον does introduce a series of events in chronological sequence in Rev. 19:11–21. My point is that a pattern is established in 19:11–21—I.E., visions that are clearly in chronological sequence are introduced by καὶ εἶδον. That fact that 20:1 is introduced by καὶ εἶδον suggests that we should at least consider whether the events in 20:1–3 follow chronologically after those in 19:11–21. There is nothing in 20:1–6 that suggests anything but such a sequence. It is White's amillennialism that has produced this hermeneutical device (recapitulation) and not the straightforward exegesis of Revelation 19:11–20:10. As Blomberg notes, the very content of the section makes it "impossible to insert a literary seam in between Revelation 19:20–21 and 20:1 as amillennial and postmillennial perspectives are forced to do. Chapter 19 ends with the eternal punishment of two-thirds of the unholy trinity of chapters 12 to 13: the first Beast and the false prophet. But what is the fate of the dragon, I.E., Satan, the third individual and chief person of this demonic trio? This question is not answered until 20:1–3. But, given that there is no logical or chronological break before verse 4, the millennium

that is described in the rest of chapter 20 must of necessity follow the return of Christ, with which chapter 19 concludes" (Craig Blomberg, "Eschatology and the Church: Some New Testament Perspectives," *Themelios* 23 [June 1998], 14–15). CF. R. Fowler White, "Making Sense of Rev. 20:1–10? Harold Hoehner Versus Recapitulation," *Journal of the Evangelical Society 37* (1994): 540. CF. also White's unconvincing attempt to deal with the hermeneutics of Rev. 20:1–3 in "On the Hermeneutics and Interpretation of Revelation 20:1–3: A Preconsummationist Perspective," *Journal of the Evangelical Theological Society* 42 (March, 1999), 53–66. For further discussion favoring chronological sequence in these verses, CF. Robert L. Thomas, *Revelation 8–22: An Exegetical Commentary* (Chicago: Moody, 1995), 527–41, 580–81; Harold W. Hoehner, "Evidence from Revelation 20," in *A Case for Premillennialism: A New Consensus*, eds. Donald K. Campbell and Jeffrey T. Townsend (Chicago: Moody, 1992), 247–52.

[20]This untenable view is that of the postmillennialists. Boettner writes, "We hold…that the binding of Satan is a process continuing through this dispensation as evil is more and more suppressed, as the world is more and more Christianized…." CF. Loraine Boettner, *The Millennium* (Philadelphia: Presbyterian and Reformed Publishing Co., 1957), 127. Chilton writes, "The Lord *began* [italics mine] 'binding the strong man' during His earthly ministry; having successfully completed His mission, He is now plundering Satan's house and carrying off his property." CF. David Chilton, *The Days of Vengeance* (Ft. Worth: Dominion Press, 1987), 500. Chilton's view seems to be a refinement of Boettner's. As Hughes points out, however, the binding is an act that occurs prior to the thousand years. It does not, as Boettner and Chilton imply, continue throughout the thousand years. CF. James A. Hughes, "Revelation 20:4–6 and the Question of the Millennium," *The Westminster Theological Journal 35* (Spring, 1973), 281, N. 2.

[21]CF. Joseph Seiss, *Lectures on the Apocalypse*, 3 vols. (9TH ed., New York: Charles C. Cook, 1906), 3:270–82; Rene; Pache, *The Future Life*, trans. Helen I. Needham (Chicago: Moody, 1962), 61–96; Robert A. Morey, *Death and the Afterlife* (Minneapolis: Bethany House, 1984), 72–93; C. Fred Dickason, *Angels Elect and Evil* (rev. ed., Chicago: Moody, 1995), 233.

[22]CF. *Theological Dictionary of the New Testament*, see "ᾅδης," by J. Jeremias, I (1964), 146–49.

[23]According to Josephus, the Pharisees held to the idea of a spatial separation in the underworld (Josephus, *Jewish Antiquities* 18.14, trans. Louis H. Feldman, in *Josephus*, 10 vols., The Loeb Classical Library [New York: G.P. Putnam, 1930], 9:12–13). CF. *Theological Dictionary of the New Testament*, 1:147.

[24]On the interpretation of Eph. 4:8–9 as referring to the abode of the dead, CF. *Theological Dictionary of the New Testament*, see "κατώτερος," by F. Büchsel, 3 (1965): 641–42; *Theological Dictionary of the New Testament*, see "μέρος," by J. Schneider, 4 (1967): 597–98; Homer A. Kent, Jr., Ephesians: *The Glory of the Church*, Everyman's Bible Commentary (Chicago: Moody, 1971), 69–70; Wilhelm Bousset, *Kyrios Christos*, trans. John E. Steely (Nashville: Abingdon, 1970), 65. For alternate views, however, CF. F.F. Bruce, *The Epistles to the Colossians, to Philemon, and to the Ephesians*, New International Commentary on the New Testament (Grand Rapids: Eerdmans, 1984), 343–44, N. 56; *Theological Dictionary of the New Testament*, see "καταβαίνω," by J. Schneider, 1 (1964): 523; W. Hall Harris III, "The Ascent and Descent of Christ in Ephesians 4:9–10," *Bibliotheca Sacra* 151 (1994): 198–214.

[25]CF. the discussion in Seiss, *Lectures on the Apocalypse*, 3:270–82; and Morey, *Death and the Afterlife*, 84–87.

[26]CF. *A Hebrew and English Lexicon of the Old Testament,* eds., Francis Brown, S.R. Driver, and Charles A. Briggs (London: Oxford University Press, 1953), see "תֹּפֶת," 1075; *International Standard Bible Encyclopedia*, see "Topheth," by J.F. Prewitt, 4 (1988), 876–77.

[27]Seiss, *Lectures on the Apocalypse*, 3:279–80.

[28]*Theological Dictionary of the New Testament*, see "γέεννα," by J. Jeremias, 1 (1964), 657–58.

[29]*Theological Dictionary of the New Testament*, see "ἄβυσσος," by J. Jeremias, 1 (1964), 9–10.

[30]In one text (I.E., Rom. 10:7) the term *abyss* may be a synonym for sheol or hades, but even there it may refer to the prison of spirits, CF. 1 Pet. 3:19. Cranfield says the Abyss equals sheol in Rom 10:7. CF. C.E.B. Cranfield, *A Critical and Exegetical Commentary on the Epistle to the Romans*, International Critical Commentary, 2 vols. (Edinburgh: T. & T. Clark, 1979), 2:525.

³¹The Bible speaks of angels who are imprisoned today: (1) There are apparently demons in the Abyss (Luke 8:28–31). (2) Certain demons are kept in Tartarus (2 Pet. 2:4; NASB mistakenly reads "hell") in "eternal bonds" (Jude 6) because of their sin in Genesis 6. The demons of Tartarus, unlike those of the Abyss, will never be released (CF. Rev. 9:1–3). Tartarus should probably be understood as a different place than the Abyss. CF. Dickason, *Angels*, 233; *Exegetical Dictionary of the New Testament*, see "ταρταρόω," 3:336.

³²*Theological Dictionary of the New Testament*, 1:10.

³³Seiss, *Lectures on the Apocalypse*, 3:270. Charles writes, "The abyss is regarded only as a temporary abode of punishment." CF. R.H. Charles, *The Revelation of St. John*, International Critical Commentary, 2 vols. (Edinburgh: T. & T. Clark, 1920), 2:141.

³⁴The Greek text is difficult to explain. It literally reads "and a great chain upon his hand" (καὶ ἅλυσιν μεγάλην ἐπὶ τὴν χεῖρα αὐτοῦ). E.R. Craven suggests that the chain is looped over the angel's hand or arm. CF. John Peter Lange, "The Revelation of John," trans. E. Moore, ed. E.R. Craven, in *Commentary on the Holy Scriptures*, ed. J.P. Lange, 25 vols. (reprint ed., Grand Rapids: Zondervan, 1960), 25:349. Swete (*The Apocalypse of St. John*, 256) suggests that the chain lies on the angel's hand "ready for use as soon as he comes upon the criminal."

³⁵CF. Swete, *The Apocalypse of St. John*, 256; Mounce, *The Book of Revelation*, 361, N. 4.

³⁶CF. Charles, *The Revelation of St. John*, 2:141.

³⁷One of the more recent warnings of this kind comes from Vern Sheridan Poythress, "Genre and Hermeneutics in Rev. 20:1–6," *Journal of the Evangelical Theological Society* 36 (March, 1993), 41–54. As much as the present writer admires Dr. Poythress's obvious gifts, he cannot help but conclude that his "new" approach is simply another attempt to somehow find amillennialism in the passage. His attack on literalism is really as old as amillennialism itself. The point that literalists make is one that Poythress acknowledges, I.E., symbols have referents. It should be added that the symbols of the Revelation are intended to symbolize *something* literal or actual.

³⁸One of the more well known literalists says, "One need scarcely insist upon the symbolic character of the scene, for that seems evident...." Cf. Walter Scott, *Exposition of the Revelation of Jesus Christ* (4TH ed., London: Pickering & Inglis, N.D.), 396.

³⁹Josephus, *Jewish Antiquities* 1.50–51, in *Josephus*, 10 vols., The Loeb Classical Library (New York: G. P. Putnam, 1930): 4:25. For this illustration, the writer is indebted to William Kelly, *Lectures on the Book of Revelation* (London: G. Morrish, 1874), 409–10.

⁴⁰After hearing the writer preach upon Rev. 19:17–21 (Oct. 17, 1993), Professor Donald Bloesch remarked that he had never heard anyone in the Presbyterian Church or the United Church of Christ preach from the book of Revelation. Dr. Bloesch hastened to add that he has preached from the Revelation.

⁴¹Walvoord pointedly addresses the issue: "The question has been raised as to how an angel who is an immaterial being can lay hold on Satan who is also an immaterial being. Such a query is born of unbelief." Cf. John F. Walvoord, *The Revelation of Jesus Christ* (Chicago: Moody, 1966), 291.

⁴²Seiss, *Lectures on the Apocalypse*, 3:269.

⁴³Martin Kiddle, *The Revelation of St. John*, Moffatt New Testament Commentary (New York: Harper, 1940), 399.

⁴⁴Scott, *Exposition of the Revelation of Jesus Christ*, 396.

⁴⁵Kelly, *Lectures on the Book of Revelation*, 412–13.

⁴⁶Mounce, *The Book of Revelation*, 361, N. 6.

⁴⁷Mounce, *The Book of Revelation*, 361. On the significance of the names here in Revelation, CF. Seiss, *Lectures on the Apocalypse*, 3:264–67.

⁴⁸*Theological Dictionary of the New Testament*, see "δράκων," by W. Foerster, 2 (1964): 281–83.

⁴⁹Charles, *The Revelation of St. John*, 2:141.

[50] *Theological Dictionary of the New Testament*, see "ὄφις," by W. Foerster, 5 (1967): 580.

[51] *A Greek-English Lexicon of the New Testament*, eds. William F. Arndt, F. Wilbur Gingrich, and Frederick W. Danker (2D. ed., Chicago: University of Chicago Press, 1979), see "διάβολος," 182.

[52] *Theological Dictionary of the New Testament*, see "διάβολος," by W. Foerster, 2 (1964): 71–73.

[53] Beasley-Murray, *The Book of Revelation*, 285.

[54] *Theological Dictionary of the New Testament*, 2:79; CF. *Theological Dictionary of the New Testament*, see "σατανᾶς," by W. Foerster and K. Schaferdiek 7 (1971): 151–65.

[55] *A Greek-English Lexicon of the New Testament* (Arndt, Gingrich, and Danker), see "σατανᾶς," 744.

[56] Donald Grey Barnhouse, *Revelation: An Expository Commentary* (Grand Rapids: Zondervan, 1971), 378–79.

[57] Mounce, *The Book of Revelation*, 362.

[58] Beasley-Murray, *The Book of Revelation*, 285.

[59] E.G., Hendriksen, *More Than Conquerors*, 225–26; Lenski, *The Interpretation of St. John's Revelation*, 574–75; Garlington, "Reigning With Christ," 69–72.

[60] Harry R. Boer, an amillennial scholar, admits, "The binding of the strong man in the Synoptic Gospels, on which Augustine based his entire position, bears no recognizable relationship to the thrust of the amillennial view. That thrust is that the binding of Satan applies only to his ability to deceive the nations. But where are the nations in the pericopes that refer to the binding of the strong man? They are not to be seen. What is very much in view is the local sufferers from demon possession and Satan's inability to prevent Jesus from healing them; what is not at all in view is the now blessedly undeceived nations." CF. "What About the Millennium?" *The Reformed Journal* 25 (Jan., 1975), 29.

[61]Cf. the discussion in Walvoord, *The Revelation of Jesus Christ*, 292–93.

[62]So Hendriksen, *More Than Conquerors*, 228.

[63]Hendriksen, *More Than Conquerors*, 226. In context, however, the deception of Satan that is interrupted is the future deception of the nations (16:13–14) by the Beast, the false prophet, and Satan (Cf. 19:20). It is not a deception that ended at the cross allowing the worldwide missionary effort. Hendriksen and those who follow him do not see the contradiction of their position here. He asserts that Satan was bound at the cross to end his deceptions, yet he earlier says (P. 219) that it is only at Christ's second coming that "his power to deceive on earth shall cease forever."

[64]Contrary to the amillennial exegesis of Hughes, the deception of 20:3 is not defined by 20:7–8. Hughes identifies 20:7–8 as the deception referred to in 20:3. This cannot be, for John says that Satan is imprisoned in order that he might not deceive the nations "any longer" (ἔτι). This cannot refer to the deception of 20:7–8, because that is after the thousand years. The deception described in 20:3 refers to something antecedent to the thousand years—the events in 19:11–21. Cf. James A. Hughes, "Question of the Millennium," 281–83; Richard A. Ostella, "The Significance of Deception in Revelation 20:3," *The Westminster Theological Journal* 37 (Winter, 1975), 236–38. Ostella argues that the discontinuance of deception in Rev. 20:3 "is a critically decisive exegetical point…which ultimately demands the conclusion that the millennium involves an extension of redemptive history subsequent to the parousia."

[65]Boer, "What About the Millennium?" 28.

[66]Kurt Koch, *Christian Counseling and Occultism* (Grand Rapids: Kregel, 1965), 290.

[67]*Theological Dictionary of the New Testament*, see "εὐαγγελίζομαι," by G. Friedrich, 2 (1964): 710, 722.

[68]J. Dwight Pentecost, *Your Adversary the Devil* (Grand Rapids: Zondervan, 1969), 183.

[69]Oscar Cullmann, *Christ and Time*, trans. Floyd V. Filson (Philadelphia: Westminster, 1964), 84, 144–46.

3: Binding of Satan

[70]"To Illustrate Plus," *Leadership 19* (Spring, 1998), 79, 81.

[71]J. Oswald Sanders, *Satan is No Myth* (Chicago: Moody, 1975), 137.

[72]Swete, *The Apocalypse of St. John*, 257. The recapitulation theory, I.E., the amillennial theory that Rev. 20:7–10 recapitulates the events of 19:11–21, founders on the question of the deception of the nations. According to this view the binding of Satan (20:3) took place at the cross, and from that time the nations are protected from Satanic deception, allowing the gospel message to be disseminated worldwide. However, in 19:20 the battle of Armageddon ends the future deception of the nations by the false prophet. Furthermore, the recapitulation theory assumes that the final defeat of Satan (20:7–10) takes place at the time of the defeat of the Beast and the false prophet (19:19–21), whereas 20:10 presupposes that the Beast and the false prophet are defeated before Satan and are present in the lake of fire before him. It is simply wrong to posit a wrenching chronological break between chapters 19 and 20. "Narrative progression seems hard to evade." CF. Paul A. Rainbow, "Millennium as Metaphor in St. John's Apocalypse," *Westminster Theological Journal* 58 (1996), 211, N. 8. Rainbow is responding to R. Fowler White, "Reexamining the Evidence for Recapitulation in Rev. 20:1–10," *Westminster Theological Journal 51* (1989), 319–44.

[73]This question is raised as a major problem for premillennialists by White. CF. R. Fowler White, "Reexamining the Evidence for Recapitulation in Rev. 20:1–10," *The Westminster Theological Journal 51* (Fall, 1989), 323–24.

[74]CF. George Eldon Ladd, *A Commentary on the Revelation of John* (Grand Rapids: Eerdmans, 1972), 262–63; James Moffatt, "The Revelation of St. John the Divine," in *The Expositor's Greek Testament*, 5 vols. (London: Hodder & Stoughton, 1910; reprint ed., Grand Rapids: Eerdmans, 1970), 5:471.

[75]White notes that the term "nations" (τά ἔθνη) generally refers to unbelievers in contrast to the saints (2:26; 5:9; 7:9; 10:11; 11:2, 9, 18; 12:5; 13:7; 14:6, 8; 16:19; 17:15; 18:3, 23; 19:15). As he admits, however, four other times—five, including 20:3—the term does refer to the saints (15:4; 21:24, 26; 22:2). CF. White, "Making Sense of Rev. 20:1–10," 540–41.

[76]Walvoord, *The Revelation of Jesus Christ*, 302; CF. the discussion in Thomas, *Revelation 8–22*, 410–11.

[77] For the thoughts developed here, CF. Seiss, *Lectures on the Apocalypse*, 3:285–89.

[78] CF. Lynn Harold Hough, "The Revelation of St. John the Divine: Exposition," in *The Interpreter's Bible*, 12 vols. (New York: Abingdon, 1957), 12:517.

[79] There are, of course, impersonal "evils" in nature, such as storms, earthquakes, volcanic eruptions, and disease. My point, however, is that the most tragic evils in the world are caused by deliberate, wicked choices of personal beings. CF. Hough, "Revelation," 517–18.

[80] Seiss, *Lectures on the Apocalypse*, 3:284–86.

[81] Seiss, *Lectures on the Apocalypse*, 3:286–87.

[82] CF. Beasley-Murray, *The Book of Revelation*, 287.

[83] Daniel Defoe, *Adventures of Robinson Crusoe*, forward by Clyde S. Kilby (Chicago: Moody, 1965), 194. Significantly, many of these Christian elements have been deleted from later editions. CF. Daniel Defoe, *Robinson Crusoe* (Garden City: Doubleday, 1945), 150.

[84] *Oxford Dictionary of the Christian Church*, see "St. Boniface," 187.

[85] For this illustration I am indebted to Chilton, *Days of Vengeance*, 497.

[86] This illustration was told to me on July 23, 1996 by Mrs. Gwenneth Schwab at Conference Point on Lake Geneva, Wisconsin.

[87] Packer, "The Devil's Dossier," 24.

❧

THE FOURTH LAST THING:

The Millennial Kingdom Of Christ
Revelation 20:4-6

❧

In the film *Grand Canyon* (1991), an immigration attorney breaks out of a traffic jam and tries to bypass it by taking another route. His new route takes him along streets that seem progressively darker and more deserted. Then comes the predictable nightmare: the man's fancy sports car stalls in one of those alarming inner-city neighborhoods whose streets are terrorized by armed teenage gangsters. He manages to phone for a tow truck, but before it arrives five young street toughs surround his car and threaten him with considerable bodily harm. Just in time, the tow truck shows up and its driver—an earnest, genial man named "Simon"—begins to hook up the sports car. The young toughs protest: the tow truck driver is interrupting their payday. So the driver takes the group leader aside and attempts a five sentence introduction to morality. "Man," he says, "the world ain't s'pposed to work like this. Maybe you don't know that, but this ain't the way it's supposed to be. I'm s'pposed to be able to do my job without askin' you if I can. And that dude is s'pposed to be able to wait with his car without you rippin' him off. Everything's s'pposed to be different than what it is here."[1]

❧

As Cornelius Plantinga, professor of systematic theology at Calvin Theological Seminary, has written, "Central in the…Christian understanding of the world is a concept of the way things are supposed to be. They ought to be as designed and intended by God." The way things are supposed to be includes peace on earth, justice for all mankind, mutual respect and goodwill among people, and widespread concern for the good of one's neighbor.[2]

As everyone knows, however, "things are not that way at all. Human wrongdoing…mars every adult's workday, every child's schoolday, every vacationer's holiday." Plantinga asks his readers to think of the corrupt influences of sin. "A moment's reflection yields memories and images of wrongdoing so commonplace that we are likely to accept them as normal." A criminal in an old 1940s movie hangs up a telephone receiver; before exiting the phone booth, he rips the page he had consulted from the phone book and pockets it. A third grader distributes party invitations in a manner calculated to let the omitted classmates clearly see their exclusion. A man driving a car cuts someone off and then, to assure him that the move was intentional, offers him the hand signal that is known world wide. Two old flames meet at a high school reunion and begin to intimately chat with nostalgia and boozy self-pity over what might have been. Although each is happily married to someone else, somehow the two grads end the evening in a hotel room.

The Bible assures us that God hates sin. He hates it because it violates His laws. He also hates it, Plantinga astutely observes, because it breaks the peace, because it interferes with the way things are supposed to be. "Sin offends God not only because it bereaves or assaults God directly, as in impiety and blasphemy, but also because it bereaves and assaults what God has made." Sin spoils everything God has made. It adulterates a marriage. It befouls a stream. It uses an excellent mind to devise an ingenious tax fraud.

The great writing prophets of the Bible knew that "sin has a thousand faces."[3] They looked on in hope to a new age in which human wickedness would be straightened out, the foolish would be made wise, and the wise humble. They dreamed of a time when the Lord Himself would be present to teach man His ways, when He would sort out the differences between peoples, and warfare between nations would end (Isa. 2:2–4). They spoke of a time when a great anointed Son of David would judge and rule the earth (Isa. 11:1–9). He would treat all classes of people fairly, and would immediately crush all wickedness. They prophesied that the desert places would flower as new streams of water appeared, the blind would see, the deaf would hear, and the lame would leap for joy (Isa. 35). People would go to sleep without weapons in their laps (Isa. 32:14–20). They would work in peace and honesty. A wolf would lie down with a lamb (Isa. 11), and all nature would be fruitful, benign, and filled with wonder. All nature and all mankind would look to God, lean on God, and delight in God (Isa. 42:1–12; 60; 65:17–25; Joel 2:24–29).[4]

When Jesus Christ appeared on the scene He came to fulfill all these dreams of the prophets. At His first coming He died upon the cross to provide forgiveness for sins and reconciliation with God. At His second coming He will reign upon the earth, and restore things to the way they are supposed to be.

In Revelation 19 and 20 John describes, in chronological order, a series of events that will transpire at the time of our Lord's return. First, He will return as a warrior-king to make war against His enemies (Rev. 19:11–16). Second, He will destroy the armies of Antichrist and cast him into the lake of fire (19:17–21). Third, Satan will be imprisoned in the Abyss for a thousand years and Christ will reign upon the earth for one thousand years—a "millennium." The term *millennium* is from two Latin words: *mille* (1,000) and *annus* (year).

Before beginning an exposition of the passage it will be necessary to briefly define a few terms that relate to the history of the interpretation of our passage.[5] There are, broadly speaking, three interpretations of the text.[6]

THREE APPROACHES TO REVELATION 20:1–6

THE PREMILLENNIAL VIEW

According to the premillennial view Christ returns prior to the thousand years and reigns upon the earth. His return is "pre"—"prior to" or "before"—the millennium. This view has also been known as "chiliasm," because of the Greek words for "thousand years" in our passage. A straightforward reading of the passage leads to this view, and it is the interpretation of the early church so far as is known.[7] No writer for the first 200 years of church history advanced any other view.[8] Most modern commentators agree that the apostle John here teaches the premillennial advent of Christ, although they do not all agree that he was correct.[9]

THE AMILLENNIAL VIEW

According to the amillennial view there will be no future reign of Christ on earth.[10] It is not really precise to say that amillennialsits do not believe in a millennium. They do not believe in a *future* millennium. They believe that the millennium is *now*.[11] The thousand years are a symbol of the present reign of the saints in heaven. Satan, the amillennialists argue, was bound during Christ's first advent, and the first resurrection takes place when a person is born again or when a believer dies and goes to heaven.[12]

This view was unknown, so far as we know, in the early, post-apostolic church.[13] However, war was declared on the premillennial view by the formidable Alexandrian scholars, Dionysius (died c. AD264),[14] Clement (c. 150–c. 215)[15], and Origen (c. 185–c. 254).[16] They accused the premillennialists of being Judaistic and literalistic,[17] charges which are repeated until the present time.[18]

Sadly, it was the great Augustine (354–430)[19] who developed the amillennial interpretation which replaced premillennialism for hundreds of years. Augustine says that he was at one time a premillennialist, but he abandoned the view because he objected to the carnal way some premillennialists were describing life in the millennial kingdom as a time of gluttonous and drunken banqueting.[20]

THE POSTMILLENNIAL VIEW

According to the postmillennial view, Christ returns after the thousand-year period, which may be literal or may refer to an indefinite yet very long period of time. Proponents argue that chapter 19 (the rider on the white horse) does not describe the second advent of Christ but rather the victorious preaching of the gospel in the present age. The thousand years describes the present age during which the gospel will make great inroads and the world will be Christianized. This age will culminate in a very long period of spiritual prosperity, increasing peace, and economic well being. This long period is what is known as the millennium. Only after the thousand years does Christ return to earth.

Postmillennialists also like to claim Augustine as their father.[21] A number of very able theologians of the past have held the view.[22] It has not been very popular in the twentieth century, but there is a small and growing group of Christians in our day who have embraced the viewpoint.[23]

In this chapter our passage will be expounded from the premillennial point of view because I believe that interpretation is the true one and the only one that is theologically meaningful.[24] A number of reasons for accepting the premillennial view will be presented in the following pages, but our primary purpose is to expound the message of the text rather than to argue a theological point.

THE MILLENNIAL KINGDOM: THE REIGN OF CHRIST UPON THE EARTH (VERSES 4–5)

THE VICTORIOUS CHRIST

In his vision[25] John sees thrones and people sitting upon them, and "they reigned with Christ for a thousand years" (v. 4). Verse 6 says they "will reign with Him." The great millennial hymn of Isaac Watts (1674–1748) expresses the age long hope of the people of God:

Jesus shall reign wher-e'er the sun
Does his successive journeys run;
His kingdom spread from shore to shore,
Till moons shall wax and wane no more.

From north to south the princes meet
To pay their homage at His feet;
While western empires own their Lord,
And savage tribes attend His word.

To Him shall endless prayer be made,
And endless praises crown His head;
His name like sweet perfume shall rise
With every morning sacrifice.[26]

The promise of the angel Gabriel to Mary will at last be fulfilled, "the Lord God will give Him the throne of His father David; and He will reign over the house of Jacob forever; and His kingdom will have no end" (Luke 1:32–33).[27] The age-long request of the church will be granted, "Thy kingdom come, Thy will be done, on earth as it is in heaven" (Matt. 6:10). The promise of Jesus to His own will be honored, "Blessed are the gentle, for they shall inherit the earth" (Matt. 5:5). The earth they inherit will be changed from its present condition (Isa. 35). The answer to the apostles' question—"Lord, is it at this time You are restoring the kingdom to Israel?" (Acts 1:6)—will then be given. Israel shall be converted (Rom. 11:26) and returned to her land (Isa. 14:1), and her temple and rituals shall be restored (Ezek. 40–48).[28] The Lord Jesus Christ will dwell in Jerusalem (Zech. 8:3), and the nations will call that city "the city of the Lord, the Zion of the holy One of Israel" (Isa. 60:14; 2:3; Psalm 2:6; 48:2; 110:2). This king, says the author of the epistle to the Hebrews, will be characterized by a love of righteousness and a hatred for lawlessness (Heb. 1:8–9). There will be no frustrated United Nations trying to sort out the differences between different nations with different political philosophies and ideologies. The thousand years will be a "Christocracy,"[29] wherein the "King of kings and Lord of lords" (Rev. 19:16) will rule the nations with a "rod of iron" (19:15).[30] He will rule with complete power and authority.

In 1991 military thugs overthrew the government of President Jean-Bertrand Aristide of Haiti. President Aristide went into exile, but most nations still considered him the legally elected ruler of the country. He was restored in 1994, yet for the time of his exile he had authority of a kind but no power. The Lord Jesus Christ will have authority and power.

Alexander Woollcott met G.K. Chesterton (1874–1936) for lunch at a London restaurant. Chesterton expounded on a variety of philosophical topics, including the relationship between power and authority. "If a rhinoceros were to enter this restaurant now, there is no denying he would have great power here. But I should be the first to rise and assure him that he had no authority whatever."[31] When Jesus Christ reigns on earth, the great Chesterton would surely agree, He will have both the power and the authority to do so.

All dissension among nations will be solved, and war will be nonexistent. "And He will judge between the nations," says Isaiah the prophet (2:4), "and will render decisions for many peoples; and they will hammer their swords into plowshares"—their tanks and machine guns will be melted down and turned into trucks and tractors—"and their spears into pruning hooks. Nation will not lift up sword against nation, and never again will they learn war."[32] The poor and the needy will be given special protective care (Psalm 72:4, 12, 13), and every human being will be tenderly guarded. "A bruised reed He will not break, and a dimly burning wick He will not extinguish; He will faithfully bring forth justice" (Isa. 42:3).[33] The moral virtue of truth will be exalted in every phase of the kingdom. In contrast to the rulers of today, who seem able to justify almost any sort of untruth on the ground of "political expediency," the coming King will "faithfully bring forth justice" (Isa. 42:3). Jerusalem will be called "the City of Truth" (Zech. 8:3).[34]

4: Millennial Kingdom of Christ

The text says that Satan is the deceiver of the nations (v. 3), so it is not surprising to find governments often using deceit as a deliberate policy both to their own citizens and toward each other. Such cynicism is not new. Over 23 centuries ago Plato (427–347 BC) had Socrates say, "Then if anyone at all is to have the privilege of lying, the rulers of the State should be the persons; and they, in their dealings either with enemies or with their own citizens, may be allowed to lie for the public good. But nobody else should meddle with anything of the kind; and although the rulers have this privilege, for a private man to lie to them in return is to be deemed a more heinous fault...."[35]

During the millennium Satan, "the father of lies" (John 8:44), will be in the abyss where he can deceive the nations no longer, and the earth will be ruled by Him who is called "Faithful and True" (Rev. 19:11).

Their Identity

The Redeemed of the Ages. As John looks he sees two groups[36] of people reigning with Christ: one group to whom judgment is given and another group made up of the martyrs of the tribulation. Of the first group he writes, "And I saw thrones, and they sat upon them, and judgment was given to them." To whom does this refer? Of whom does John say that "they sat" and "judgment was given to them"? The standard exegetical procedure is to look in the preceding context (nearest antecedent) for their identity. They are not the devil (v. 2), nor the angel (v. 1), nor the beasts and their armies (19:19–21). The nearest possibility is found in 19:14: "the armies which are in heaven, clothed in white linen, white and clean." It refers to God's redeemed people.[37]

In light of the prophecy in Daniel 7:18—"But the saints of the Highest One will receive the kingdom"—I would conclude that this includes the Old Testament saints. Because of Matthew 19:28, where Jesus says to His disciples, "In the regeneration when the Son of Man will sit on His glorious throne, you also shall sit upon twelve thrones, judging the twelve tribes of Israel," I would argue that the apostles are included. I would also argue, because of 1 Corinthians 6:2–3[38] ("the saints will judge the world [and] we shall judge angels") that the saints of the present age, the church, are included (CF. also Rev. 2:26–27; 3:21; 5:10).[39] The occupants of the thrones, then, are the redeemed of all the ages. They are the Messiah's assessors, His assistants in the work of judging.[40] They are the King's associate justices in the affairs of the kingdom.

These thrones should not be thought of as mere ceremonial positions; these are not make-believe judges.[41] The kingdom will begin on earth after the defeat of the Lord's enemies, and there will be many crucial matters needing to be settled without delay.[42] Throughout the millennial kingdom human life will continue with the possibilities of sin and error (CF. Ps. 72:4. 9, 14; Isa. 65:20; Zech. 14:17), though greatly restrained and controlled. There will be need for judicial activity then as well as now. These justices will not be marked by the prejudice and fallibility so characteristic of our present judicial system.[43]

The Martyrs of the Tribulation. John sees another group in his vision, "the souls"[44] of the tribulation martyrs,[45] those who refused to worship the Antichrist or go along with his cause.[46] During the holocaust days of tribulation, they identified with Jesus Christ by proclaiming Him and obeying Him. John has in mind the martyrs of the tribulation, but the tribulation martyrs will be but the final group of those faithful Christians who loved Christ more than life. With great courage they took to heart the words of their Savior, "Do not fear those who kill the body, but are not able to kill the soul" (Matt. 10:28).

The stories of the martyrs are almost without number, and this text tells of their special place in the heart of God, for they are singled out for special mention. There was a modern martyr, an Anglican, James Hannington of Oxford and Uganda. He toiled shiningly for Christ in Eastern Equatorial Africa until his work was cut short by violent death. "I felt," he wrote in his diary just before the end, "that they were coming upon me to murder me; but I sang

'Safe in the Arms of Jesus,' and laughed at the agony of my situation." That is the spirit of martyr Christianity—safe in the arms of Jesus, and laughing at the agony.[47]

Their Resurrection. In standing against the Beast the martyrs paid the penalty of death. If they received death from the state, what will they receive from God? The answer is quick and dramatic. The martyrs—and all of God's people—will receive life and a place in the government of Christ's kingdom.[48] The verb "they came to life" is the key interpretive problem of the passage and the entire millennial question. What does it mean?

When I say that this is the key problem I do not mean that it is a difficult problem. Actually, it is a very easy problem, unless an exegete is trying to force the verse to say something it does not say. Some say the verb refers to the new birth of the soul.[49] This is impossible as a careful reading of the verse will show. These people came to life after they were beheaded.[50] They were put to death *because* they were born again. Their new birth came before their martyrdom, not after. If this verse refers to the new birth, then the martyrs were beheaded before they were born again.[51]

Others say it refers to the death of the Christian and his entrance into heaven—"they came to life" means they died![52] Others say it speaks of a symbolic resurrection, that the influence of the martyrs lives in the hearts of all succeeding generations.[53] This, of course, is a farce. What kind of a hope and reward does this offer the souls under the altar? The Scriptures do promise a recompense of the sacrifices of devotion of the saints, and it is to be given at "the resurrection of the righteous" (Luke 14:14). In point of fact, as most modern interpreters[54] agree, the verb speaks here of bodily resurrection. Our text speaks of that future day when all of God's people will rise bodily from the dead. This shall take place at the beginning of the millennium.

There are four reasons for saying this: First, the immediate context requires it. In verse 5 the very same verb occurs, and almost everyone concedes that it there means physical resurrection. If one is spiritual, then the other must be spiritual. On the other hand if one is physical, then the other must be physical.[55] If not, then language can be twisted to mean anything.[56] Second, the context of the book demands it. In Revelation 2:8 it is used of the physical resurrection of the Lord Jesus Christ, and in 13:14 it is used of the Beast who was physically wounded and was physically resuscitated. Third, the use of the term "resurrection" in verse 5 also demands it. This word occurs 42 times in the New Testament, 39 times outside of this chapter. In 38 of those places it clearly means physical resurrection. In all but one place it refers to bodily resurrection (Luke 2:34).[57] This strongly suggests that such is the meaning intended here. Finally, this is the interpretation of the earliest interpreters of the Revelation. Later interpreters adopted what is called a spiritualizing method of interpretation, the allegorical method. When they did they put an end to all trustworthy exegesis of the Revelation.[58]

They "came to life." In a very real sense believers are more truly alive in heaven than they are on earth. Nevertheless, the New Testament teaches that salvation is not complete until the resurrection of the body. At that moment the soul will be reunited with the body—a real body, the same body, yet a changed body. The believer in his body will then be incorruptible and immortal (1 Cor. 15:52–54).

When he was a young man, Dwight L. Moody was called upon to preach a funeral sermon. He searched through the Gospels to find one of Christ's funeral sermons. He said, "I searched in vain. Our Lord broke up every funeral He ever attended. Death could not exist where He was!"[59] One day all of God's dead people are going to rise in new bodies. And those who are alive at that time are also going to receive glorified, resurrection bodies as their salvation is brought to perfection (1 Cor. 15:51–52).

Their Millennial Reign

The Purpose of Their Reign. What is the purpose of the millennial reign of Christ? Well, the Old Testament predicts the restoration of Israel and the establishment of the reign of the Davidic Messiah (CF. Dan. 7; Ezek. 36–37). One reason for the millennium, then, is to fulfill the Old

4: Millennial Kingdom of Christ

Testament covenant promises of God. Other commentators suggest that in the millennium there will be within our geography and within our history the vindication of the cause of Christ. The very world where He was rejected will see the manifestation of His glory. Furthermore, some scholars suggest, God is the Creator (Rev. 4), and in the millennium He shall be proven to be the Lord of the world and of history.[60]

Yet none of these things is the emphasis of this passage. What John draws attention to is those who reign with Christ. One of the early premillennialists was Tertullian (c. 160–c. 225), the noted teacher from North Africa. The reason he found the millennial hope so necessary is in order that Christians might be rewarded on the very scene of their suffering and striving.[61] It is the fate of believers in this life to be judged by the ungodly world powers. Jesus told His disciples that they would be brought before courts, governors, and kings and scourged for His sake (Matt. 10:17–18). Many would be beaten and killed. He also promised authority over cities in His kingdom to those who were faithful (CF. Luke 19:11–27). In short, the time of Christ's coming is the time of reward (Rev. 11:18).[62]

It is only at the Lord's appearing that He will give crowns or rewards to His people. "In the future there is laid up for me the crown of righteousness, which the Lord, the righteous Judge, will award to me on that day; and not only to me, but also to all who have loved His appearing" (2 Tim. 4:8). The apostle Peter adds, "And when the Chief Shepherd appears, you will receive the unfading crown of glory" (1 Pet. 5:4). Likewise in Revelation 2:26 we are told that it is in the end that the Lord will give His people "authority over the nations." It is at the time of the Lord's second advent, not today in heaven or on earth, that is the time of enthronement for the saints.[63]

Henry C. Morrison, after serving for 40 years on the African mission field, headed home by boat. On that same ship also sailed Theodore Roosevelt. Morrison was quite dejected when, on entering New York harbor, President Roosevelt received a great fanfare as he arrived home. Morrison thought he should get some recognition for 40 years in the Lord's service. Then a small voice came to him and said, "Henry—you're not home yet."[64] Mr. Morrison's real fanfare did not come when he died and went to heaven, either. It is yet to come in the millennial kingdom.

The Basis of Their Reign. The basis of their entrance into the millennial kingdom is their saving relationship to Jesus Christ. Only those who have been born again can enter the kingdom, Jesus told Nicodemus (John 3:3). However, the new birth is not mentioned in our text at all. What is mentioned is the faithfulness of the martyrs. Their obedience is stated both positively and negatively:[65] positively, they were faithful in proclaiming Jesus Christ in obedience to God's

Word;[66] negatively, they did not cave in to the pressures of the world system of the Beast.

In one of Jesus' kingdom parables (Luke 19:11–27) He speaks of differences of reward in the kingdom. One would have authority over ten cities (v. 17), another would have authority over five cities (v. 19). When our Lord describes rewards He does so in terms of tangible, visible honor in the kingdom. The reward for these martyrs is going to take place in the visible, historical, and temporal scene of their martyrdom.[67] Reward will apparently depend on degrees of faithfulness in this present life.

The Time of Their Reign. By now it is clear that I believe that the reign described in Revelation 20:4–6 is future, following the second advent of Jesus Christ.[68] It will be during the time of Satan's imprisonment in the abyss. It will follow the believers' bodily resurrection from the dead. It is marked out in our passage as taking place between the resurrection of the righteous and the resurrection of the unrighteous.[69]

It is often asserted that we should not base our views of prophecy on such a symbolical and difficult passage. I would argue that it is not a difficult passage. Furthermore, I would argue that it is the central New Testament passage on the chronology of events of the end time. I would also argue that it is the theological prejudice of our dear postmillennial and amillennial brethren that gives them such difficulty with this passage.

The Place of Their Reign. Where do they reign? It is
quite evident that they reign upon the earth, yet we are told
by some that this text nowhere states that they reign upon
the earth.[70] To say this is to read the passage with blinders
on, ignoring both the near context and the broader context
of the book. First, in Revelation 5:10 it says of God's people
that "they will reign upon the earth."[71] Second, the clear
implication of 19:11–16 is that Christ returns to earth to
defeat the nations. Third, after the thousand years Satan
is to be released, and he will again attack God's people.
Verse 9 clearly says the saints are living "on the broad plain
of the earth." Finally, the Old Testament looks forward to
an earthly kingdom of the kind described here (cf. Ps. 2:8;
Dan. 7:14; Ezek. 36–37).[72]

The Subjects of Their Reign. Those who occupy the
thrones are not sham rulers. Their offices are real, and
there are genuine tasks that go along with them. The life
of the believer in the millennium is not a life of idleness.
It will be a busy life.[73] But whom do they judge and rule?
Our text does not say, so I confess my answer is somewhat
speculative.[74] The subjects of God's resurrected saints must
be the believing Gentiles and Jews who pass through the
tribulation and are alive at the second advent.

There are a number of lines of evidence in support of
this conclusion.[75] First, as has just been suggested, the rewards of Christ are not empty offices. It would be empty

recognition of their service to reign over a world of which they were the sole inhabitants.[76] Second, there are no unbelievers alive to enter the kingdom (John 3:3–5). They have either been killed in the great battle in chapter 19 or they have faced Christ at the judgment of the nations described in Matthew 25:31–46, at which time they have been denied entrance into the kingdom.[77] Since those ruled are not unbelievers, they must be believers. There will be saved Jews and Gentiles who enter the millennium in natural bodies, marry and have children, and carry on normal lives during that time. Life will be greatly improved, yet they will grow old and die. Their children will be confronted with the gospel and will have to choose whether or not they will embrace the Messiah as their Savior (CF. Isa. 65:18–25).

Some have been offended at the thought of unglorified people in their earthly bodies walking the same earth with the Lord's immortal ones in their resurrection glory. One writer calls this "a *mixum gatherum*," I.E., a mixed gathering.[78] Yet such a thing has already happened. The Lord Jesus Christ in His resurrection body spent 40 days before His ascension instructing His disciples, who had unglorified bodies (CF. Acts 1:3).[79]

The Length of Their Reign. John says they "reigned with Christ for a thousand years" (v. 4). The millennium is an intermediate kingdom. It is a transitional phase—an interlude, "an intermezzo of history"[80]—that leads up to the eternal kingdom described in chapter 21. Amillennialists tell their premillennial brethren that the number 1,000 should not be taken literally. Rather, they assert, it is a symbolical number standing for a complete period, a very long period of indeterminate length.[81] They argue that our passage is the only one in the Bible to speak of a millennium. Furthermore, they assert, in a book full of symbolical numbers we should expect to take this one symbolically as well.

In response, it should be pointed out, first of all, that while this is the only passage to describe the length of Christ's earthly kingdom, it is not the only passage to speak of that kingdom, as has been seen. Furthermore, although some of the numbers in Revelation are symbolic, that does not mean they have no literal meaning. For example, in chapters 2 and 3 there are letters written to seven churches. All interpreters agree that the number *seven* is used to suggest that these churches are in some way representative. Yet, it can be pointed out, there were seven actual churches in Asia Minor for whom Christ had a message. Additionally, whenever the number 1,000 is found in Revelation it refers to something definite.[82] For example, the 144,000 Israelites (Rev. 7:4–8; 14:1, 3) must be understood literally because John states that they are made up of 12,000 from each of the 12 tribes of Israel. When the two witnesses (Rev. 11:3) are granted authority for 1,260 days, the preceding verse interprets this literally to refer to 42 months of 30 days each.[83] Furthermore, whenever the word "year" is used with a number (Old Testament) or a numeral (New Testament) it always refers to literal years.[84] Likewise, in Revelation whenever there is a reference to time periods like days or months they should always be taken literally. There is no reason that we should not make the same application to years.[85] The only safe course is to take the numbers of Revelation at face value unless there are textual or contextual reasons for not doing so.[86]

The Quality of Their Reign. The reign of Christ's assessors or assistants will introduce a change in the world's history. The nations of the earth will be under the administration of immortal rulers whose commands they will be required to obey. There will be a rule "with a rod of iron." There will be a sudden collapse of all the usual haunts of sin, a rooting out of all the nurseries of iniquity, the clearing away of the marshes and bogs of crime. The pictures on the "People" page in *Time* Magazine will not be the lawbreakers and shallow, immoral celebrities. There will be a revolution in business customs, culture, newspaper writing, book making, science, and education.[87] The little phrases "with Christ" (v. 4) and "with Him" (v. 6) suggest that for the first time this earth will have a perfect government.

A Stark Contrast: The Fate Of Those Who Are Unbelieving
(verse 5)

The Second Resurrection Is A Resurrection Of The Unbelieving Dead

A stark contrast faces the reader in verse 5. John sees a group of people who do not rise at the coming of Christ. They do not sit on thrones and they do not reign with Christ for a thousand years. These are the "rest of the dead," a phrase filled with great sadness. The "rest of the dead" are unbelievers who have died in their sins without a savior. At the end of verse 5 John speaks of the "first resurrection," the resurrection he has been describing in verse 4, the resurrection of believers unto eternal life. The expression "first resurrection"[88] suggests that there will be a "second,"[89] and this is confirmed in verses 12–13 where people are raised to face God in judgment.[90]

The first resurrection is selective. Only the saints rise. The second resurrection will be absolutely universal. All unbelievers—those without Christ—will rise.[91] The first resurrection restores believers to bodily life for their millennial reign. The second brings the "rest of the dead" before the great white throne in verse 11.[92] John here anticipates the terrible judgment scene that begins at verse 11 when all who have rejected the truth will be raised bodily to face God.

The First Resurrection Is A Resurrection Of The Believing Dead

The resurrection of verse 4, John tells us, is "the first resurrection."[93] In John 5:29 our Lord distinguishes between "a resurrection of life" and "a resurrection of judgment." The first resurrection[94] is the "resurrection of life." In Luke 14:14 it is called "the resurrection of the righteous," and in Hebrews 11:35 it is called "a better resurrection." The Dutch have a wonderful word for resurrection that captures the meaning exactly. It is *oopstanding*. At the resurrection, believers in their glorified bodies will stand up, they will be raised from the dead.[95]

An Interpretive Beatitude: The Blessings Of Those Who Participate In The First Resurrection (verse 6)

In verse 6 those who participate in the first resurrection are pronounced "blessed and holy." This is the "big idea" or main lesson of the whole paragraph. The term *blessed* introduces the fifth of seven beatitudes in Revelation (1:3; 14: 13; 16:15; 19:9; 20:6; 22:7, 14). The word means "happy" or "good," and was used in Greek literature to mean extraordinary good fortune. It can have the sense of "fortunate" (Acts 26:2), of being "better off" (1 Cor. 7:40).[96] In our passage the source of spiritual prosperity and well being is God. It is He who bestows spiritual grace upon these resurrected ones in the form described in this verse.[97]

The term *holy*[98] occurs several times in Revelation, but this is the only one of the seven beatitudes that has the term.[99] It speaks of the privileged position of those who participate in the first resurrection.[100] It focuses especially on the priestly position of God's people in the millennial age. During the thousand-year reign both the royal and priestly character of God's immortal ones comes forth in complete glory.[101]

THEY SHALL ESCAPE THE SECOND DEATH

There are three reasons why those who rise are blessed.[102] First, they shall escape "the second death." The "second death" is described in verse 14 and in 21:8. To suffer the "second death" is to be cast into the lake of fire where the Beast and the false prophet are. It is a place that was prepared for the devil and his angels (CF. Matt. 25:41). The first death may be defined as physical death, the death of the body, and the second death occurs when the soul is cut off from the presence of God.

THEY SHALL SERVE AS PRIESTS OF GOD AND OF CHRIST

The second blessing of the first resurrection is that those who rise will serve as "priests of God and of Christ." The linking of God and Christ together, coupled by their being worshipped together in 5:13, clearly indicates that in the book of Revelation Christ is regarded as the equal of

God.[103] The term "priest" suggests worship and service. The millennial saints are viewed as the means by which Christ's redemptive work is mediated throughout the world. The work of the gospel will continue throughout the millennial period. The millennial earth will not be a deathless earth, and there will be those who carry the message of life to the lost.[104]

They Shall Reign With Christ For A Thousand Years

The saints will not only have a priestly work, they will also have a regal work to do. These blessed and holy immortals shall share the transcendent glory of their Messiah King.

Let me make one further observation on verse 6. This verse is an interpretive beatitude; it is not part of the vision, it interprets the vision. What is striking is that the thousand years are found in *both* the vision and the interpretation.[105] If the thousand years were to be interpreted in a spiritualized or allegorical way John would tell us here. If the thousand years were a symbol of something else, then surely John would tell us in his interpretation. He would speak perhaps of the saints living in heaven for a long time. But the thousand years are retained in the interpretation which suggests that by "a thousand years" John means 1,000 actual years.

Furthermore, in verse 4 the phrase "they came to life and reigned" is in the past (aorist) tense. But in the interpretation (v. 6) the future tense is used. In other words, in his interpretation John says the privileges he saw in the vision of verse 4 are yet future! As Professor Everett Harrison of Fuller Seminary remarked long ago, "That nails the argument for premillennialism down tight!"[106]

Conclusion

"Everything's s'pposed to be different than what it is here." This world is not what it is supposed to be, and the King of kings is coming to change it. All those who reign will tell the truth and will praise other public officials in the millennium. Public telephone books will be left intact. Highway overpasses will be graffiti-free. Tow truck drivers and erring motorists will be serene on inner-city streets. The former gang members—provided they were converted prior to Christ's return—will all go to law school—if there are law schools in the millennium![107] P.T. Barnum (1810–91), the famous showman, delighted in showing to visiting clergymen an exhibit he called "The Happy Family," in which lions, tigers, and panthers squatted around a lamb, without a predatory smack of the lips. Dexter Fellows, the Barnum press agent, declared that when a minister asked Barnum if the group ever gave any trouble, the showman replied: "Apart from replenishing the lamb now and then, they get along very well together."[108] No, the world is not what it is supposed to be, but a day is coming, says the prophet Isaiah, "when the wolf will dwell with the lamb, and the leopard will lie down with the kid, and the calf and the young lion and the fatling together; and a little boy will lead them" (11:6).

The Lord God has given us this passage not to give us ammunition with which to fight over the millennial question but to encourage His people to remain firm in the faith. Our time is coming, and we shall reign with Christ. Two Christians, a man and a woman, were talking about their faith in Christ. The woman was thrilled about her assurance of safety in the Savior and she said, "I have taken a one way ticket to heaven, and I do not intend to come back." The man replied, "You are going to miss out on a lot. I have taken a return ticket, for I am not only going to meet Christ in Glory, but I am coming back with Him in power and great glory to the earth."[109]

There is a warning in our passage for all who think they can change this present order with the sword or with social action. As with our Lord Jesus Christ, final victory comes only through death and resurrection.[110]

All believers need to take seriously the phrase "the rest of the dead" (v. 5). The "first resurrection" will include all who have put their faith in Jesus Christ as personal Savior. All of these will rise one day to serve in Christ's kingdom.

But "the rest of the dead"—those who reject Christ—will have no part in the millennial kingdom. Their destiny is the lake of fire. The goal of teachers and preachers of Scripture is to urge men and women and boys and girls to come to Christ, to embrace eternal life. It is sobering to think that every week as God's Word is proclaimed people are addressed who are still on the road that leads to "the second death."

NOTES

[1] For this summary of the scene from *Grand Canyon* I am indebted to Cornelius Plantinga, Jr.'s erudite volume, *Not the Way It's Supposed to Be: A Breviary of Sin* (Grand Rapids: Eerdmans, 1995), 7–8.

[2] In these introductory remarks I am closely following the thoughts of Plantinga, *Not the Way It's Supposed to Be*, 7–27.

[3] Plantinga, *Not the Way It's Supposed to Be*, 9.

[4] Plantinga, *Not the Way It's Supposed to Be*, 9–12. For a fuller discussion of the prophets' description of the Messianic kingdom, CF. Alva J. McClain, *The Greatness of the Kingdom* (Chicago: Moody, 1959), 217–54.

[5] Robert G. Clouse, "The Christian Hope: A History of the Interpretation of the Millennium," in *New Testament Essays in Honor of Homer A. Kent, Jr.* (Winona Lake, IN: BMH Books, 1991), 203–17.

[6] The three views are ably presented in Millard J. Erickson, *Contemporary Options in Eschatology: A Study of the Millennium* (Grand Rapids: Baker, 1977), 55–106; Robert G. Clouse, ed., *The Meaning of the Millennium: Four Views* (Downers Grove: IVP, 1977); Darrell L. Bock, ed., *Three Views on the Millennium and Beyond* (Grand Rapids; Zondervan, 1999). Clouse's work includes four views in that he chooses to have a representative from two different

schools of premillennialism. These two schools (historic premillennialism and dispensational premillennialism) do not differ significantly, however, in their exegesis of Rev. 20:1–6.

[7]In making this assertion I claim no patristic support for later developments in premillennialism such as the tenets of classic dispensationalism; E.G., the distinction between Israel and the church and the pretribulational rapture. CF. Alan Patrick Boyd, "A Dispensational Premillennial Analysis of the Eschatology of the Post-Apostolic Fathers (Until the Death of Justin Martyr)," (Th.M. thesis, Dallas Theological Seminary, 1977), 88–92.

[8]Those writers who spoke to the subject were without exception premillennial. They include Papias (C. AD60–130), Barnabas (70–132), Irenaeus (C. 135–C. 200), Justin Martyr (C. 100–65), Tertullian (C. 150–225), and Hippolytus (C. AD170–235). See Hans Bietenhard, "The Millennial Hope in the Early Church," *Scottish Journal of Theology* 6 (1953), 12–30. This comment should be qualified in that Justin Martyr conceded to Trypho, after affirming his own premillennialism, that "many who belong to the pure and pious faith, and are true Christians, think otherwise." See *Dialogue with Trypho* 80, in *The Ante-Nicene Fathers*, vol. 1, eds. Alexander Roberts and James Donaldson, revised A.C. Coxe (1884; reprint ed., Grand Rapids: Eerdmans, 1967), 239. Relevant documentation is as follows: Papias' views are found in Irenaeus *Against Heresies* 5.33.3–4, in *The Ante-Nicene Fathers*, 1:562–63. CF. also: *The Epistle of Barnabas* 15.3–9 in *The Apostolic Fathers*, 2 vols., trans. Kirsopp Lake, in The Loeb Classical Library (Cambridge: Harvard University Press, 1912), 1:395–97; Irenaeus, *Against Heresies* 5.28–36, in *The Ante-Nicene Fathers*, 1:556–67; Tertullian *Against Marcion* 3.24 in *Tertullian*, 2 vols., trans. Ernest Evans (Oxford: Clarendon Press, 1972), 1:247; Tertullian *On the Resurrection of the Flesh* 19, 25, in *The Ante-Nicene Fathers*, 3:558–59, 563.

9See R.H. Charles, *The Revelation of St. John*, 2 vols., International Critical Commentary (Edinburgh: T. & T. Clark, 1920), 2:182–86; Martin Kiddle, *The Revelation of St. John*, Moffatt New Testament Commentary (New York: Harper, 1940), 390–97; Hans Lilje, *The Last Book of the Bible*, trans. Olive Wyon (Philadelphia: Muhlenberg, 1957), 248–53; T.R.F. Glassen, *The Revelation of John* (Cambridge: Cambridge University Press, 1965), 111–13; Mathias Rissi, *Time and History: A Study on the Revelation* (Richmond: John Knox, 1966), 13–14; G.B. Caird, *The Revelation of St. John the Divine*, Harper New Testament Commentary (New York: Harper, 1966), 248–56; John F. Walvoord,

The Revelation of Jesus Christ (Chicago: Moody, 1966), 282–300; George Eldon Ladd, *A Commentary on the Revelation of John* (Grand Rapids: Eerdmans, 1972), 259–68; G.R. Beasley-Murray, *The Book of Revelation*, New Century Bible (London: Oliphants, 1974), 287–97; J. Massyngberde Ford, *Revelation*, Anchor Bible (New York: Doubleday, 1975), 349–54; Robert H. Mounce, *The Book of Revelation*, New International Commentary on the New Testament (rev. ed., Grand Rapids: Eerdmans, 1998), 360–71; F.F. Bruce, "Revelation," in *The International Bible Commentary*, ed. F.F. Bruce (rev. ed., Grand Rapids: Zondervan, 1986), 1624; David E. Aune, *Revelation 17–22*, Word Biblical Commentary (Nashville: Nelson, 1998), 1084, 1104–8; Jurgen Roloff, *The Revelation of John: A Continental Commentary*, trans. John E. Alsup (Minneapolis: Fortress, 1993), 222–29; Merrill C. Tenney, *Interpreting Revelation* (Grand Rapids: Eerdmans, 1957), 154–63; J. Ramsay Michaels, *Interpreting the Book of Revelation* (Grand Rapids: Baker, 1992), 142–47; *Theological Dictionary of the New Testament*, see "χιλιάς," by E. Lohse, 9 (1974): 470–71; J. Ramsay Michaels, "The First Resurrection: A Response," *Westminster Theological Journal* 39 (1976), 100–9; Jack S. Deere, "Premillennialism in Revelation 20:4–6," *Bibliotheca Sacra* 135 (1978), 58–73; Jeffrey L. Townsend, "Is the Present Age the Millennium?" *Bibliotheca Sacra* 140 (1983), 206–24; Harold W. Hoehner, "Evidence From Revelation 20," in *A Case for Premillennialism: A New Consensus*, eds. Donald K. Campbell and Jeffrey L. Townsend (Chicago: Moody, 1992), 235–62.

[10]Examples of commentators who are amillennial include: Henry Barclay Swete, *The Apocalypse of St. John* (London: Macmillan, 1906), 260–63; R.C. H. Lenski, *The Interpretation of St. John's Revelation* (Minneapolis: Augsburg, 1943), 564–90; William Hendriksen, *More Than Conquerors* (Grand Rapids: Baker, 1939), 221–32; Leon Morris, *The Revelation of St. John*, Tyndale New Testament Commentaries (Grand Rapids: Eerdmans, 1969), 233–38; Michael Wilcock, *I Saw Heaven Opened* (Downers Grove: IVP, 1975), 187–94; Philip Edgcumbe Hughes, *The Book of the Revelation* (Grand Rapids: Eerdmans, 1990), 208–16; G.K. Beale, *The Book of Revelation*, The New International Greek Testament Commentary (Grand Rapids: Eerdmans, 1999), 972–1021. In addition to the commentaries, see W. J. Grier, *The Momentous Event* (London: The Evangelical Bookshop, 1945; reprint ed., London: Banner of Truth, 1970), 103–24; Jay Adams, *The Time is at Hand* (rev. ed., Greenville: A Press, 1966); G.C. Berkouwer, *The Return of Christ* (Grand Rapids: Eerdmans, 1972), 291–322 and *passim*; William E. Cox, *Amillennialism Today* (Philadelphia: Presbyterian & Reformed, 1975), 7–12, 99–111 and *passim*; Anthony A. Hoekema,

The Bible and the Future (Grand Rapids: Eerdmans, 1979), 223–38. Cf. also the following essays in *Westminster Theological Journal*: James A. Hughes, "Revelation 20:4–6 and the Question of the Millennium," 35 (Spring, 1973), 281–302; Meredith G. Kline, "The First Resurrection," 37 (Spring, 1975), 366–75; Idem., "The First Resurrection: A Reaffirmation," 39 (Fall, 1976), 110–19; Philip Edgcumbe Hughes, "The First Resurrection: Another Interpretation," 39 (Spring, 1977), 315–18; R. Fowler White, "Reexamining the Evidence for Recapitulation in Rev. 20:1–10," 51 (1989), 319–44.

[11]Various amillennialists have suggested new terminology to replace the term *amillennialism*. For example, Adams suggested "realized millennialism," Poythress preferred "preconsummationism," and Hendriksen called himself a "nunc millennialist;" that is, "one who believes that the millennium is *now*." Cf. Adams, *The Time is at Hand*, 9; Vern S. Poythress, *Understanding Dispensationalists* (2D. ed., Phillipsburg, Presbyterian and Reformed, 1994), 36; William Hendriksen, "Review of George Eldon Ladd, *A Commentary on the Revelation of John*," *Westminster Theological Journal* 35 (1973), 353.

[12]Postmillennial and amillennial writers are quick to point out that premillennialists differ with each other on a number of details (cf. Hoekema, *The Bible and the Future*, 187–88). On the key exegetical points in Rev. 20:4–6, however, it is the postmillennialists and amillennialists who lack a consensus, not the premillennialists. To cite just two examples, there is substantial difference of opinion on the nature of the first resurrection and on the thousand-year reign. The first resurrection has been interpreted as the regeneration of the sinner (e.g., Augustine, *City of God* 20.6), the death of the believer (Hoekema, 233), and the resurrection of Christ (e.g., P.E. Hughes, *Revelation*, 316–17). The reign of the saints has been explained as the present spiritual reign of Christ in the hearts of believers (Cox, *Amillennialism Today*, 64), the present reign of disembodied saints in heaven (e.g., Hoekema, *The Bible and the Future*, 231–33), and the present church age during which believers rule in this world as kings and priests (e.g., Wilcock, *I Saw Heaven Opened*, 192).

[13]It is not uncommon for amillennial scholars to sift through the early fathers in pedantic fashion and announce that only a few were premillennial. Cf. Grier, *The Momentous Event*, 19–27; Albertus Pieters, "Chiliasm in the Writings of the Apostolic Fathers," *The Calvin Forum* 4 (August and September, 1938), 9–11, 37–39. It is an argument from silence that works against them. In point of fact

the only fathers who addressed the millennial question were without exception premillennial.

[14]Dionysius' allegorical approach to the Revelation is known through Eusebius *The Ecclesiastical History* 7.25, The Loeb Classical Library, 2 vols. (Cambridge: Harvard University Press, 1932), 2:197–209.

[15]Clement does not refer directly to Chiliasm in his writings, yet he was probably unfavorable to it due to the allegorical interpretation that had grown up in Alexandria. Cf. Bietenhard, "The Millennial Hope," 20. Beginning with Philo (c. AD20–c. AD50), the Jewish philosopher and exegete, and on into the Christian era, Alexandrians sought a way to make the Old Testament compatible with Platonic thought. Furthermore, the doctrine of an earthly millennium seemed crass to the ascetic world view of these fathers. Cf. Justo L. Gonzalez, *A History of Christian Thought*, 3 vols. (Nashville: Abingdon, 1970), 1:83, 84.

[16]Origen *On Principles* 2.11.2, in *The Ante-Nicene Fathers*, vol. 4, eds. Alexander Roberts and James Donaldson, revised by A.C. Coxe (1885; reprint ed., Grand Rapids: Eerdmans, 1965), 297. Bietenhard ("The Millennial Hope," 21) wrote, "A Greek dualism of above and below replaced the [New Testament] contrast between this world and the world to come.... The basic principle that Scripture must be interpreted according to the Spirit and not the flesh was a right principle, but Origen's application of it was disastrous, for he identified the spiritual with neo-Platonic philosophy."

[17]To many students of Revelation, under the sway of the rigid metaphysical dualism of Plato, the premillennial doctrine of a divine kingdom established on earth, having political and physical aspects, seems to be sheer materialism. Yet their theological views, suggests McClain (*The Greatness of the Kingdom*, 519–20), may involve practical and humorous inconsistencies. McClain illustrates: "During a church banquet a group of preachers were discussing the nature of the Kingdom of God. One expressed his adherence to the premillennial view of a literal kingdom to be established on earth among men. To this a rather belligerent [overweight] preacher snorted, 'Ridiculous! Such an idea is nothing but materialism.' When asked to state his own view, he replied, 'The Kingdom is a *spiritual* matter. The Kingdom of God has *already* been established, is *within you*. Don't you gentlemen know that the Kingdom is not eating and drinking, but righteousness and peace and joy in the Holy Spirit?' And then the speaker reached hungrily across the table and speared another enormous piece of fried

chicken! Nobody tried to answer him. As a matter of fact, no answer was necessary; he had answered his own argument.… If the Kingdom of God can exist
now on earth in [an overweight] preacher full of fried chicken, without any
reprehensible materialistic connotations, perhaps it could also exist in the same
way among men on earth who will at times be eating and drinking under more
perfect conditions in a future millennial kingdom."

[18]For example, see Berkouwer, *The Return of Christ*, 294, 308; Lenski, *The Interpretation of St. John's Revelation*, 570–71.

[19]Augustine *The City of God* 20.6–14, trans. Marcus Dods, in *A Select Library
of the Nicene and Post-Nicene Fathers of the Christian Church*, vol. 2, ed. Philip
Schaff (1886; reprint ed., Grand Rapids: Eerdmans, 1956), 425–35. Schaff (426,
n. 5) wrote, "Augustine…revolutionized the prevailing ante-Nicene view of the
Apocalyptic millennium by understanding it of the *present* reign of Christ in
the Church."

[20]Expanding on the prophecies of Isaiah 11 and 35, Irenaeus (*Against Heresies*
5.33.3) wrote, "The days will come, in which vines shall grow, each having ten
thousand branches, and in each branch ten thousand twigs, and in each true
twig ten thousand shoots, and in each one of the shoots ten thousand clusters,
and on every one of the clusters ten thousand grapes, and every grape when
pressed will give five and twenty metretes of wine. And when any one of the
saints shall lay hold of a cluster, another shall cry out, 'I am a better cluster,
take me; bless the Lord through me.' In like manner [the Lord declared] that
a grain of wheat would produce ten thousand ears, and that every ear should
have ten thousand grains, and every grain would yield ten pounds of clear,
pure, fine flour…" Eusebius (*Ecclesiastical History* 3.28.2–6) charges that the
heretic Cerinthus taught that there would be an earthly kingdom "given up
to the indulgence of the flesh, I.E., eating and drinking and marrying, and to
those things which seem a euphemism for these things, feasts and sacrifices and
the slaughter of victims." How much of Eusebius' commentary is dispassionate
and how much is fueled by anti-chiliasm we do not know. Bietenhard ("The
Millennial Hope," 17) says that Cerinthus was "one of the first exponents of the
so-called *chiliasmus crassus*."

[21]See Loraine Boettner, *The Millennium* (Philadelphia: Presbyterian and Reformed, 1957), 10.

[22]E.G., David Brown, *Christ's Second Coming: Will It Be Premillennial?* (Robert Carter, 1876; reprint ed., Grand Rapids: Baker, 1983); Charles Hodge, *Systematic Theology*, 3 vols. (New York: Scribners, 1872; reprint ed., Grand Rapids: Eerdmans, 1975), 3:858–59 and *passim*; A.A. Hodge, *Outlines of Theology* (1879; reprint ed., Grand Rapids: Zondervan, 1972), 568–69; A. H. Strong, *Systematic Theology* (Old Tappan: Revell, 1907), 1010–15. See also Benjamin Breckinridge Warfield, "The Millennium and the Apocalypse," in *Biblical Doctrines* (New York: Oxford University Press, 1929; reprint ed., Grand Rapids: Baker, 1981, 643–64.

[23]Postmillennial commentaries are rare, but at least three are currently available: Albert Barnes, *Notes on the New Testament Explanatory and Practical: Revelation* (1851; reprint ed., Grand Rapids: Baker, 1949), 419–32; David S. Clark, *The Message from Patmos: A Postmillennial Commentary on the Book of Revelation* (reprint ed., Grand Rapids: Baker, 1989), 119–32; David Chilton, *The Days of Vengeance* (Ft. Worth: Dominion Press, 1987), 481–519. See also: J. Marcellus Kik, *An Eschatology of Victory* (Nutley: Presbyterian & Reformed, 1975), 177–233; Boettner, *The Millennium*; John Jefferson Davis, *Christ's Victorious Kingdom* (Grand Rapids: Baker, 1986), 83–99; Keith A. Mathison, *Postmillennialism: An Eschatology of Hope* (Phillipsburg: Presbyterian and Reformed, 1999); Allan R. Ford, "The Second Advent in Relation to the Reign of Christ," *The Evangelical Quarterly* 23 (1951), 30–39; Greg L. Bahnsen, "The Prima Facie Acceptability of Postmillennialism," *The Journal of Christian Reconstruction* 3 (Winter, 1976–77), 48–105; Martin G. Selbrede, "Reconstructing Postmillennialism," *The Journal of Christian Reconstruction* 15 (Winter, 1998), 146–224; Vern Crisler, "The Eschatological *A Priori* of the New Testament: A Critique of Hyper-Preterism," *The Journal of Christian Reconstruction* 15 (Winter, 1998), 225–56.

[24]Missionary theologian (and amillennialist) Harry R. Boer complained, "The Reformed view of the millennium [amillennialism] suffers from a suspicious peculiarity. It appears to mean little or nothing in the life of the Church. Where is the joy, the comfort, the triumph of knowing that Satan is bound, even if only partially? Who is thrilled about living in the millennium? When and where are we told about its blessing and its power?" See "What About the Millennium?" *The Reformed Journal* 25 (Jan., 1975), 26–27. In another place he asserts that his denomination, the Christian Reformed Church, "continues to live in a state of near if not complete eschatological unawareness." See "The Reward of the Martyrs," *The Reformed Journal* 25 (Feb., 1975), 8.

[25]The commentators commonly point to the intertestamental literature and to the theology of the rabbis as the source of John's idea of an intermediate kingdom. In the intertestamental literature the doctrine is taught in the second century AD in the books of 1 Enoch and Jubilees, in the first century AD in the Psalms of Solomon and the Sibylline Oracles, in the early first century AD in the Assumption of Moses and in 2 Enoch, and in the late first century AD in 2 Baruch and 4 Ezra. The Rabbinic authorities are as follows: Eliezer ben Hyrcanus (AD90) suggested a thousand years; Joshua (AD90), two thousand years; Eleazar ben Azariah (AD100), 70 years; Akiba (AD135), 40 years; Jose of Galilee (AD110), 60 years; Dasa (AD180), 600 years; Eliezer ben Jose of Galilee (AD150), 400 years. The intertestamental literature is conveniently catalogued in R.H. Charles, *Eschatology: The Doctrine of a Future Life in Israel, Judaism and Christianity* (2ND. ed., London: Adam and Charles Black, 1913; reprint ed., New York: Schocken Books, 1963), 219–20, 239–40, 270–71, 273, 301–2, 315, 324–37. The list of the rabbis comes from Ford, *Revelation*, 353. The sources of John's conception of the millennium, however, lie elsewhere than in contemporary Jewish speculations. His sources are twofold: (1) the Old Testament prophecies in Ezekiel 36–37 with its description of the resurrection of Israel and the restoration of the nation to the land, and Daniel 7 with its description of the Son of Man's temporal kingdom over earthly nations and peoples; and (2) a vision from God. Cf. Beasley-Murray, *The Book of Revelation*, 288; Deere, "Premillennialism in Revelation 20:4–6," 59.

[26]Isaac Watts, "Jesus Shall Reign," in *Hymns of Truth and Praise* (Ft. Dodge: Gospel Perpetuating Publishers, 1971), 196.

[27]The Kingdom of the Messiah lasts forever, but the millennium lasts for only a thousand years. As Culver has demonstrated, the millennium is within that future kingdom and is the initial stage of it. See Robert Duncan Culver, *Daniel and the Latter Days* (rev. ed., Chicago: Moody, 1977), 49–52. Culver follows George N.H. Peters, *The Theocratic Kingdom*, 3 vols. (New York: Funk & Wagnalls, 1884; reprint ed., Grand Rapids: Kregel, 1972), 2:630–31.

[28]It is true that Rev. 20 says nothing about "a conversion and return of the Jews, of the rebuilding of Jerusalem, of a restoration of the temple and temple worship, of an initial renewal of the earth" (Herman Bavinck, *The Last Things*, trans. John Vriend [Grand Rapids: Baker, 1996], 115). Many biblical texts do, however, say something about such a conversion of Israel (E.G., Isa. 14:1–2; Jer. 31:33–34; ROM. 11:26–27), and the apostles—after a 40-day seminar on

the kingdom with Christ—clearly expected it (Acts 1:6). This is true of the other elements mentioned by Bavinck (rebuilding of Jerusalem [Isa. 2:3; Ezek. 43:1–7; Zech. 14:4–11; Ps. 110:2], restoration of the temple and temple worship [Ezek. 40:1–46:24], the renewal of the earth [Isa. 32:13–15; 35:1–2; Ezek. 36: 4–11]). Every systematic theologian must fit the pieces of the prophetic puzzle together, and the premillennialists have done it most successfully.

[29]See Berkouwer, *The Return of Christ*, 317.

[30]Seiss argues that the "rod of iron" cannot be understood as an instrument of destruction but only as a tool for gracious and merciful care. Surely he is wrong as is indicated by the context of Rev. 19:15, the context of Rev. 2:27, and the context of Ps. 2:9. The example of David in 1 Sam. 17:34–36 demonstrates that shepherding involves violently dealing with predators. Cf. Joseph A. Seiss, *Lectures on the Apocalypse*, 3 vols. (9TH ed., New York: Charles C. Cook, 1906), 3:292–94; S. Lewis Johnson, Jr., *The Old Testament in the New* (Grand Rapids: Zondervan, 1980), 12–19.

[31]As told by Clifton Fadiman, ed., *The Little, Brown Book of Anecdotes* (Boston: Little, Brown and Co., 1985), 117.

[32]Isaiah 2:4 is inscribed on the well-known statue (donated by the Soviet Union) on display at the United Nations in New York. Significantly, the following part of the verse is omitted: "And He will judge between the nations, and will render decisions for many peoples." It is the Warrior-King of Rev. 19 and not the United Nations who will bring peace to the earth!

[33]"As long as men live in the flesh on earth, there will be differences in abilities and needs" (McClain, *The Greatness of the Kingdom*, 226).

[34]McClain, *The Greatness of the Kingdom*, 222–23.

[35]Plato, *The Republic* 3.189, in *Great Books of the Western World*, ed., Robert Maynard Hutchins, vol. 7: *Plato*, trans. Benjamin Jowett (Chicago: Encyclopedia Britannica, 1952), 326.

[36]Some see only one group: the martyrs (E.G. Morris, *The Revelation of St. John*, 236). However, the martyrs are not mentioned until later in the verse after John has already seen the thrones and their occupants (Deere, "Premillennial-

ism in Revelation 20:4–6," 63). Charles argues that the text is unintelligible and ungrammatical with two clauses coming between εἶδον and its accusative τὰς ψυχὰς. Ladd argues that we should add an additional εἶδον ["and I saw the souls"] to bring out the force of the Greek idiom. Charles' also adds an εἶδον to the text, but radically reconstructs the verse in the process (Charles, *The Revelation of St. John*, 2:182–83; Ladd, *A Commentary on the Revelation of John*, 263).

[37]Culver, *Daniel and the Latter Days*, 219. Cf. John Peter Lange, *The Revelation of John*, trans. Evelina Moore, in Commentary on the Holy Scriptures, 25 vols. (reprint ed., Grand Rapids: Zondervan, 1960), 25:350.

[38]Mounce argues that because the text is silent about the identity of the occupants of the thrones we should not speculate. I would object that the rest of the Bible is not silent, and surely the unity of Scripture would require that texts such as Daniel 7:18; Matt. 19:28; 1 Cor. 6:2–3; and Rev. 3:21 not be so readily dismissed. Mounce's own suggestion is that the occupants are a heavenly court (Mounce, *The Book of Revelation*, 365).

[39]Other occupants have been suggested: (1) The twenty-four elders [Dusterdieck, Scott, Walvoord]. They are a representative group, however, while the occupants are individuals. (2) God and Christ and the seven angelic assessors and the apostles [Bullinger]. The phrase "and judgment was given to them" (αὐτούι καὶ κρίμα ἐδόθη) excludes God and Christ, and 1 Cor. 6:3 would preclude angels. See Friedrich Dusterdieck, *Critical and Exegetical Handbook to the Revelation of John*, trans. Henry E. Jacobs (6TH ed., New York: Funk & Wagnalls, 1884), 464; Walter Scott, *Exposition of the Revelation of Jesus Christ* (4TH ed., London: Pickering & Inglis, N.D.), 400; Walvoord, *The Revelation of Jesus Christ*, 296; E. W. Bullinger, *The Apocalypse* (3RD. ed., London: Eyre & Spottiswoode, 1935; reprint ed., Grand Rapids: Kregel, 1984), 613.

[40]In the judgment scene in Daniel 7:22 judgment is passed in favor of the saints. Here, however, the phrase αὐτούι καὶ κρίμα ἐδόθη indicates those to whom the right has been given to act as judges, not those in whose favor judgment is given. Cf. Caird, *The Revelation of St. John the Divine*, 252.

[41]Seiss, *Lectures on the Apocalypse*, 3:337–38. Seiss remarks that there will be no sinecures, offices requiring little or no work, in the kingdom.

[42]Bullinger (*The Apocalypse*, 612) suggests that those on the thrones judge or vindicate those who shall have a part in the first resurrection. In point of fact, however, those on the thrones will themselves be part of the first resurrection.

[43]McClain, *The Greatness of the Kingdom*, 484–85.

[44]Some scholars (Swete, *The Apocalypse of St. John*, 262; Hendriksen, *More Than Conquerors*, 230–31; Grier, *The Momentous Event*, 116) make much of the term τὰς ψυχὰς, and they argue that our text describes disembodied believers presently reigning with Christ in heaven. Others (Seiss, *Lectures on the Apocalypse*, 3:305; Berkouwer, *The Return of Christ*, 304) argue that the term means no more than individuals, persons in the body (Acts 2:41; 7:14; 27:37). I think it is best to take the term as referring to disembodied souls as in 6:9. John first sees the souls, and he then sees them raised from the dead in their resurrection bodies. Cf. Scott, *Exposition of the Revelation of Jesus Christ*, 400.

[45]Warfield's great exegetical skills left him when he wrote on Rev. 20:4–6. As one example, he says here that these are "not literal martyrs" (Warfield, "The Millennium and the Apocalypse," 652). However, John speaks of actual martyrs, for those who refused to worship the Beast were put to death (13:15). Cf. Isbon T. Beckwith, *The Apocalypse of John* (London: Macmillan, 1991; reprint ed., Grand Rapids: Baker, 1979), 740.

[46]Some commentators see three groups in v. 4 (Seiss, *Lectures on the Apocalypse*, 3:303; Bullinger, *The Apocalypse*, 615): (1) the saints, (2) the tribulation martyrs, and (3) the living survivors of the Beast's reign. They point out that τὰς ψυχὰς ("the souls") is in the accusative case while οἵτινες ("those who") is in the nominative. Their argument is that τὰς ψυχὰς cannot be the antecedent of οἵτινες and that οἵτινες is the subject of an entirely new sentence. There are two objections to this view: (1) The phenomenon *constructio ad sensum* ("without following any fixed rules")—in this case, the relative used without formal agreement with its antecedent—is not uncommon in Revelation [1:15, 19, 20; 5:6; 11:4, 9, 11, 15; 14:7; 17:3; 19:1; cf. F. Blass and A. Debrunner, *A Greek Grammar of the New Testament and Other Christian Literature*, trans. Robert W. Funk (Chicago: University of Chicago Press, 1961), 74, FL 134; 147, FL 282; 155, FL 296]. (2) The following statement, "they came to life," governs both groups and cannot refer to living saints. Cf. Ladd, *A Commentary on the Revelation of John*, 265; Deere, "Premillennialism in Revelation 20:4–6," 65. In this verse, then, οἵτινες introduces a relative clause which emphasizes a characteristic

quality of its antecedent, and the καὶ serves as an explicative ("namely," CF. Mounce, *The Book of Revelation*, 365, N. 8). Incidentally, the distinction between the martyrs and the living survivors of the tribulation is supported by Swete, Lenski, and Barclay. CF. Swete, *The Apocalypse of St. John*, 259; Lenski, *The Interpretation of St. John's Revelation*, 581; William Barclay, *The Revelation of John*, 2 vols. (rev. ed., Philadelphia: Westminster, 1976), 2:192.

[47]James S. Stewart, *The Wind of the Spirit* (Nashville: Abingdon, 1968), 54.

[48]Deere, "Premillennialism in Revelation 20:4–6," 65.

[49]Augustine, *City of God* 20.6; Kik, *An Eschatology of Victory*, 181–82; Cox, *Amillennialism Today*, 99–100; Wilcock, *I Saw Heaven Opened*, 192.

[50]John sees the souls "of those who had been beheaded" (τῶν πεπελεκισ-μένων, perfect passive participle of πελεκίζω). The instrument of capital punishment in republican Rome was the πελεκύς, I.E., the double-edged ax. By the time Revelation was written the ax had been superceded by the sword (Acts 12:2), but capital punishment was still referred to informally as "beheading." See Charles, *The Revelation of St. John*, 2:183; Swete, *The Apocalypse of St. John*, 258.

[51]Seiss, *Lectures on the Apocalypse*, 3:306.

[52]Lenski, *The Interpretation of St. John's Revelation*, 581; Hendriksen, *More Than Conquerors*, 230; Morris, *The Revelation of St. John*, 237; Hoekema, *The Bible and the Future*, 233. Morris lamely remarks that this is not the usual word for resurrection. In point of fact there is no Greek word that exclusively means "to rise from the dead." Mounce (*Revelation*, 366, N. 10) notes that other words used for rising from the dead (ἀνίστημι, ἐγείρω, ἀναζάω) are used with other meanings in different contexts. James A. Hughes ("Revelation 20:4–6," 290–92) argues that the verb ἔζησαν is a constative rather than an ingressive aorist and describes the present intermediate state ("they lived"). It must be a constative aorist, he argues, in that ἐβασίλευσαν ("they reigned") is constative. However, there is no rule of grammar that says ἔζησαν cannot be ingressive while ἐβασίλευσαν is constative (Deere, "Premillennialism in Revelation 20:4–6," 66). Recognized grammarians such as Turner and Robertson take ἔζησαν as ingressive while they understand ἐβασίλευσαν to be constative. See A.T. Robertson, *A Grammar of the Greek New Testament in the Light of*

Historical Research (Nashville: Broadman, 1943), 833; James Hope Moulton, *A Grammar of New Testament Greek*, 4 vols., vol. 3: *Syntax*, by Nigel Turner (Edinburgh: T. & T. Clark, 1963), 71.

[53]Swete, *The Apocalypse of St. John*, 263. CF. Seiss, *Apocalypse*, 3:308.

[54]E.G., Seiss, *Lectures on the Apocalypse*, 3:306; Charles, *The Revelation of St. John*, 2:183–84; Caird, *The Revelation of St. John the Divine*, 253–54; Beasley-Murray, *The Book of Revelation*, 295; Walvoord, *The Revelation of Jesus Christ*, 297; Ladd, *A Commentary on the Revelation of John*, 265–66; Thomas, *Revelation 8–22*, 416–17; Mounce, *The Book of Revelation*, 366.

[55]James Hughes ("Revelation 20:4–6," 301–2) argues that v. 5 is also a spiritual resurrection. This presents him with a real dilemma. The word "until" ($\H{\alpha}\chi\rho\iota$) suggests that the rest of the dead rise after the thousand years. If coming to life means going to heaven, then after the thousand years the unbelieving dead live spiritually in heaven! Hughes is aware of his dilemma, but he fails to resolve it. He cites the use of $\H{\alpha}\chi\rho\iota$ in Rom. 5:13 where it is used as an improper preposition with the meaning "before" (See also Hoekema, *The Bible and the Future*, *236*). In Rev. 20:5, however, it is used as a conjunction with the aorist subjunctive and has the force of a future perfect, "until, to the time that." CF. *A Greek-English Lexicon of the New Testament*, eds. William F. Arndt, F. Wilbur Gingrich, and Frederick W. Danker (2D. ed., Chicago: University of Chicago Press, 1979), see "$\H{\alpha}\chi\rho\iota$," 129; Deere, "Premillennialism in Revelation 20:4–6," 68–9.

[56]Henry Alford, *The Greek Testament*, 4 vols. (Chicago: Moody, 1958), 4:732. Certainly it is possible to speak of a spiritual reality and a literal reality in the same context. Jesus does in John 5:25–29. The two passages are different, however. In the gospel the context provides the clues that the Lord was speaking in two senses, whereas there is nothing in Rev. 20:4–5 to indicate a change in meaning. See Ladd, *A Commentary on the Revelation of John*, 266.

[57]In Luke 2:34 ἀνάστασις is used in its etymological sense of "rising."

[58]Charles, *The Revelation of St. John*, 2:185. Postmillennial scholar John Jefferson Davis (*Christ's Glorious Kingdom*, 95) concedes, "On this point the premillennial school appears to have the better argument." To understand the resurrection of v. 5 as a bodily resurrection, says Swete (*The Apocalypse of St. John*, 259),

is "to interpret apocalyptic prophecy by methods of exegesis which are proper to ordinary narrative." Isbon T. Beckwith (*The Apocalypse of John* [New York: Macmillan, 1919; reprint ed., Grand Rapids: Baker, 1979], 738) is on much sounder ground when he writes, "Apocalyptic prophecy is not allegory, and in our passage it is not possible upon any sound principles of exegesis to take the first resurrection as different *in kind* from that of 'the rest.'" It is anti-chiliastic prejudice and party loyalty, not biblical exegesis, that continues to provide the impetus for scholars to engage in hermeneutical experimentation to find excuses to ignore the clear teaching of this text. Amillennial scholar Harry R. Boer confesses, "In terms of the traditional interpretation of the thousand years as a literal reality, whether in the a- or pre- or post-millennial sense of the word, no other view than the premillennial is possible for an exegesis that puts scripture above the harmonistic demands of doctrine or tradition" ("The Reward of the Martyrs," 7).

[59]Adapted from Paul Lee Tan, *Encyclopedia of 7,700 Illustrations*, 1142.

[60]Mounce, *The Book of Revelation*, 369; Roloff, *The Revelation of John*, 225.

[61]Tertullian *Against Marcion* 3.24. Cf. Bietenhard, "The Millennial Hope in the Early Church," 15.

[62]The New Testament's teaching on reward may be outlined as follows: (1) There will be differences in reward for believers depending on degrees of faithfulness in this life (Matt. 5:19; Mark 10:40; Luke 19:11–27; 1 Cor. 3: 14–15), (2) the time of reward will be the Second Advent of Christ, and (3) the manifestation of reward will be during the millennial kingdom (Matt. 19:28; Rev. 2:26–27; 20:4–6). For an unconvincing rejection of the idea of degrees of reward, see Craig L. Blomberg, "Degrees of Reward in the Kingdom of Heaven?" *Journal of the Evangelical Theological Society* 35 (1992): 159–72. See the judicious remarks of Darrell L. Bock, "Periodical Reviews," *Bibliotheca Sacra* 150 (1993): 106–7. Blomberg's main objection to degrees of reward is expressed in his question, "If the heavenly aspect of eternal life represents perfection, is it not fundamentally self-contradictory to speak of degrees of perfection?" In response Bock points out that Blomberg confuses ontology with function. In the kingdom the resurrected people of God will be equal to each other in glorified sinlessness but different from each other in function and responsibility.

[63]Seiss, *Lectures on the Apocalypse*, 3:311–12.

[64]Michael P. Green, ed., *Illustrations for Biblical Preaching* (Grand Rapids: Baker, 1989), 306.

[65]Deere, "Premillennialism in Revelation 20:4–6," 64–65.

[66]The phrase "the testimony of Jesus" (διὰ τὴν μαρτυρίαν ᾽Ιησοῦ) should here be understood as an objective genitive: the martyrs had been beheaded because of the testimony they had borne to the Lord Jesus (Ladd, *A Commentary on the Revelation of John*, 265).

[67]Amillennialism makes the promise of reward in the kingdom almost meaningless. Boer ("The Reward of the Martyrs," 9–10, 28), writes, "But it is not history that John records, nor is it an anticipated event in time and space in a historical framework called the millennium.… The reign of the martyrs…is a purely figurative way of recognizing the service the martyrs rendered to God.… At the close of the heroic-tragic spectacle of Revelation the martyrs as chief actors in the unfolding drama are called to the center of the stage to receive the grateful applause and recognition of the Lord and of the church on whose behalf they suffered and died. Having enjoyed their moment of glory, they then disappear and melt away into the whole body of the redeemed in the new heaven and the new earth (Rev. 21, 22)."

[68]Boer ("The Reward of the Martyrs," 28) appears to believe that the reward of the martyrs is at the second advent when for a "moment of glory" they receive the grateful applause of the Lord and the church. On this point and on the binding of Satan ("What About the Millennium? 27) Boer appears to be an amillennial futurist.

[69]Culver, *Daniel and the Latter Days*, 23. Culver's extended definition of the millennium (P. 23–100) is the best in English and should be consulted.

[70]Cf. Bavinck, *The Last Things*, 115; Grier, *The Momentous Event*, 105; Mounce, *The Book of Revelation*, 360; F.F. Bruce, "Revelation," 1624.

[71]The United Bible Societies editors give the future tense (βασιλεύσουσιν, 5:10) an "A" rating. Cf. Barbara Aland *et al*, *The Greek New Testament* (4TH ed., Stuttgart: Deutsche Bibelgesellschaft, 1993), 844.

[72]Deere, "Premillennialism in Revelation 20:4–6, 69.

[73]Seiss, *Lectures on the Apocalypse*, 3:338.

[74]Gundry, for example, offers a different answer than the one offered here. He suggests that some of the wicked who survive the tribulation and Parousia will enter the millennium. See Robert H. Gundry, *The Church and the Tribulation* (Grand Rapids: Zondervan, 1973), 166–67.

[75]Deere, "Premillennialism in Revelation 20:4–6," 69.

[76]Caird, *The Revelation of St. John the Divine*, 251.

[77]Cf. Stanley D. Toussaint, *Behold the King: A Study of Matthew* (Portland: Multnomah, 1980), 288–92. Whether the "goats" go directly to hell or are sent first to Hades to await the second resurrection Jesus does not say. It is clear that their ultimate destiny is "eternal fire."

[78]Grier, *The Momentous Event*, 107.

[79]Ladd, *A Commentary on the Revelation of John*, 268.

[80]Berkouwer, *The Return of Christ*, 292.

[81]Grier, *The Momentous Event*, 104–5; Hoekema, *The Bible and the Future*, 227; Lenski, *The Interpretation of St. John's Revelation*, 577.

[82]Hoehner, "Evidence from Revelation 20," 249.

[83]Hoehner ("Evidence from Revelation 20," 249) also cites the 7,000 killed in an earthquake (11:13), the carnage covering 1,600 stadia (14:20), and the length of the New Jerusalem of 12,000 stadia (21:16).

[84]Deere, "Premillennialism in Revelation 20:4–6," 70. As Deere notes, it is futile to argue for a symbolic meaning of "a thousand years" on the basis of Psalm 90:4 or 2 Peter 3:8. These texts do not say that a thousand years are a day; rather, they point to God's transcendence in respect to time.

[85]For days, cf. 1:10; 2:10, 13; 4:8; 6:17; 7:15; 8:12; 9:6, 15; 10:7; 11:3, 6, 9, 11; 12:6, 10; 14:11; 16:14; 18:8; 20:10; 21:25. For months, cf. 9:5, 10, 15; 11:2; 13:5; 22:2. Cf. Hoehner, "Evidence from Revelation 20," 249.

[86]John J. Davis, *Biblical Numerology* (Grand Rapids: Baker, 1968), 155.

[87]Seiss, *Lectures on the Apocalypse*, 3:327–29.

[88]Kline has argued on the basis of certain texts (Rev. 21:1, 4; HEBREWS 8:7, 8, 13; 9:1, 15, 18; 10:9; 1 Corinthians 15:45) that "first" (ἡ πρώτη) refers to the present world order. The first resurrection, then, is the death of the Christian. As Deere ("Premillennialism in Revelation 20:4–6," 72, N. 55) notes, however, Kline has begged the question. The key term here is not the adjective "first" but the noun "resurrection." Significantly, Kline does not discuss the New Testament usage of this term. See Meredith G. Kline, "The First Resurrection," *Westminster Theological Journal* 37 (1975), 366–75; Idem., "The First Resurrection: A Reaffirmation," *Westminster Theological Journal* 39 (1976), 110–19. For further interaction with Kline's position, CF. J. Ramsay Michaels, "The First Resurrection: A Response," *Westminster Theological Journal* 39 (1976), 100–9.

[89]CF. Lenski, *The Interpretation of St. John's Revelation*, 586; Hendriksen, *More Than Conquerors*, 232. Most commentators agree that a "first resurrection" implies a "second." They do not agree, of course, on the nature of the two resurrections.

[90]For Bavinck (*The Last Things*, 115) to say that "John…does not know of a physical resurrection that precedes the millennium and a second that follows it" is to willfully ignore the text.

[91]Mounce, *The Book of Revelation*, 370.

[92]Caird, *The Revelation of St. John the Divine*, 254.

[93]Hughes concludes that both the first and second resurrections are physical, but the first resurrection is Christ's resurrection, and the second resurrection is the general resurrection of all men at the Parousia. However, there is nothing in the present context about Christ's resurrection; it is all about the resurrection of the martyrs and those who sit upon the thrones. See Philip Edgcumbe Hughes, "The First Resurrection: Another Interpretation," *Westminster Theological Journal* 39 (1977), 315–18; Idem., *The Book of the Revelation*, 213–16.

[94]The first resurrection takes place in stages. Only some of the participants are mentioned in Rev. 20:4–5. The stages or orders of the first resurrection are: (1)

Jesus Christ (1 Cor. 15:23–24), (2) certain saints after His resurrection (Matt. 27:52–53), (3) the church age saints prior to the tribulation (1 Thess. 4:13–18), (4) the two witnesses in the middle of the tribulation (Rev. 11:11), and (5) the Old Testament saints and tribulation martyrs at the second advent (Dan. 12:1–3). Cf. Seiss, *Lectures on the Apocalypse*, 3:321–24; Roy L. Aldrich, "Divisions of the First Resurrection," *Bibliotheca Sacra* 128 (1971), 117–19; Deere, "Premillennialism in Revelation 20:4–6," 71–72.

⁹⁵Ray C. Stedman, *God's Final Word: Understanding Revelation* (Grand Rapids: Discovery House, 1991), 324.

⁹⁶*Exegetical Dictionary of the New Testament*, see "μακάριος," by G. Strecker, 2:376–77.

⁹⁷*International Standard Bible Encyclopedia*, see "Bless," by A.C. Myers, 1 (1979), 523.

⁹⁸*International Standard Bible Encyclopedia*, see "Holiness," by E.F. Harrison, 2 (1982), 725–29.

⁹⁹*Theological Dictionary of the New Testament*, see "ἅγιος," by O. Procksch, 1 (1964), 110, n. 71.

¹⁰⁰The context—resurrection—assumes, of course, the acquired holiness or complete sanctification and glorification of those who reign with Christ (1 John 3:2). The thrust of v. 6, however, is to emphasize the position and privilege of the resurrected ones.

¹⁰¹Dusterdieck, *Critical and Exegetical handbook to the Revelation of John*, 465.

¹⁰²Swete, *The Apocalypse of St. John*, 260.

¹⁰³Swete, *The Apocalypse of St. John*, 260.

¹⁰⁴Caird, *The Revelation of St. John the Divine*, 255–56; cf. Charles, *The Revelation of St. John*, 2:186. Charles wrote, "These facts suggest that the priestly offices of the blessed in the Millennial Kingdom have to do with the nations, who are to be evangelized during this period (14:6–7; 15:4)."

[105]Walvoord, *The Revelation of Jesus Christ*, 293.

[106]As quoted by S. Lewis Johnson, Jr. "The Millennial Kingdom of Christ" (cassette tape, Dallas: Believers' Chapel, 1989–90). Dr. Johnson was my teacher when I studied the Greek text of the Revelation at Dallas Seminary in 1969. Dr. Harrison made this remark when Lewis Johnson was his student in a class on the Revelation at Dallas in the 1940s.

[107]Plantinga, *Not the Way It's Supposed to Be*, 11.

[108]As told by Tan, *Encyclopedia of 7,700 Illustrations*, 800.

[109]Adapted from Tan, *Encyclopedia of 7,700 Illustrations*, 798.

[110]J. Ramsey Michaels, *Interpreting the Book of Revelation* (Grand Rapids: Baker, 1992), 143.

THE FIFTH LAST THING:

THE RELEASE OF SATAN AND MAN'S FINAL REBELLION
REVELATION 20:7-10

༺ ❀ ༻

"One of the profoundest facts in the entire realm of history" has been the universal sense of guilt among men.[1] Whatever the differences among the ancient, pagan religions of man—and they are many—they were united in their recognition that man had offended his gods, and their anger must be appeased. The teachers of every branch of the Christian church agree on the problem. John Henry Newman writes, "The human race is implicated in some terrible aboriginal calamity. It is out of joint with the purposes of its Creator."[2] The fact of guilt is a permanent theme in the world's great literature. Think of Lady Macbeth, overcome with remorse over her complicity in the murders committed by her husband, viewing the imagined blood stains on her hand: "Out, damned spot! out, I say!"[3] And everywhere in Scripture we are indicted, "Both Jews and Greeks are all under sin…that every mouth may be closed, and all the world may become accountable to God…for all have sinned and fall short of the glory of God" (Rom. 3:9, 19, 23).

༄

Yet mankind in these early years of the 21ST century is in a state of denial—rejecting all that his forebears have told him about his sin. "Nothing," says Anglican Bishop D.R. Davies, "is so sinister in our world today as the decline in the sense of sin, the dissipating of the sense of guilt." This modern tendency was foreseen by H.G. Wells in his ghoulish story, *The Island of Dr. Moreau*. The scientist, Dr. Moreau, sought to produce a new race of beings by the process of vivisecting animals. He did extensive surgery upon various kinds of animals—trying to humanize them—reshaping their bodies, molding their brains, and teaching them rudimentary ideas of morality. But gradually the beast inside would begin to creep back, and they would commit violent and cruel acts, for which they felt no remorse. What the story shows is that a man without guilt would be an inconceivable monstrosity.[4]

Yet several forces in our modern world—liberal Protestant theology, aggressive secularism, ethereal humanism, revived paganism, and psychological Freudianism—have contributed to this modern trend. Man is basically good, we are told. Suppressed guilt feelings are the source of neurosis; therefore guilt feelings must be transcended. As a result, the language of sin—the Biblical assertions that unbelief, rebellion against God, and transgression of His commandments are blameworthy—has been replaced by the language of sociology and therapy. "There was a time when we were afraid of being caught doing something sinful in front of our ministers," observes a character in one of Peter De Vries' short stories. "Now we are afraid of being caught doing something immature in front of our therapists."[5]

Shortly before his death Roman Catholic Archbishop Fulton J. Sheen was interviewed by *Christianity Today*. In the interview he asserts, "The modern world does not believe in sin…. The ministers and priests [have] stopped talking about sin. The lawyers picked it up and it became a 'crime.' The psychiatrists reached for it and it became a 'complex.'… It used to be that we Catholics were the only ones in the world who believed in the immaculate conception of the Virgin Mary. Today every American believes he is immaculately conceived. [If he does something wrong] he is not a sinner; he is [just] sick."[6]

One caveat should be added here. Not all counseling or therapy is wrong—it is often very helpful to talk our problems out with a responsible, mature Christian elder, pastor, or counselor, and there may be occasions when a Christian will need medical help from a physician with psychiatric training. What needs to be said, however, is that our modern society has rejected the Biblical explanation of evil. It has rejected the Biblical terminology of sin for a new moral vocabulary that is largely psychological. Therapy is deadly when it encourages us to think of ourselves as helpless victims instead of the full-scale sinners and responsible moral beings that we really are.

Some time ago the *Wall Street Journal* placed an advertisement in the *New York Times*. It was a reprint of one of their editorials entitled, "When was the last time you had a good conversation about sin?" The editorial recounted the roll call of sinful behavior we see daily on television news and then commented, "Sin isn't something that many people, including most churches, have spent much time talking about or worrying about through [recent] years....But we will say this for sin: it at least offered a frame of reference for personal behavior. When the frame was dismantled, guilt wasn't the only thing that fell away; we also lost the guidewire of personal responsibility....Everyone was left on his or her own. It now appears that many wrecked people could have used a road map."[7]

Human history—whether we speak collectively of the nations, or individually of our own personal lives—is the tragic tale of our offenses against Almighty God. The Bible tells us that the proper way to deal with our sins is to confess them, to bring them out in the open before God for His forgiveness (1 John 1:9). The wrong approach is to suppress our sense of sin, for that is the sure and certain road to damnation.[8]

Verses 7 through 10 of Revelation 20 are all about the reality of sin in man. The passage contains a prophecy of the very last sins that will be committed by mankind in history, and it shows the inevitable outcome of that sin. The lesson, the "big idea" of Revelation 20:7–10 is that God will use Satan in the closing events of world history to prove once and for all the depravity[9] and moral corruption of the heart of man.

The Release Of Satan From The Abyss (verse 7)

The Time Of His Release

The passage looks ahead to a specific moment in history. It describes events to take place "when the thousand years are completed," at the end of the millennium.[10] Any one thousand-year period is a millennium; however, because of the preeminence of the one thousand-year period in our passage—it is the one thousand-year period in the future when Jesus Christ shall reign upon the earth—it is called *the* millennium.[11]

A Description of the Millennium

The millennial age, the Scriptures assure us, will be a golden age for human beings.[12] It will begin with the return of Jesus Christ to defeat His enemies and reign upon the earth (Rev. 5:10). During this period Satan will be imprisoned in the abyss and will have absolutely no influence upon human life (20:1–3). Associated with the Lord Jesus

183

in His reign will be His redeemed of the ages. In their glorified, resurrected bodies these immortal ones will the associates of the King of kings (20:4–6). It will be an era marked
by a spirituality unknown in human history (CF. Joel 2:28).
It will be a time when the absolute moral standards of God
will be imposed on all of society (Isa. 8:20; 32:5; 40:4; 42:3;
Mal. 4:4). The Messiah shall rule with a rod of iron (Rev.
19:15), and everyone will be held responsible for his moral
actions (Ezek. 18:3–29). There will be no warfare; it will be
an era of world-wide peace (Ps. 46:9; Mic. 4:3). The environmental crimes of man shall be righted, and beauty shall
reign in nature (Isa. 30:23–25; 35:1–10). The slums of the cities shall be healed (Isa. 61:4; Ps. 72:16), and physical disease
and deformity will disappear (Isa. 33:24; 35:5–6; Mal. 1:8).
Everything worthwhile in human life will be fostered (Isa.
42:3). All international power shall be vested in Jesus Christ
who shall judge between the nations (Isa. 2:2, 4). As King
of the Jews, Christ shall reign from Jerusalem, the city of
David (2 Sam. 5:7, 9; Ps. 110:2; Isa. 2:2–4; 60:14, 18; Zech.
8:3), called by Ezekiel (38:12) the "navel of the earth."

The Inhabitants of the Millennium

To understand the passage better it is important to know
one more thing about the millennium: there will be two
kinds of humanity living on the earth at that time. There
will be, first of all, the resurrected, glorified immortal

people of God. They will walk the earth in sinless perfection having bodies like that of the glorified Christ (CF. Phil. 3:21; 1 John 3:2). However, there will also be a group of people in their natural bodies. They will be born-again believers (CF. John 3:3–5) converted to Christ during the time of the tribulation, but they will not yet have their resurrection bodies.[13] Human life for them will continue with the natural processes of marriage (Jer. 33:11), procreation, birth (Zech. 8:5), and growth (Isa. 60:22). Disease and deformity shall be divinely controlled (CF. Isa. 33:24; 35:5–6; Mal. 1:8). The length of human life will be greatly prolonged (Isa. 65:20–22) and only shortened if a person is incorrigible in his sins. Children born during this time will be sinners just as today, with sinful natures and sinful tendencies, and they will have to turn to Christ for salvation or be lost in their sins. No doubt part of the work of those who serve in the priestly office and reign with Christ will be to evangelize the nations.[14] Remembering these truths will help the student understand, in part at least, why Satan is released at the end of the millennium.

THE PURPOSE OF HIS RELEASE

In verse 3 John says that after the thousand years Satan "must be released for a short time." The Greek particle translated "must" means "it is necessary." It was often used with the sense of "divine destiny or unavoidable fate."[15] It

The Seven Last Things

here suggests divine necessity—what A.T. Robertson calls the "sad necessity."[16]

For reasons in the purpose and plan of God it is necessary that he be released. What then are the reasons? Two are implied in the text.[17] The first reason is to demonstrate the incorrigibility of Satan. No sooner is he released than he demonstrates that neither his plans nor his nature have changed.

Some time ago the following remarks were made by an Italian writer best known for his book on the life of Christ:

> The Christian…should feel for [Satan] as the most supremely unfortunate of created beings, the leader and symbol of all enmity and division, yet the archangel who once was nearest to God. Perhaps only our love can help him to save himself, help him become again what he once was, the most perfect of heavenly spirits. If Satan can be freed from the hatred of Christians, men would be forever freed from Satan….Is it not possible that Christ redeemed men so that, following this precept to love their enemies, they may one day be worthy of conceiving the redemption of the most ominous and stubborn enemy of all?….We must approach Satan in a spirit of mercy and justice, not in order to become his admirers or imitators but with the hope of freeing him from himself and ourselves thereby from him. Perhaps he awaits only a sign of our mercy to find once again in himself the

strength to renounce his hatred, that is, to free the whole world from the dominion of evil.[18]

There is not the slightest hint in Scripture to support such remarks. Nowhere are believers told to love the devil, nor is it suggested that Christians can redeem Satan or anyone else, nor is it their duty to show him mercy. This passage suggests that Satan is an evil rebel—and the Christian's deadly enemy—to the very end.

Regrettably the same kind of humanistic indifference to Scripture is to be found in writers professing to be evangelical. L'Engle writes, "I know a number of highly sensitive and intelligent people in my own communion who consider as a heresy my faith that God's loving concern for his creation will outlast all our willfulness and pride. No matter how many eons it takes, he will not rest until all of creation, including Satan, is reconciled to him, until there is no creature who cannot return his look of love with a joyful response of love....I cannot believe that God wants punishment to go on interminably any more than does a loving parent. The entire purpose of loving punishment is to teach, and it lasts only as long as is needed for the lesson. And the lesson is always love."[19]

A long prison term frequently reforms the conduct of criminals. Even though their hearts remain unchanged, they nevertheless refrain from the kind of behavior that got them imprisoned. Satan's one thousand-year prison sentence does not reform him even in appearance. He is still evil within, and he immediately seeks to seduce others.[20]

The second reason for Satan's release is to demonstrate the depravity of the heart of man. Just as in the book of Genesis where Satan was allowed to enter the first paradise, so he is allowed to enter the last paradise of this present world. Just as he was allowed to enter Eden to expose the nature of man's heart, so in the restoration of paradise—the millennial earth—he is permitted to do it again.[21] The great aim of God in this as in all things is not to glorify man, but to glorify Himself.[22] In this final chapter of the world's history it is again demonstrated that man perpetually embraces evil unless sustained by sovereign grace.

In these events are seen some elements of a premillennial philosophy of history.[23] One of the reasons for the continuation of history is God's purpose to demonstrate man's utter ruin in sin and his total responsibility for the evil state of the world.[24] The apostle Paul says that the day will come when "every mouth" will be stopped (Rom. 3:19). Yet up until this very moment men's mouths have never been stopped because they either suppress their sense of sin or else excuse themselves. In Eden the man blamed the woman, and the woman blamed the serpent (Gen. 3:12–13). The next excuse came in the days after Cain killed Abel when great violence broke out in the earth. Had God approached men at that point they would probably have said, "It's your fault. You let Cain get away with it. If you had only punished him no one would ever have done such a thing again." So, God said, "I'll institute human government and capital punishment." "Whoever sheds man's blood, by man his blood shall be shed" (Gen. 9:6).

Man did not improve. Perhaps his excuse would be, if asked, "Well, we need to be inspired with promises and hope." And thus, the Lord gave the great promises to Abraham (Gen. 12, 15, 17). Man did not improve. Perhaps his excuse then, had he been asked, would be, "Yes, we have government, but we don't know how to apply it. We don't know what you want us to do. We have promises, but we need guidelines." And so, God gave them the Law of Moses with the ten commandments. Again man failed the test. If quizzed he would have probably said, "Well, the law is too abstract. If only we could see a flesh and blood example of what you want." So God sent the Lord Jesus Christ into the world. He lived a perfect life and exposed their terrible moral failure, so they killed Him. Possibly men would then say, "Well, we need power to follow your Word." And the Lord gave the Holy Spirit to His followers. Yet today the world is in terrible shape, and a church marked by power in many ways is also marked by failure and unbelief in others.

Men still have excuses. In many recent crimes reported in the press the excuses have been sociological and psychological in nature. The evil behavior of people, criminals and non-criminals, is blamed on poverty, drugs, bad chromosomes, insecurity, narcissism, self-pity, sexual repression, anxiety, morbidity, insensitivity, paranoia, etc.

A few years ago a group of teenage boys in New York's Central Park attacked a young woman jogger. She was raped, stabbed, beaten, and left for dead. When caught the young men claimed they were out for a night of "wilding." They lived on the edge of Harlem, yet their backgrounds were normal. Four of the youths lived in a building with a doorman. One was enrolled in a parochial school. Another had just received an A on a book report. Yet the inevitable excuses of our therapeutic society were quickly given. The boys were "damaged…in pain inside." They were "letting out their anger." One psychologist said, "Society has not been nice to these kids." So the criminals are the true victims. They are not depraved—just deprived.[25]

Charles Colson visited a model correctional institution in Europe. The psychiatrist explained that 71-percent of the inmates had been classified as mentally abnormal since they had committed particularly heinous crimes. Since people are inherently good, said the doctor, anyone who does evil must be mentally ill. So inmates with this "illness" were sent to her institution to be cured. A few days after Colson's visit, a convicted rapist was given permission for a short furlough under the escort of a 26-year old female guard. Part of his therapy was to attend a movie with a woman, a step on his road to "normalcy." Not far from the prison gates, the inmate battered and murdered the young woman. Charles Colson concluded, "Violent tendencies are not an illness. Criminal behaviors are not symptoms of a disease. We cannot explain away awful acts through sociological factors or odd chromosomes or poverty or germs or drugs. While these can surely be factors in criminal behavior, the root cause of crime has not changed since Cain. It is sin." He adds, "The Bible teaches that men and women's natures are inherently depraved. Without restraints, sin will emerge and wreak its havoc on whatever crosses its path."[26]

More recently there are those who will blame evil behavior on Satan. Even this is given a uniquely modern twist. We are told that these people—ensnared in cults and abusive situations—are totally innocent. They are not responsible.

And so, at last, during the millennial kingdom, God places man in a world without Satan. It will be a world where Jesus Christ actually lives on the earth in a physical, visible—albeit glorious—body. It will be a perfect environment where disease is curtailed. It will be a world where man's accountability and responsibility are clearly spelled out. Surely, in such a world, man will live an upright, moral life. Well, no! The millennial kingdom will clearly show that the problem is with the total depravity of the human heart. The problem, man will be conclusively shown, is not with the environment, with his chromosomes, with his victim status, or with the devil. It is with himself.

THE GATHERING OF THE NATIONS AGAINST THE SAINTS (VERSE 8)

THE SEDUCTION OF THE NATIONS

John apparently is not told who will release Satan. Perhaps it will be the same angel that will imprison him in the abyss as the millennial age begins (v. 1–2). Regardless, he will no sooner be released than he will seek "to deceive the nations," and verses 7–8 make it clear that he will be successful ("the number of them is like the sand of the seashore"). It is apparent that the population of the earth will grow tremendously during the thousand years. It is also apparent that many of those who will be born to Christian parents will not acknowledge Christ as Savior, but will remain in unbelief. Christ will rule with a rod of iron, and many will chafe under His rule.[27] And when Satan seeks to seduce them into rebellion, they will readily follow him.

The words of Psalm 66:3 prophetically anticipate the millennial reign of Christ.[28] The psalmist writes, "Because of the greatness of Thy power Thine enemies will give feigned obedience to Thee." Jesus will rule with a rod of iron, and many will yield external obedience to the king, but their hearts will be filled with rebellion.[29]

About the turn of the century, a man rushed down to make a New York ferry; just as the ferry was pulling out, he jumped and landed on the rail of the boat. He sat there exhausted, breathing heavily. After a few minutes, he stood up and walked toward the center of the boat. A fellow-passenger said, "You almost missed it." "Yes," he said, "but I'll get there now in time for the third race." "The third race? Where do you think you're going?" "Why, over to the race track." "Well," said the other man, "you're on the Methodist Church chartered Sunday-school picnic boat." The man went over to the captain and said, "Captain, I'll give you $500 if you'll put me back." The captain said, "Look, buddy, it took us twenty minutes to get out here; it would take us twenty minutes to turn around and go back, and another twenty minutes to get out here—that's an hour. There are 2,000 children on this ferry and that amounts to two thousand hours of their picnic time. You're on this boat till we get back at nine o'clock tonight." "Oh well," said the man, "where's the bar?" "It's closed for the day," replied the captain. No bar, nothing but children prattling and singing hymns and choruses—all day this man had to live in that atmosphere. When the boat docked at nine o'clock that night, the race-track man was first off—to get to the nearest bar. That, says Donald Grey Barnhouse, is a picture of what the millennium is going to be like for millions of people on this earth. They hate righteousness. Their hearts are deceitful and wicked. They will despise the Christ whom they see with their own eyes.[30]

In another passage the apostle John tells Christians, "Do not love the world" (1 John 2:15). By "world" John means the principles and ways of pagan society.[31] The world system will reemerge in the millennium, with unconverted people craving the pleasures and pastimes and culture of a sinful world.

THE DESCRIPTION OF THE NATIONS

Satan's seductive propaganda appeals to unbelievers in nations all over the earth. John specifically mentions the names of two nations, "Gog and Magog." In Ezekiel 38:2 Gog is from the land of Magog in "the remotest parts of the north" (38:6). The identity of Gog and Magog in Ezekiel's day is debated; many feel they were the Scythians or the Goths, fierce and wild tribes to the north who were viewed with horror by the civilized world.[32] In later Jewish writings "Gog and Magog" becomes an expression to describe all the rebellious nations of Psalm 2.[33] In Ezekiel's prophecy of the end times Gog is the Antichrist who comes against Israel as they are settling in the land prior to the beginning of the millennium.[34] In John's Revelation Gog and Magog come against Israel at the end of the millennium.[35]

How can Gog and Magog be used of the battle in chapter 19 and again appear in this battle at the end of the millennium?[36] The most likely explanation is that Antichrist is Gog and is defeated at the second coming. During the millennium his defeat becomes the stuff of legends among the nations, like Napoleon's defeat at Waterloo. Now, at the end of the millennial kingdom, in Revelation 20:8, the Gog and Magog "legend" is applied to a new historical situation when Satan leads the new "Gog and Magog."[37] Satan meets his "Waterloo"—his "Gog and Magog," if you will. Just as Antichrist fulfills the Gog and Magog prophecy at the beginning of the millennium, so the rebellious millennial nations fulfill it as well at the end of the thousand years.

THE MOBILIZATION OF THE NATIONS

In any case the nations are mobilized for war. The events described here "enshrine deep insight into the resilience of evil." The lesson is that "no matter how far human society progresses it can never reach a point where it is invulnerable to such attacks."[38] As one reads of the rebellion he is tempted to say, "This is incredible. Will human beings who have lived on earth with the King of kings and Lord of lords actually mobilize for war against Him?" If one finds this incredible he does not understand the depravity of the human heart.

There are other illustrations of such depravity in the Bible:[39] Is it not incredible that, after ten supernatural plagues which he confessed to be sent by God, Pharaoh would array his armies against the people of Israel who are visibly defended by the pillar of cloud (Exod. 14)? It is equally incredible that, after the earth opened up and swallowed Dathan and Abiram (Num. 16; Ps. 106:17) and the fire of God had struck dead 250 of their fellow rebels, one day later the people grumbled against Moses and Aaron and said, "You have killed the people of the Lord" (Num. 16: 41). The events in our passage are simply true to what the Bible says about the evil in the heart of man.

The noted historian, Arnold J. Toynbee, says that history records 21 civilizations.[40] These are 21 attempts by civilized man to make a success of systematic living, independently of God. The remarkable thing about them is that every one of them is a complete and utter failure.[41] Even Western civilization is crumbling today. Why? One astute observer of the world scene, Prof. Reinhold Niebuhr, said that democracy could only develop in those societies where the Christian doctrine of original sin flourished.[42] As modern civilization suppresses this doctrine and loses its understanding of right and wrong it will falter. It is significant that even the civilization of the millennial kingdom will end in failure. The problem will not be the government. It will not be the environment. It will not be the educational programs. It will not be false religions and Satanic influence. The problem will be the heart of man!

THE SURROUNDING OF THE CITY BY THE ENEMY (VERSE 9)

THE FOCUS OF THEIR ATTACK

The armies of Satan come up "on the broad plain of the earth." This can be rendered "on the breadth of the land" (CF. Isa. 8:8; Hab. 1:6) and refers to the land of Israel.[43] The focus of Satan's attention is "the camp of the saints" and "the beloved city," the city of Jerusalem.[44] It is rightly called "beloved" because for a thousand years it has been the seat of Christ's kingdom and the spiritual center of the earth (CF. Isa. 60:14, 18; 62:3, 7; Jer. 31:6).[45]

The term "camp" denotes a military camp of an army on the march (Ex. 16:13) or engaged in battle (Heb. 11:34). The verse distinguishes the camp from the city. The saints are gathered in the camp in order to defend the city[46] from attackers.[47] This would suggest that the rebellion comes as no surprise to the King of kings.

What kind of temptation does Satan use to seduce the nations to come in battle against the Son of God? One of the older and more thoughtful commentators[48] suggests that it is one of the oldest temptations of all—namely anti-Semitism, the hatred of Gentiles against the Jews. The Bible is clear that Israel will enjoy a special place during the millennium (Isa. 60:10–12; 61:5–6). Think how the unconverted Gentiles will be galled to serve the Jewish nation. Satan goads them, "Why should the Jew have first place? Assert your racial superiority. Go up and destroy Jerusalem and build a metropolis of your own."

According to Zechariah 14:16–19 the nations will be required to make an annual fall (the month of Tishri 15–21)[49] pilgrimage to Jerusalem for the Feast of Tabernacles. It is very possible that the nations will gather for war at that time. They might think that such a large gathering would arouse little suspicion at a time when large numbers of visitors are expected in the city anyway. And so they go up, not for worship, but for war.[50]

THE NATURE OF THEIR DESTRUCTION

When man sinned in the Garden he declared a cosmic civil war in the universe. God did not create man to be free. He created him to be free and dependent upon Himself. Almighty God will not surrender His supremacy in this universe to Satan or to rebellious man. His holiness demands that He say an eternal "No!" to the rebellion of His creatures. "No, you will not triumph!"[51] As one reads of these great armies surrounding the city he is prepared for a great prolonged battle, but none comes; instead, the wicked millions are immediately destroyed. The power of

God is so great that there is not even the appearance of a battle.[52]

An unknown Jew or Jews, writing in the second century before Christ, composed the so-called *Sibylline Oracles*,[53] in which we find a description of the last battle that is similar to the one we find here. He describes "the kings of the nations"[54] throwing themselves against the land of Israel, "bringing retribution upon themselves." He says that the "accursed kings" shall each place his throne in a ring around the city with his infidel people by him. "With witless mind" they cast their spears against the Holy One. He says that then God shall speak with a mighty voice unto all "the undisciplined, empty-minded people, and judgment shall come upon them." "Fiery swords" shall fall from heaven down to the earth. "God shall judge with war and sword, and with fire and cataclysms of rain."[55]

During the Crimean War (1853–56) there was a famous battle between the English cavalry and the Russian cannoneers. The British officers made a terrible miscalculation and sent a brigade of 600 cavalry up a valley right into the Russian guns. It was a terrible blunder—the Russians could not believe their eyes as the horsemen rode into the trap—and the English soldiers were decimated. Alfred Lord Tennyson immortalized the event with his poem "The Charge of the Light Brigade."

"Forward the Light Brigade!
Charge for the guns!" he said:
Into the valley of Death
Rode the six hundred.

Cannon to the right of them,
Cannon to the left of them,
Cannon in front of them
Volley'd and thunder'd;
Storm'd at with shot and shell,
Boldly they rode and well,
Into the jaws of Death,
Into the mouth of Hell
Rode the six hundred.[56]

The captain of the Devil's army, Satan himself, makes a terrible blunder at the end as he leads his forces—the "Dark Brigade"—into the jaws of death and into the mouth of Hell.

THE CASTING OF THE DEVIL INTO THE LAKE OF FIRE (VERSE 10)

THE DESTINY OF THE DEVIL

In another passage (John 14:2) Jesus promises His disciples, "I go to prepare a place for you," the heavenly city in which God's people shall live throughout eternity. In yet another place (Matt. 25:41), we read that the lake of fire was "prepared for the devil and his angels." The same word, *prepare,* is used of both places. The devil is taken and summarily thrown into his eternal home. There he joins the Beast and the false prophet who were put there a thousand long years before.

Revelation 20:10 touches upon a number of important theological matters. For one thing, it demonstrates that the Devil is not God, nor is he a rival to God. In the end he is seen to be the creature that he is. "The mystery of the devil, like the mystery of evil itself, lies hidden in the depths of the mystery of God's purpose for His creation." The passage does seem to suggest that it is not the function of the devil to originate sin in man but to reveal it and develop its latent possibilities.[57] Other theological matters touched on are the nature of hell and the question of annihilation.

THE NATURE OF HIS PUNISHMENT

This is the fourth chapter in the downfall of Satan. The first chapter was the Cross when Christ took from him the ability to terrorize mankind with the fear of death. The second chapter is his expulsion from heaven in the middle of the tribulation (Rev. 12). The third chapter is when he is cast into the Abyss at the beginning of the millennium (Rev. 20:2). Now, finally, he is thrown into the lake of fire (Rev. 20:10). A lake is a body of water from which there is no outlet. There is no release from hell. It goes on "forever and ever." "There is no intermission and no end."[58]

The lake of fire is a terrible picture. It is, of course, picturesque language, but it describes a real fact in the spiritual world.[59] An older lady once asked me after a meeting in McKinney, Texas if I believed in a literal hell, and I assured her that I did. "Is it literal fire?" she asked. Of the exact nature of that fire, of course, one cannot speak.

Literal fire would quickly burn up an ordinary human body. Of course, those in hell do not have ordinary human bodies. They will be resurrected bodily, and just as the blessed have bodies uniquely suited for glory, these have bodies uniquely suited for judgment. I was born in Sydney, a small steel mill city in Nova Scotia, eastern Canada. I remember the story of a man who fell into molten steel. His body was annihilated immediately. Yet, in hell people are never burned up—they are there "forever and ever." It is a dreadful place of torment, and the Bible uses the most dreadful picture in the human language to describe it.[60]

Verse 10 is an important one for those who teach the doctrine of annihilation, the doctrine that the lost do not suffer eternally but are destroyed. It is important to note who the devil's companions are. The Beast and the false prophet were cast into the lake of fire one thousand years before, and they are still there! They have not been annihilated. They still exist in that awful place.[61]

Conclusion

This passage demonstrates that the believer's three great enemies in the spiritual warfare—the world, the flesh, and the devil—exist up to the very end of this present world. The world system, the pagan mindset of collective rebellion against the will of God, re-emerges in the millennial kingdom in spite of the righteous rule of the Lord Jesus Christ. The devil is an evil being who is incorrigible. He shall act hatefully and murderously toward the people of God until the end. Believers should be wary of this evil being who seeks their destruction. So also the flesh: the doctrines of original sin and total depravity are true. The human heart is deceitful and corrupt, and those who face God at the last judgment will have nothing to say. There is only one way to escape: men and women must confess their sins to Him and embrace Christ as their Savior. Only those who believe in Christ as Savior are forgiven their sins.

This generation is trying hard to suppress its sense of sin, but "out of sight" does not mean "out of mind." Thankfully, God has given people consciences, and He has sent His messengers to talk to them about their sins and their need of forgiveness. There is no thicket in which they can hide themselves from the storms of self-accusation; there is no shore that cannot be washed by the recurrent tides of the brooding awareness of their sins.[62]

The problem with this world is the human race. I am not talking about the fashionable social sins that everyone likes to denounce—environmental damage, sexism, crime, racism, nuclear arms, etc.—modern people have a keen eye for the sins of society. I am writing, rather, about my own personal package of disobedience and rebellion against God, and my hateful behavior toward neighbors, fellow employees, family, and friends. People too readily suppress their own actual, individual sin and guilt.

Many years ago a correspondent for the *London Times* wrote a series of articles on a number of the same social problems that face us now. He ended each article with the question, "What's wrong with the world?" G.K. Chesterton (1874–1936) read a number of the articles and then wrote this famous reply:

> Dear Editor:
> What's wrong with the world?
> I am
> Faithfully yours,
> G.K. Chesterton.[63]

At the base of all of the world's problems is the sinfulness of man.

Further, the lesson of all these people who are to be born in the millennial age should be contemplated. No doubt, many will embrace the faith of their parents, but many will not. This is another reminder that born-again people do not propagate born-again children. Every child born into this world has to make his own decision to accept or reject Christ. Parents and grandparents must be encouraged to faithfully place the claims of Christ before the children in their care.

Finally, all should remember that two eternal "homes" have been "prepared" for God's creatures. For the devil and his angels God has prepared the lake of fire; for His own redeemed people Christ has prepared the heavenly city. The challenge which preachers must place before those to whom they proclaim God's Word is: "In which of these homes will you spend eternity?"

NOTES

[1]D.R. Davies, *Down Peacock's Feathers: Studies in the Contemporary Significance of the General Confession* (New York: Macmillan, 1944), 36. In this introduction I have borrowed a number of thoughts from Davies, 36–43.

[2]John Henry Newman, *Apologia Pro Vita Sua*, ed. M. Svalgic (London: Oxford University Press, 1967), 217.

[3]William Shakespeare, *The Tragedy of Macbeth* 5.1.37, in the Yale Shakespeare (rev. ed., New Haven: Yale University Press, 1954), 86.

[4]H. G. Wells, *The Island of Dr. Moreau*, in *Seven Science Fiction Novels of H.G. Wells* (New York: Dover, N.D.), 77–182.

[5]Quoted by Thomas G. Long, "God Be Merciful to Me, A Miscalculator," *Theology Today 50* (July, 1993): 166.

[6]David Kucharsky, "Bottom-Line Theology: An Interview With Fulton J. Sheen," *Christianity Today* (June 3, 1977): 10.

[7]*The New York Times* (Jan. 8, 1992). Quoted by Long, "God Be Merciful," 167.

[8]Davies, *Down Peacock's Feathers*, 44.

[9]I am here referring to original sin in the narrow sense, that is the sinful state in which we are born. It is the sinful disposition or inclination to evil that is the inward root of all personal sins. CF. Charles Hodge, *Systematic Theology*, 3 vols. (New York: Charles Scribner, 1872; reprint ed., Grand Rapids: Eerdmans, 1975), 2:227; Louis Berkhof, *Systematic Theology* (4TH ed., Grand Rapids: Eerdmans, 1949), 244.

[10]It should be noted that this paragraph does not begin with καὶ εἶδον ("and I saw," CF. 19:17, 19; 20:1, 4, 11, 12; 21:1). Charles says that "our author here forsakes the apocalyptic style and adopts the prophetic. Likewise, Govett asserts that "the present paragraph is not vision, but pure prophecy." CF. R.H. Charles, *The Revelation of St. John*, 2 vols., International Critical Commentary (Edinburgh: T. & T. Clark, 1920), 2:187; Robert Govett, *The Apocalypse: Expounded by Scripture*, 4 vols. (London, 1861; reprint ed., Miami Springs: Conley & Schoettle, 1981), 4:268.

[11]J.A. Seiss, *Lectures on the Apocalypse*, 3 vols. (9TH ed., New York: Charles C. Cook, 1906), 342.

[12]CF. Alva J. McClain, *The Greatness of the Kingdom* (Chicago: Moody, 1959), 217–54; John F. Walvoord, *The Revelation of Jesus Christ* (Chicago: Moody, 1966), 301–2.

[13]Walvoord, *The Revelation of Jesus Christ*, 302.

[14]This is suggested by Charles, *Revelation*, 2:143, 154, 186. Remarkably, it is denied by Seiss, *Apocalypse*, 3:346.

[15]*A Greek-English Lexicon of the New Testament*, eds. William F. Arndt, F. Wilbur Gingrich, and Frederick W. Danker (2D. ed., Chicago: University of Chicago Press, 1979), see "δεῖ," 172.

[16]A.T. Robertson, *Word Pictures in the New Testament*, 6 vols., vol. 6: *The General Epistles and the Revelation of John* (Nashville: Broadman, 1933), 6:458.

[17]Cf. Govett, *The Apocalypse: Expounded by Scripture*, 4:213–15; Seiss, *Lectures on the Apocalypse*, 3:351–52; Ford C. Ottman, *The Unfolding of the Ages* (New York: Baker & Taylor, 1905), 429–30; Walvoord, *The Revelation of Jesus Christ*, 303; G. R. Beasley-Murray, *The Book of Revelation*, New Century Bible (London: Oliphants, 1974), 291; Robert H. Mounce, *The Book of Revelation*, New International Commentary on the New Testament (rev. ed., Grand Rapids: Eerdmans, 1998), 363, 371. Govett suggests two other reasons: (1) To display the omniscience of God, His foreknowledge of all future actions—those of man and Satan as well as His own. (2) To justify eternal punishment. It has been suggested by some that God's punishments are remedial and reformatory and lead to repentance (E.G. Michael Paternoster, *Thou Art There Also: God, Death, and Hell* [London: SPCK, 1967], 50–51), but one thousand years in prison have not changed Satan. When released his love of violence and rebellion are shown to be undiminished.

[18]Giovani Papini, *The Devil*, trans. Adrienne Foulke (New York: E.P. Dutton, 1954), 16–17. See 211–21 for Papini's defense of the view that the devil will ultimately be redeemed. The suggestion that Satan might eventually be saved goes back at least as far as Origen (AD185–253). See Origen, *De Principiis* 3.6.5, in *The Ante-Nicene Fathers*, 10 vols. eds. Alexander Roberts and James Donaldson (1885; reprint ed., Grand Rapids: Eerdmans, 1994), 4:346. The suggestion has been embraced by some modern writers. Paternoster cites the aphorism of W.H.G. Holmes (*The Alphabet of Holiness* [London: Mowbray, 1943], 66), "Mercy could reach Satan, if he could accept it." Paternoster himself (*Thou Art There Also: God, Death, and Hell*, 38–55) defends the view.

[19]Madeleine L'Engle, *The Irrational Season* (New York: Seabury, 1977), 97. As Bruce says in another context, "The person who says, 'I could not have a high opinion of God who would (or would not) do this or that,' is not adding anything to our knowledge of God; he is simply telling us something about himself" (F.F. Bruce, *The Epistle to the Hebrews* [rev. ed., Grand Rapids: Eerd-

mans, 1990], 79). L'Engle confesses her problem with the biblical doctrine of hell when she says, "I cannot believe…"

[20]Govett, *The Apocalypse: Expounded by Scripture*, 4:268.

[21]Beasley-Murray, *The Book of Revelation*, 291.

[22]Govett, *The Apocalypse: Expounded by Scripture*, 4:213.

[23]McClain, *The Greatness of the Kingdom*, 527–31.

[24]I am here following James Mongomery Boice, "Will There Really Be a Golden Age?" *Eternity* (Sept., 1972), 28, 30; Idem., *The Last and Future World* (Grand Rapids: Zondervan, 1974), 26–30. CF. Donald Grey Barnhouse, *Teaching the Word of Truth* (Grand Rapids: Eerdmans, 1940), 178–87; Idem., *Revelation: An Expository Commentary* (Grand Rapids: Zondervan, 1971), 386.

[25]Charles Colson, "You Can't Cure the Wilding Sickness," *Christianity Today* (Sept. 8, 1989), 80.

[26]Charles Colson, "The Wilding Sickness," 80.

[27]Surprisingly, a number of amillennial scholars have a problem with this aspect of the premillennial doctrine. If Christ must rule with a rod of iron, they argue, then surely Satan is still deceiving them for, otherwise, why would they need such an authoritative rule? One wonders how writers who affirm the doctrine of the total depravity of man can make such an objection. CF. W. J. Grier, *The Momentous Event* (Belfast: The Evangelical Bookshop, 1945; reprint ed., London: Banner of Truth, 1970), 107; Jay E. Adams, *The Time Is at Hand* (rev. ed., Greenville: A Press, 1987), 84, N. 1.

[28]CF. Arthur G. Clarke, *Analytical Studies in the Psalms* (Kansas City: Walterick, 1949), 167.

[29]S. Lewis Johnson, Jr. "The Final Rebellion" (cassette tape, Dallas: Believers' Chapel, 1989–90). I am indebted to Johnson for a number of the thoughts expressed in this chapter.

[30]Donald Grey Barnhouse, *Let Me Illustrate* (Westwood: Revell, 1967), 223–24.

[31]C.H. Dodd, *The Johannine Epistles*, Moffatt New Testament Commentary (London: Hodder and Stoughton, 1946), 41. Cf. *Theological Dictionary of the New Testament*, see "κόσμος," by H. Sasse, 3 (1965): 893.

[32]Cf. Edwin M. Yamauchi, *Foes From the Northern Frontier: Invading Hordes From the Russian Steppes* (Grand Rapids: Baker, 1982), 22–27; Govett, *The Apocalypse: Expounded by Scripture*, 4:272–76.

[33]For documentation in the Talmud, cf. Henry Barclay Swete, *The Apocalypse of St. John* (London: Macmillan, 1906), 264–65; Charles, *The Revelation of St. John*, 2:189; G.B. Caird, *The Revelation of St. John the Divine,* Harper's New Testament Commentaries (New York: Harper and Row, 1966), 256.

[34]The chronology of the invasion of Ezek. 38–39 is understood differently by various scholars. There are at least six views: (1) The invasion takes place before the tribulation (D.L. Cooper). (2) The invasion takes place in the middle of the tribulation (J.D. Pentecost, L. Wood). (3) The events take place at the end of the tribulation (Feinberg, Kelly). (4) The events of Ezek. 38–39 are spread over a period of time with ch. 38 being fulfilled in the middle of the tribulation and ch. 39 being fulfilled at its end (Hoehner). (5) The invasion takes place at the end of the millennium (Ellison, Davidson, Mounce, Tanner, Kline) (6) Ezekiel's prophecy is fulfilled in two events, one in Rev. 19:17–21 and one in Rev. 20:7–10 (Alexander, Caird). Cf. David L. Cooper, *When Gog's Armies Meet the Almighty* (Los Angeles: Biblical Research Society, 1940), 80–81; J. Dwight Pentecost, *Things to Come* (Grand Rapids: Dunham, 1958), 350–52; Leon Wood, *A Commentary on Daniel* (Grand Rapids: Zondervan, 1973), 309; Charles Lee Feinberg, *The Prophecy of Ezekiel* (Chicago: Moody, 1969), 218; William Kelly, *Lectures on the Book of Revelation* (London: G. Morrish, 1874), 448; Harold W. Hoehner, "The Progression of Events in Ezekiel 38–39," in *Integrity of Heart, Skillfulness of Hands*, eds. C.H. Dyer and R.B. Zuck (Grand Rapids: Baker, 1994), 82–92; H.L. Ellison, *Ezekiel, The Man and His Message* (Grand Rapids: Eerdmans, 1956), 133–34; A.B. Davidson, *The Book of the Prophet Ezekiel*, Cambridge Bible for Schools and Colleges, rev. A. W. Streane (Cambridge: Cambridge University Press, 1916), 301; Mounce, *The Book of Revelation*, 371; J. Paul Tanner, "Rethinking Ezekiel's Invasion by God," *Journal of the Evangelical Theological Society 39* (March, 1996): 29–46; Meredith G. Kline, "Har

Megedon: The End of the Millennium," *Journal of the Evangelical Theological Society 39* (June, 1996): 207–222; Caird, *The Revelation of St. John the Divine*, 256. Kline (P. 220), rather triumphantly, announces that his essay "spells the end of premillennialism." For a full and satisfying discussion of the problem, see Ralph H. Alexander, "Ezekiel," *The Expositor's Bible Commentary*, 12 vols., ed. Frank E. Gaebelein (Grand Rapids: Zondervan, 1986), 6:937–40.

[35]Walvoord (*The Revelation of Jesus Christ*, 303–4) notes a number of differences between the invasions in Ezekiel 38 and Revelation 20: (1) In Ezekiel the invaders come from the north, while in Revelation they come from the "four corners of the earth." (2) In Ezekiel the invasion comes at the beginning of Christ's reign, while in Revelation it comes at the end. (3) In Ezekiel the invaders are led by Gog, while in Revelation they are led by Satan. (4) The invaders in Ezekiel fall upon the mountains, and their bodies are burned, whereas in Revelation they surround Jerusalem and are consumed with fire from heaven. CF. T.B. Baines, *The Revelation of Jesus Christ* (5TH ed., London: G. Morrish, 1911), 270–71.

[36]This duplication of the invasions of Gog and Magog is recognized by a number of commentators. CF. Charles, *The Revelation of St. John*, 2:188–89; Caird, *The Revelation of St. John the Divine*, 256.

[37]"Anyone whom Gog's hat fits may wear it" (Caird, *The Revelation of St. John the Divine*, 256).

[38]Caird, *The Revelation of St. John the Divine*, 257.

[39]CF. Govett, *The Apocalypse: Expounded by Scripture*, 4:277.

[40]Arnold J. Toynbee, *A Study of History*, 12 vols. (New York: Oxford University Press, 1934–61). See especially volumes 1, 4, and 5. The 21 civilizations are: Egyptian, Andean, Sinic, Minoan, Sumerian, Mayan, Syriac, Indic, Hittite, Hellenic, Arabic, Iranian, Hindu, Mexican, Yucatec, Babylonian, Orthodox Christian (in Russia), Orthodox Christian (outside Russia), Far Eastern (in Japan and Korea), Far Eastern (main body outside Japan), and modern Western civilization.

[41]Davies, *Down Peacock's Feathers*, 78–79.

[42]"Man's capacity for justice makes democracy possible; but man's inclination to injustice makes democracy necessary." See Reinhold Niebuhr, *The Children of Light and the Children of Darkness* (New York: Scribner's, 1960), xiii. See also William H. Willimon, *Sighing for Eden: Sin, Evil, and the Christian Faith* (Nashville: Abingdon, 1985), 108–9.

[43]Cf. Govett, *The Apocalypse: Expounded by Scripture*, 4:277; Charles, *The Revelation of St. John*, 2:190. Mounce (*The Book of Revelation*, 373), on the other hand, takes the phrase to refer to a large staging area for Satan's armies.

[44]Most commentators regard the city as the earthly city. Cf. Friedrich Dusterdieck, *Critical and Exegetical Handbook to the Revelation of John,* Meyer's Commentary on the New Testament (New York: Funk & Wagnalls, 1884; reprint ed., Winona Lake: Alpha Publications, 1979), 467. Beasley-Murray (*The Book of Revelation*, 298) argues, however, that the city is the heavenly Jerusalem, which has descended from heaven to the earth during the millennial age.

[45]Cf. Charles, *The Revelation of St. John*, 2:190; William Henry Simcox, *The Revelation of St. John the Divine*, Cambridge Bible for Schools and Colleges (Cambridge: Cambridge University Press, 1910), 126–27; George Eldon Ladd, *A Commentary on the Revelation of John* (Grand Rapids: Eerdmans, 1972), 270.

[46]It is a plain evasion of the context for Swete (*The Apocalypse of St. John*, 265) to identify the city as the universal church. Cf. Dusterdieck, *Critical and Exegetical Handbook to the Revelation of John*, 467.

[47]Dusterdieck, *Critical and Exegetical Handbook to the Revelation of John*, 467.

[48]Govett, *The Apocalypse: Expounded by Scripture*, 4:269–70.

[49]Tishri is the seventh month of the Jewish year, corresponding to our September/October.

[50]Govett, *The Apocalypse: Expounded by Scripture*, 4:278–82.

[51]Davies, *Down Peacock's Feathers*, 41–42.

[52]Leon Morris, *The Revelation of St. John*, Tyndale New Testament Commentaries (Grand Rapids: Eerdmans, 1969), 239.

[53]Sibyl (Σίβυλλα) was an old woman to whom the Greeks looked for oracular utterances of divine or quasi-divine inspiration. The original Sibylline oracles have all perished, and the Sibylline oracles now available were written by Jewish and Christian authors between 160 BC and the fifth century AD. The third book, quoted here, may have been written by one Aristobulus (C. 160 BC). He circulated his work under the name of Sibyl in order to commend his monotheistic views to his pagan readers. CF. R.H. Charles, "The Sibylline Oracles," in *The Apocrypha and Pseudepigrapha of the Old Testament*, 2 vols., vol. 2: *Pseudipigrapha* (Oxford: Clarendon Press, 1913), 368–70; *International Standard Bible Encyclopedia*, see "Pseudipigrapha," by G.E. Ladd, 3 (1986), 1043.

[54]Antichrist's forces include the kings of the earth (19:18–19), but there is no mention in Rev. 20:7–10 of the "kings of the nations." Those who reign during the millennial age are Christ and His redeemed and glorified associates. It is millennial people, not millennial kings, who are deceived by Satan at the end of the one thousand years. CF. Govett, *The Apocalypse: Expounded by Scripture*, 4:282.

[55]*The Sibylline Oracles* 3.662–70. There are parts of this passage that also parallel John's description of the Second Advent (E.G., line 697: "the beasts shall eat their fill of flesh," CF. Rev. 19:21).

[56]Alfred Tennyson, *The Complete Poetical Works of Alfred Tennyson* (Boston: Houghton, Mifflin, 1881), 354–55.

[57]Beasley-Murray, *The Book of Revelation*, 298.

[58]Morris, *The Revelation of St. John*, 240.

[59]Ladd, *A Commentary on the Revelation of John*, 270.

[60] "*Poena damni* (the punishment of the damned) is inextricably linked with *poena sensus* (punishment of the senses). To speak of torment is to understand immediately, without necessarily having to say so explicitly, that it is a painful experience." CF. Trevor P. Craigen, "Eternal Punishment in John's Revelation," *The Master's Seminary Journal* 9 (Fall, 1998), 191–201 (esp. P. 198). "What other

kind of torment is there besides conscious torment?" Gomes asks. "Torment, by its very nature, demands a sentient (I.E., feeling) subject to experience it" (Alan W. Gomes, "Evangelicals and the Annihilation of Hell, part 1" *Christian Research Journal* (Spring, 1991), 18).

[61]It is common for those who deny eternal punishment to allegorize this text and treat the Beast and the false prophet not as individual persons but as symbols of the world in its varied hostility to God (CF. Swete, *The Apocalypse of St. John*, 267; Edward William Fudge, *The Fire That Consumes* [rev. ed., Carlisle: Paternoster, 1994], 192–93; John R.W. Stott, "Response," in *Evangelical Essentials*, by David L. Edwards and John Stott [Downers Grove: IVP, 1988], 318). Four observations are in order: (1) The fact that the Beast and the false prophet are "tormented" would argue against the allegorical exegesis of Fudge and Stott. The verb suggests they are actual persons as in the traditional futurist exegesis. (2) The Old Testament passages that form the backdrop of John's "Beasts" (Daniel 2 and 7) suggest that the apostle is speaking of *recurring* individuals who culminate in supreme manifestations of their type, rather than mere symbols. (3) Stott does not comment on the devil's pain. Even if he were right that the Beast and the false prophet are symbols, the devil is "thrown into the lake of fire and brimstone" and *he* suffers forever and ever. If this text says that there will be eternal conscious suffering by one sentient being—even if that being is the devil—it is hard to see why human beings would be a special case. (4) Fudge, unlike Stott, seems to depersonalize the devil, but concludes that "there is no easy solution" to the text's meaning. It is a difficult text for Fudge because he is rejecting what the text clearly teaches. CF. D.A. Carson, *The Gagging of God* (Grand Rapids; Zondervan, 1996), 527; Alan W. Gomes, "Evangelicals and the Annihilation of Hell, part 2" *Christian Research Journal* (Summer, 1991), 11–13.

[62]Davies, *Down Peacock's Feathers*, 41.

[63]Michael P. Green, ed., *Illustrations for Biblical Preaching* (Grand Rapids: Baker, 1989), 341–42.

The Last Judgment And The End Of The World
Revelation 20:11–15

Philip of Macedon (382–36 BC), father of Alexander the Great, had a slave to whom he gave a standing order. The man was to come in to the king every morning of his life, no matter what the king was doing, and to say to him in a loud voice, "Philip, remember that you must die!"[1]

Death is the one certain fact in all of our lives. Many things are probable, much is questionable, but nothing is certain, except ultimate death, sooner or later.[2] Death is the most democratic institution on earth.[3] "It comes to all men, regardless of color, education, wealth, or rank. It allows no discrimination, tolerates no exceptions. The mortality rate of mankind is the same the world over: one death per person."[4]

"It is appointed for men to die once" (Heb. 9:27). With that verdict there can be no dissent. "And after this comes judgment." The idea of a final tribunal, a Great Assize before which all men must appear and at which they will be assigned their eternal destiny, did not originate in the ghoulish imaginations of medieval artists and writers, and when the writer of Hebrews refers to a post-mortem judgment, he is not introducing some novel idea. Earlier in his letter (6:1–2), he listed "eternal judgment" as one of the elementary teachings of the Scriptures.

The idea that there will be a future judgment is found in the Old Testament (Gen. 18:25; Ps. 96:13; Eccles. 12:14; Dan. 12:2) and the New Testament (Acts 17:31; 2 Tim. 4: 1; Heb. 9:27). It is significant that the most solemn and searching preacher of judgment is Jesus Christ Himself.[5] In 12 out of 36 of His parables He depicts men as judged, condemned, and punished for their sins. In discussing the rich man and Lazarus He draws back the curtain on the existence of men in the afterlife to show the rich man in torment, suffering an anguish that has no relief and no end (Luke 16:19–31).[6]

As startling as it may seem, of the 12 uses of the term hell[7] in the New Testament, in every case but one (James 3:6) the person who uses it is the Lord Jesus Christ.[8] Commenting on the consequences of hatred, He warns of the guilty going to a "fiery hell" (Matt. 5:22). He warns those who were His followers in name only that one day He would say to them, "I never knew you; depart from me, you who practice lawlessness" (Matt. 7:23). In His last public teaching He outlines the details of the judgment of the nations in His parable of the sheep and the goats. All humanity will be divided into two classes: believers (the sheep) and unbelievers (the goats). To the group on His left hand, He will say, "Depart from Me, accursed ones, into the eternal fire which has been prepared for the devil and his angels" (Matt. 25:41). He concludes His parable with this description of punishment, "And these will go away into eternal punishment, but the righteous into eternal life" (v. 26).

In light of the teaching of Jesus, it is remarkable that Christian preachers and teachers are so reticent to talk about the last judgment and hell. There has been a modern resurgence in Universalism, the belief that all men will ultimately be saved.[9] Even in Bible-believing circles there has been the emergence of conditionalism,[10] the belief that hell means annihilation, not eternal punishment.[11] As for the man in the street, the only references to hell that he hears are the glib use of the term in ordinary conversation, the media, and literature. A Russian writer rightly diagnoses the ailment, "It is remarkable," he says, "how little people think about hell or trouble about it. This is the most striking evidence of human frivolity."[12]

Revelation 20:11–15 is the central passage, the *locus classicus*, of Scripture on the doctrine of the last judgment of the wicked. These verses clearly state that after death people will face God in judgment, and if their names are not found in the register of the redeemed ("the book of life") they will be thrown into the lake of fire.

The Vision Of A Great White Throne (verse 11)

A Description Of The Throne

John introduces the next event in his survey of the last things with the expression "and I saw," a phrase that marks out the chronology of the sequence of events at the end. Here he sees "a great white throne." He has seen other thrones in his visions, but this one differs from both the throne in heaven in Revelation 4:2[13] and the millennial throne on earth in Revelation 20:4 and 6, (CF. 3:21).[14] The fact that the throne is "great"—great in size—conveys the grandeur of its authority.[15] Its great size also suggests that the occasion is great, for this is the final settling of the affairs of this earth.[16] The whiteness of the throne suggests the purity and complete and invincible justice of the One who sits upon it.[17] The fact that it is a "throne" suggests that sovereign decisions will be meted out.

The Occupant Of The Throne

Though the Judge on the throne is not named, surely He is the Lord Jesus Christ, the Son of God.[18] Jesus said, "For not even the Father judges anyone, but He has given all judgment to the Son" (Jn. 5:22), and Jesus reaffirmed that He acts on behalf of the Father (Jn. 5:30). Paul says to the Athenians that God "has fixed a day in which He will judge the world in righteousness through a Man whom He has appointed, having furnished proof to all men by raising Him from the dead" (Acts 17:31). The despised and crucified Nazarene is "to judge the living and the dead," Paul writes in 2 Timothy 4:1. Jesus will judge the living at His second advent just before the millennium (Matt. 25:31); now He will judge the dead.[19]

The Setting Of The Throne

At first the throne is the only thing John sees. He sees nothing of the glories either of heaven or of the millennial kingdom. The single focus of the universe will be God's throne.[20] He says that "earth and heaven fled away" from the presence of Him who sat on the throne. When he writes that "earth and heaven fled away" from the presence of Him who sat on the throne, he means that it is as if they fled in dismay before the moral grandeur of God the Son because they were unfit for His continual presence. The thought is that this present universe has been contaminated beyond the possibility of cleansing.[21]

Scientists debate how the world will end. Most today agree that the universe is running down. In his popular work, *The Universe and Dr. Einstein*, Lincoln Barnett wrote the following:

> The universe is thus progressing toward an ultimate "heat-death," or as it is technically defined, a condition of "maximum

entropy".... No energy can be used because all of it will be uniformly distributed through the cosmos. There will be no light, no life, no warmth—nothing but perpetual and irrevocable stagnation. Time itself will come to an end. For entropy points the direction of time. Entropy is the measure of randomness. When all systems and order in the universe have vanished, when randomness is at its maximum, and entropy cannot be increased, when there no longer is any sequence of cause and effect, in short when the universe has run down, there will be no direction to time—there will be no time. And there is no way of avoiding this destiny. For the fateful principle known as the Second Law of Thermodynamics, which stands today as the principal pillar of classical physics left intact by the march of science, proclaims that the fundamental processes of nature are irreversible. Nature moves just one way.[22]

The Scriptures assert, however, that this present universe will be annihilated before the laws of physics are fulfilled. The universe will not run down, it will burn up.[23] The apostle Peter fills in some of the details when he writes, "the heavens will pass away with a roar and the elements will be destroyed with intense heat, and the earth and its works will be burned up...the heavens will be destroyed by burning, and the elements will melt with intense heat!" (2 Pet. 3:10, 12). And so the throne stands isolated, majestic and terrifying. None of the irrelevancies of this life are left to distract the eye from the spectacle of the Judge and His throne. Everything else will have passed away.[24]

Francis Schaeffer tells of his boyhood in Philadelphia when he would often take a short cut through the city dump. It was a place of junk, fire, and stench, but it made a vivid impression as he saw all the things people had spent their money on. He speaks of the homes of some rich people, people who had spent their lifetimes accumulating possessions, and describes one house where a non-Christian man had owned a large, gorgeous dining room table. He had it built inside the house, and he was very proud of it. When the house was sold and all his household goods were to be dispensed with they couldn't get the table out the door, so they simply chopped it up and burned the pieces.[25]

At God's throne all the material possessions and human honors will be absent. All homes, furnishings, clothing, hobbies, educations, books, and cars will be burned up. In that isolated moment people will be able to reflect on the things that really matter.

THE VISION OF THE JUDGMENT OF THE UNBELIEVING DEAD (VERSES 12–15)

THE RESURRECTION OF JUDGMENT (CF. JOHN 5:29)

John then sees "the dead...standing before the throne." Who are these people? To identify them correctly one must go back to verse 5 and the two expressions, "the rest of the dead" and "the first resurrection." At the second coming of

Christ before the millennial kingdom there will be a resurrection of believers who will be evaluated for reward at the judgment seat of Christ (2 Cor. 5:10).[26] Those who rise at that time participate in "the first resurrection," which is a bodily resurrection. What transpires in verses 12–13 is the resurrection of "the rest of the dead"—the unbelieving wicked who did not rise to reign with Christ.[27]

These verses clearly imply a bodily resurrection. Nowhere does the Bible say what kind of body these resurrected ones will have, but it is evidently a body suited to suffer in the torments of the lake of fire. The fact of two resurrections harmonizes with Jesus' teaching in John 5:28–29, where He speaks of "a resurrection of life" for those who are righteous and a "resurrection of judgment" for those who are wicked. In Revelation we are told that the two resurrections are separated by one thousand years.

THE PERSONS OF THE JUDGMENT

"The rest of the dead" are the unregenerate, those who have never been born again, unbelievers destined for the lake of fire.[28] The judgment in verses 12 and 13, then, does not include the saved.[29]

In verse 13 John writes that "the sea gave up the dead[30] which were in it, and death and Hades gave up the dead which are in them." In 6:7–8 "death and Hades" were agents of judgment.[31] Death is seen as a power stalking the land, and hades is personified as a monster opening its jaws to receive the dead. Hades is the abode of the unrighteous as they wait for the last judgment.[32] The "sea,"[33] too, is mentioned; even those lost at sea will be raised. No one will escape the last judgment.

John says that "the great and the small" will stand before God: the important and the unimportant, the powerful and the weak, the educated and the uneducated, the rich and the poor, the old and the young. The wealthy western nations and the third world nations will all be represented.

Rudyard Kipling (1865–1936) wrote that all earthly distinctions vanish before the reality of the last judgment:

> Oh, East is East, and West is West,
> And never the twain shall meet,
> Till Earth and Sky stand presently
> At God's great Judgment Seat.[34]

THE CRITERIA OF THE JUDGMENT

The evidence for judgment[35] will be supplied by "books."[36] First, "books" or records of deeds performed will be opened. The judgment of God is not arbitrary or capricious.[37] As Paul writes, God "will render to every man according to his deeds" (Rom. 2:6). The point of the verse is not salvation by works; no one is saved by works. Rather, it is "damnation by works"[38]—people are responsible for what they have done.

The teaching of Scripture that there will be a judgment is based on two great facts: (1) There is a God who created us. He is a loving God (Luke 11:42), yet He is also infinitely holy (John 17:11). (2) Man is a responsible creature, accountable to God (Gen. 2:16–17). People have a conscience and the commandments of God, and He will hold them responsible for these things.[39]

It is a sobering thing to realize that God has a record of the lives of all the billions of human beings that have ever lived—every thought, every mean act, every dirty transaction, every dishonest moment, every foul word, every treacherous betrayal, every harsh feeling or remark.[40]

God the Judge, who is omniscient, will preside with perfect knowledge of the character and history of every person who stands before Him.[41] The last judgment will be more exacting than anything provided by modern technology. If mere humans can produce instant replay, computer printouts, and a plastic disc that is capable of storing the entire *Encyclopedia Britannica*, then it should not be surprising that the Creator of the universe should have data on all His creatures. Jesus says that men shall render account for "every careless word" that they speak (Matt. 12:36), and Paul writes that "God will judge the secrets of men" (Rom. 2:16).

When he was 35 my father quit smoking cigarettes. When he was 77, 42 years later, he had a chest x-ray, and the doctor asked, "When did you quit smoking?" Dad asked him how he knew he had been a smoker and he answered, "I saw a few scars on the x-rays." All people have little secrets—and some big secrets—and they will all be known.

In Thornton Wilder's play *Our Town*, a young woman tells her brother of an incident in the life of another girl named Jane Crofut. Jane was sick, and her minister sent her a letter. On the envelope he had written: "Jane Crofut; The Crofut Farm; Grover's Corners; Sutton County; New Hampshire." But that's not all; there was more: "the United States of America; Continent of North America; Western Hemisphere; the Earth; the Solar System; the Universe; the Mind of God." The minister's lesson, of course, is that no one anywhere is forgotten by God.[42]

John then sees "another book" opened, "the book of life." It is a list of those who are saved, those who have been forgiven for all their sins. When I was born my mother was a member of a church whose minister told his congregation that God would place all of a person's good deeds on one scale and all of his evil deeds on another scale. If there were more good deeds than evil that person would go to heaven, and if there were more evil deeds than good he would go to hell.

That teaching is utterly contrary to God's Word, which teaches salvation by faith in Christ and not by religious works. No one will ever gain entrance into heaven by his or her good works. The books of deeds will only prove the sinner's utter unworthiness to enter God's eternal kingdom.

The "book of life" is a register of those who have been saved by Jesus Christ. Everyone listed in the "book of life" is a sinner. The difference between a saved person and a lost person is not his evil deeds but that a saved person has recognized his or her own sinfulness and has come to Christ for forgiveness of sins and the gift of life. When a person believes in Jesus Christ as Savior he may be confident that his name is written in the "book of life."[43]

What is the relationship between the two sets of books at the last judgment of the unsaved? They bear independent witness that the people before the Judge are not saved. The one set of books demonstrates from the deeds of a person's life that he or she is truly sinful, and when the book of life is opened and the person's name is not found, this will prove that he or she is not saved. Since the name has not been found in the book of life, the books of deeds are again consulted. The books of deeds give supporting evidence that this person is lost,[44] and his punishment will be based on the deeds done in this life.

THE JUSTICE OF THE JUDGMENT

The judgment will be perfectly just. It is twice asserted that all will be judged "according to their deeds" (v. 12, 13). This would seem to suggest that there are levels of torment in the lake of fire. This is also suggested in Matthew 10:15 when Jesus says that it will be "more tolerable for Sodom and Gomorrah in the day of judgment" than for those who have heard and rejected the Savior.

Occasionally a man is released from prison after years of imprisonment because the authorities discover that he is innocent of the crime for which he was convicted. Such an injustice will never occur in God's courtroom. No one will ever bear the penalty of another person's guilt. No one will ever be able to claim that he or she got a "bad rap." Perfect justice will be meted out by the Judge upon the great white throne.

THE EXECUTION OF THE JUDGMENT

The destruction of death and hades

The judgments are immediately executed. "Death and Hades," personified in this passage, are cast into the lake of fire. Death is the last enemy of man (1 Cor. 15:54–55), and hades is the grim receptacle of death's prey—the abode of the dead. The last vestiges of man's rebellion against God are destroyed.[45]

The punishment of unbelievers

The main test on the day of judgment is whether or not one's name is in the book of life. All those who have embraced Christ as Savior are in that book. The people raised at the second resurrection are not in that book, however, and they are cast into the lake of fire. This is the "second death."

Death has three stages. First, there is spiritual death. All are born into this world spiritually dead, "dead in [our] trespasses and sins" (Eph. 2:1). The remedy for this problem is the new birth—"You must be born again" (CF. John 3:7). The second stage is physical death. All people, saved and unsaved, die physically. The remedy for this problem is the resurrection of the body at the first resurrection. Third, there is the second death, the conscious existence in the lake of fire. For this there is no remedy.[46]

The destiny of the lost is hell, here described as "the lake of fire." The Bible teaches that it is a place. The people who go there have a form of body, and bodily existence requires that there be a locality for them to exist. The Bible also teaches that it is a place of torment. The very description, "lake of fire,"[47] suggests pain, anguish, and no hope for release.

In Revelation 19:20, John speaks of "the lake of fire which burns with brimstone" or sulfur. This speaks of its element (fire) and its fuel (sulfur). This passage teaches, furthermore, that it is a place of torment beyond this life.

In the terrible days of the German bombing of London in World War II, with fires raging in the city, an evangelist stood on the street preaching the gospel of the Son of God. A heckler broke into his sermon and said, "Listen, preacher, this is hell, the bombing of London." The Christian replied, "Sir, this is not hell. And I will give you three reasons why. One, I am a Christian, and there will be no Christians in hell. Second, there is a church building right around the corner, and there are no church houses in hell. Third, I am preaching the gospel of the Son of God, and there will be no preaching of the gospel in hell." Three weeks later the same evangelist stood in Hyde Park, preaching the gospel of Christ. When he appealed for his listeners to come to the Savior a man walked out from the crowd and took his hand. It was the heckler who said that he now wanted to accept Christ as his Savior.[48]

The Bible also teaches that hell is a place of unending torment. In verse 10 John writes that the inhabitants "will be tormented day and night forever and ever" (CF. 14:11). This strongly suggests that the lake of fire does not indicate annihilation. One thousand years after they have been thrown into the lake of fire the Beast and the false prophet are still there (CF. Rev. 19:20).[49]

There have been many arguments raised against the doctrine of an eternal hell. C.S. Lewis responds to five of them in his book *The Problem of Pain*.[50]

Objection #1: The idea of retributive punishment is wrong in itself. No, says Lewis, it is actually wrong to punish for reformatory or deterrent purposes. Unless a man deserves to be punished, we ought not to make him suffer. Lewis points out correctly that there are people who will not turn to Christ. If allowed to stay in that rebellious state unpunished they will forever think God a fool. God can forgive sin, but He cannot condone it.

Objection #2: Is not eternal punishment for transitory sin a gross disproportion? No, for a man's life is always long enough for him to become set in his directions—the wicked have chosen their path. And, it might be added, time is unrelated to the character of sin. Guilt is endless unless forgiven.

Objection #3: Isn't the language of the Bible (eternal punishment (Matt. 25:46), destruction (Matt. 10:28), banishment (Matt. 8:12)) overly intense? Surely it should be taken symbolically. Lewis acknowledges that it is symbolical language, but he points out that symbols have referents—they symbolize something actual. The Bible uses language that in the strongest way possible describes something "unspeakably horrible."

Objection #4: How can the saints in heaven have pleasure if there is a single soul in hell? This objection implies, suggests Lewis, that men are more merciful than God. Too much is said about hell that reflects little trust in the Maker of men.

Objection #5: Is not God defeated in His purposes if a single soul is ultimately lost?[51] In response to this objection it can be argued that those in hell are there of their own volition, refusing, even while being punished, to give up the selves they have chosen above God. It can also be argued that God is expressing His holiness in retribution and His mercy in saving His own people. In both cases, punishment and salvation, He will be true to His own nature.

C.S. Lewis writes, "I willingly believe that the damned are, in one sense, successful, rebels to the end; that the doors of hell are locked on the inside."[52] He adds, "In the long run the answer to all those who object to the doctrine of hell, is itself a question: 'What are you asking God to do?' To wipe out their past sins, and, at all costs, to give them a fresh start, smoothing every difficulty and offering every miraculous help? But He has done so, on Calvary. To forgive them? They [do not want to be] forgiven. To leave them alone? Alas, I am afraid that is what He does."[53]

What is particularly troubling is the assumption by annihilationists that they have a sensitivity superior to those who hold the Biblical view. They use terms such as "dreadful, awful, terrible, fearful, intolerable," of the Biblical view. As J.I. Packer suggests, the annihilationists do not have a superior spiritual sensitivity, but rather a "secular sentimentalism."[54]

A Christian girl was attending a small Baptist college, and she took a job caring for a woman, a Mrs. Payne, who was dying of cancer of the pancreas. Mrs. Payne was a very moral person, but she was not a Christian. She was not afraid of death and did not believe she needed Christ. The young Christian girl, Cynthia, cried to God, "What are you doing? This is a good woman. Is she really going to go to hell when she dies?"

She was so troubled that she spoke to one of her professors, also a Christian. He rolled up his sleeve and said, "I have ugly skin, see? The skin on my arm is dry, patchy and scaly. I look like I might have a fatal disease, but I don't. I just have a skin problem, a surface problem, you might say. Now, Mrs. Payne, she might have nice, smooth skin. She might look much better on the surface than I do. But on the inside she's got a disease so serious it's killing her. It's the same thing with her sin. She hasn't dealt with it, and it's killing her. The cancer will kill her physically, and her unforgiven sin will kill her spiritually."[55] That is an excellent analogy of what is happening in the hearts of all those who reject Jesus Christ.

CONCLUSION

There are several lessons—both theological and practical—that are suggested by this passage. First, death is the one certain fact of our existence. It compels us to make a choice between "eternal punishment"[56] and "eternal life" (Matt. 25:46).[57] Second, the doctrine of the last judgment helps people face the impermanence of this world ("earth and heaven fled away"). This is the only true evaluation of this world.[58] Third, the doctrine of the last judgment assures people that all the injustices of this life will eventually be set right. Every wrong thing will receive its appropriate penalty. Good will triumph over evil.[59] Fourth, the doctrine of the last judgment stresses man's accountability to God. One day every single person in this world will give an account to God the Son of the life they have lived.[60] Fifth, this doctrine warns people that there are those who are going to go to hell. "All have sinned," the Bible says (Rom. 3:23). All have disobeyed God, and all have contributed to the cosmic rebellion that has taken peace from the earth.

Sixth, the passage teaches that each sinner will be evaluated. One's relatives won't help. It won't help to say, "But God, my mother was a Christian. My dad prayed for me." The question each person must ask is, "Have I believed in Christ?"

Seventh, there is an absoluteness and finality about the judgment of Revelation 19:11–15. This is truly the last judgment. The Great White Throne Judgment will not be like any earthly courtroom. "There will be a Judge, but no jury; a Prosecutor, but no defender; a sentence, but no appeal. This is the final judgment of the world."[61]

Finally, true believers can face the end not as cowards shrinking from it, but with anticipation in mingled joy and solemnity. For the Christian thinks of the last judgment as the dawn of the new heaven and new earth more than the doom of this world.[62] Why do Christians think of the last judgment with confidence? Because their names are written in the "book of life." Are their names there because they were better people than the others? No, they were equally bad—the Christian is someone who has sins that condemn him. Yet before the last judgment takes place God has acquitted him.

How can that be? The answer is because of the death of Christ. At the Cross Jesus Christ bore the penalty our sins deserved. He suffered in our place. "[God] made Him who knew no sin to be sin on our behalf, that we might become the righteousness of God in Him" (2 Cor. 5:21). C.S. Lewis writes, "I said glibly…that I would pay 'any price' to remove this doctrine. I lied. I could not pay one-thousandth part of the price that God has already paid to remove the fact. And here is the real problem: so much mercy, yet still there is hell."[63] The person who believes in Christ, who embraces Christ as Savior, is registered in the book of life and does not need to appear at the Great White Throne Judgment. He has been acquitted of all crimes against God.

In the early pioneer era of California there was a wheat farmer, a Christian, whose field was next to the railroad tracks. One day when his grain was ripe and ready for harvest a train passed by and sparks from the locomotive set his field on fire. The farmer rushed toward the smoke, and part way to the fire he started another fire which he was able to control. This produced a break in his grain, so that when the blaze arrived it stopped at the break in his grain that he had burned off.

He was dejected at losing half his crop. "Why did God allow this?" he reasoned. As he walked along he noticed the charred body of a hen that had been caught in the blazing inferno. He turned over the dead hen with his foot, and five little chicks ran from underneath it. The man immediately thought of the blessing that was His in having a Savior who died for him.

The Bible tells us that the wrath of God is a consuming fire (Heb. 12:29). The fire of wrath will come. Nevertheless it will not touch those who are protected by the Lord Jesus Christ.

The full wrath of God is seen at two great moments in human history—at the Great White Throne Judgment and at the Cross of Christ, where it has already been poured out for those who trust Christ as Savior. The message with which the preacher of the gospel needs to face his listeners is this:

"At which point will you choose to face it? If you choose to come to Christ, then His substitutionary death will protect you from the last judgment." "There is therefore now no condemnation for those who are in Christ Jesus" (Rom. 8:1).[64]

NOTES

[1] Quoted by J.S. Whale, *Christian Doctrine* (Cambridge: Cambridge University Press, 1941), 170–71.

[2] Whale, *Christian Doctrine*, 172.

[3] Whale (*Christian Doctrine*, 172–73) quotes the last sentence of Sir Walter Raleigh's unfinished *History of the World*: "O eloquent, just and mighty Death! whom none could advise, thou has persuaded; what none hath dared, thou hast done; and whom all the world hath flattered, thou only hast cast out of the world and despised. Thou hast drawn together all the far stretched greatness, all the pride, cruelty and ambition of man, and covered it all over with these two narrow words: *Hic Jacet*' [here lies...]!"

[4] Fred Carl Kuehner, *Heaven or Hell?* (Washington: Christianity Today, N.D.), 24C. Kuehner does note the Biblical exceptions of Enoch (Gen. 5:24) and Elijah (2 Kings 2:11), who were taken into God's presence without dying. Others should be added, of course—namely, the generation of believers alive at the translation of the church (1 Thess. 4:17).

[5] "There is no doctrine which I would more willingly remove from Christianity than this [I.E., the doctrine of Hell], if it lay in my power. But it has the full support of Scripture and, specially, of Our Lord's own words...." CF. C.S. Lewis, *The Problem of Pain* (New York: Macmillan, 1944), 106.

[6] Kuehner, *Heaven or Hell?* 24D–E.

[7] The English word *hell* is related to the Old English *helle-* [*kel*], meaning to hide or cover. CF. Calvin D. Linton, "The Sorrows of Hell," *Christianity Today* (Nov. 19, 1971), 12.

[8.]The term γέεννα appears in the following verses: Matt. 5:22, 29, 30; 10:28; 18: 9; 23:15, 33; Mark 9:43, 45, 47; Luke 12:5; James 3:6.

[9.]For evangelical responses, see the essays by the Christianity Today Institute, "Universalism: Will Everyone Be Saved?" *Christianity Today* (March 20, 1987), 31–45.

[10.]In the contemporary debate over hell some writers distinguish between "conditional immortality" and "annihilationism." They argue that a Platonic doctrine of the immortality of the soul more than exegesis has led to the doctrine of an eternal hell. The soul of the unsaved person will in the end die, will cease to exist. (CF. Clark H. Pinnock, "The Destruction of the Finally Impenitent," *Criswell Theological Review 4* [Spring, 1990], 252). Two observations are in order: (1) The orthodox doctrine of the immortality of the soul does not affirm an absolute immortality, but a contingent immortality—the soul depends on God's continuing providential support. (2) The conditionalist viewpoint may sound more pleasant to the ear than annihilationism, but underlying annihilationism is the same belief in the mortality of the soul. In either case, conditionalism or annihilationism, the end result is the same: the souls of the wicked will be condemned to extinction. CF. Alan W. Gomes, "Evangelicals and the Annihilation of Hell, part 1" *Christian Research Journal* (Spring, 1991), 16–17.

[11.]See the discussions by J.I. Packer, "The Problem of Eternal Punishment," *Crux* (Sept., 1990), 18–25; Idem., "Evangelicals and the Way of Salvation," in *Evangelical Affirmations*, eds. Kenneth Kantzer and Carl F.H. Henry (Grand Rapids: Zondervan, 1990), 107–36. Also see the five articles on hell by members of The Master's Seminary faculty in *The Master's Seminary Journal 9* (Fall, 1998), 127–217.

[12.]Nicholas Berdyaev, *The Destiny of Man* (London: Geoffrey Bles: The Centenary Press, 1937), 338.

[13.]There are a number of differences between the two thrones: (1) The first throne, that of 4:2, was set in heaven; this one is set in space. (2) The first had a rainbow around it, a sign of covenant promises; this throne offers no promises—it offers naked justice and retribution. (3) Out of the first proceeded lightning, thunder, and voices threatening judgment upon the earth; this one is cold and austere with no further warnings to make. (4) The throne in chapter 4 was surrounded by other thrones that symbolized the varied duties of the glorified saints; this one is established with one purpose in mind and with no associates. (5) Before the first throne there were seven lamps, symbolizing the gracious works of the Holy Spirit; here the purpose is purely retributive. (6) Before the first there was a sea of glass, a symbol of refuge and peace; there is no refuge and peace offered here. (7) Connected with the first throne there was singing and joyful exultation; here there is only the administration of retributive justice. CF. J.A. Seiss, *Lectures on the Apocalypse*, 3 vols. (9TH ed., New York: Charles C. Cook, 1906), 3:355–56; W.A. Criswell, *Expository Sermons on Revelation*, 5 vols. (Grand Rapids: Zondervan, 1969), 5:83–85.

[14]The millennial throne on earth was surrounded by Messiah's assessors; this throne stands alone in space. CF. R.H. Charles, *The Revelation of St. John*, International Critical Commentary, 2 vols. (Edinburgh: T. & T. Clark, 1920), 2:192.

[15]Robert H. Mounce, *The Book of Revelation*, New International Commentary on the New Testament (rev. ed., Grand Rapids: Eerdmans, 1998), 375.

[16]Robert Govett, *The Apocalypse: Expounded by Scripture*, 4 vols. (London, 1861; reprint ed., Miami Springs: Conley & Schoettle, 1981), 4:290–91.

[17]Seiss, *Lectures on the Apocalypse*, 3:355.

[18]So: William Kelly, *Lectures on the Book of Revelation* (London: G. Morrish, 1874), 449; Walter Scott, *Exposition of the Revelation of Jesus Christ* (4TH ed., London: Pickering & Inglis, N.D.), 411; Govett, *The Apocalypse: Expounded by Scripture*, 4:291; William Hendriksen, *More Than Conquerors* (Grand Rapids: Baker, 1939), 235; John F. Walvoord, *The Revelation of Jesus Christ* (Chicago: Moody, 1966), 305; David Chilton, *The Days of Vengeance* (Ft. Worth: Dominion Press, 1987), 529–31. Not all commentators agree with this interpretation. Others have noted that elsewhere in the Revelation the phrase ὁ καθήμενοi ἐπὶ τοῦ θρόνου (4:2, 9; 5:1, 7, 13; 6:16; 7:10, 15; 19:4; 21:5) refers to the Father. Some also detect an allusion to Dan. 7:9–14. They conclude, therefore, that the Father has reserved the last judgment for Himself. CF. Charles, *The Revelation of St. John*, 2:192; Isbon T. Beckwith, *The Apocalypse of John* (New York: Macmillan, 1919; reprint ed., Grand Rapids: Baker, 1979), 748; Henry Barclay Swete, *The Apocalypse of St. John* (London: Macmillan, 1906), 267; G.B. Caird, *The Revelation of St. John the Divine*, Harper New Testament Commentary (New York: Harper & Row, 1966), 258; Alan F. Johnson, "Revelation," *The*

Expositor's Bible Commentary, 12 vols., ed. Frank E. Gaebelein (Grand Rapids: Zondervan, 1981), 12:589; Robert L. Thomas, *Revelation 8–22: An Exegetical Commentary* (Chicago: Moody, 1995), 429. Caird suggests that at this time the Son surrenders the sovereignty to God the Father (1 Cor. 15:24–28), and Johnson opines on the basis of 22:1, 3 that Jesus may share the judgment with the Father. John, however, sees only one person ("Him") on the throne in 20:11.

[19]Scott, *Exposition of the Revelation of Jesus Christ*, 411.

[20]G.R. Beasley-Murray, *The Book of Revelation*, New Century Bible (London: Oliphants, 1974), 299.

[21]Caird, *The Revelation of St. John the Divine*, 259.

[22]Lincoln Barnett, *The Universe and Dr. Einstein* (2ND. rev. ed., New York: Perennial Library, 1966), 102–3.

[23]With many I understand John's description to refer to the literal dissolution of the present universe—"the literal vanishing of the former heaven and earth into nothingness" (Charles, *The Revelation of St. John*, 2:193; CF. Walvoord, *The Revelation of Jesus Christ*, 305). Others, however, see the action as less than complete destruction. They argue that there is continuity between the geophysical and astronomical material of the old and new earth; it is simply the corruption of the curse that is burned away. The present verse poetically describes the terror of the wicked in the face of judgment. CF. Swete, *The Apocalypse of St. John*, 268; Beasley-Murray, *The Book of Revelation*, 300–1.

[24]Martin Kiddle, *The Revelation of St. John*, Moffatt New Testament Commentary (Harper: New York, 1940), 401, 402, 403.

[25]Francis A. Schaeffer, *No Little People* (Downers Grove, IL: InterVarsity, 1974), 268–69.

[26]The first resurrection takes place in stages with church age believers being resurrected at the rapture prior to the tribulation and Old Testament saints being resurrected at the beginning of the millennial kingdom (CF. Dan. 12:1–3).

[27]Seiss, *Lectures on the Apocalypse*, 3:358–59; Kelly, *Lectures on the Book of Revelation*, 451; Scott, *Exposition of the Revelation of Jesus Christ*, 412; Walvoord, *The*

Revelation of Jesus Christ, 306; Philip Edgcumbe Hughes, *The Book of the Revelation* (Grand Rapids: Eerdmans, 1990), 218; Chilton, *Days of Vengeance*, 532; Mathias Rissi, *The Future of the World* (London: SCM, 1972), 36.

[28]Not all interpreters would agree with the view offered here that the resurrection in v. 12–13 is a resurrection of the wicked. Some would argue that the text describes a general resurrection. CF. Swete, *The Apocalypse of St. John*, 268; Beasley-Murray, *The Book of Revelation*, 301; Mounce, *The Book of Revelation*, 376.

[29]As Walvoord (*The Revelation of Jesus Christ*, 306–7) notes, the Scriptures are silent concerning the judgment of saints who survive the millennium or die in the millennium. Erich Sauer, a premillennial scholar, argues that the converted nations of the millennial kingdom will also appear at the great white throne. CF. *The Triumph of the Crucified*, trans. G.H. Lang (Grand Rapids: Eerdmans, 1951), 175. Govett (*Apocalypse*, 4:296–97), a partial-rapturist, also argues that there will be believers at the great white throne.

[30]The Greeks and Romans attached great importance to burial. Many ancient peoples thought that they would be with their own people in the realm of the dead. If someone died by drowning it was believed that they would not be able to reach the dwelling place of the dead. Such thoughts would not have concerned John, however. CF. Beckwith, *The Apocalypse of John*, 749.

[31]Beasley-Murray, *The Book of Revelation*, 303.

[32]"Death…appears…in the Revelation of John under the double aspect of 'power' and of 'space'" (Rissi, *The Future of the World*, 36).

[33]Charles (*The Revelation of St. John*, 2:194–96) felt the text made no sense as it now stands. How, he wondered, could the sea give up its dead (v. 13) when it had already vanished in v. 11? This is to press John for a chronology of judgment day that is not there. John's point is that the material universe vanishes but not before its gloomy prisons have given up their dead. The order of events is decided on dramatic grounds. CF. Kiddle, *The Revelation of St. John*, 406; Leon Morris, *The Revelation of St. John*, Tyndale New Testament Commentaries (Grand Rapids: Eerdmans, 1969), 241.

[34]Rudyard Kipling, *The Ballad of East and West*, quoted by Leon Morris, *The Biblical Doctrine of Judgment* (London: Tyndale, 1960), 62, N. 3.

[35]Beasley-Murray, *The Book of Revelation*, 299.

[36]"Literal books, or rolls, are, of course, out of [the] question" (CF. Scott, *Exposition of the Revelation of Jesus Christ*, 413). While this may be true, the literal intent is obvious. There is a register or record in heaven of everything that everyone has ever done (Thomas, *Revelation 8–22*, 431).

[37]Swete, *The Apocalypse of St. John*, 268; Mounce, *The Book of Revelation*, 376; George Eldon Ladd, *A Commentary on the Revelation of John* (Grand Rapids: Eerdmans, 1972), 273.

[38]Chilton, *Days of Vengeance*, 533.

[39]John Gerstner, "The Bible and Hell, part 1," *His Magazine 28* (Jan., 1968), 34–35.

[40]Seiss, *Lectures on the Apocalypse*, 3:359.

[41]E.A. Litton, *Introduction to Dogmatic Theology*, ed. Philip E. Hughes (London: James Clarke, 1960), 592.

[42]Thornton Wilder, *Our Town*, Act 1 (1938; reprint ed., New York: Avon Books, 1957), 60–61.

[43]In Revelation 17:8 John writes that the names in the book of life were there "from the foundation of the world." In this he is in agreement with the apostle Paul (CF. Eph. 1:4).

[44]"The 'books' would be as it were the vouchers for the book of life." CF. Henry Alford, *The Greek Testament*, 4 vols., vol. 4: *Hebrews—Revelation* (rev. ed., Chicago: Moody, 1958), 735; Charles, *Revelation*, 2:194.

[45]Mounce, *The Book of Revelation*, 378.

[46]Whale (*Christian Doctrine*, 178) writes, "Death has been called the sacrament of sin because it is the effective sign of opportunities gone for ever. Death is tre-

mendous because life is, and because in it life says its last word. Little wonder that James Denney, in protesting against the modern tendency to make light of human death, should have added that 'it is the greatest thought of which we are capable, except the thought of God.' The fact which is here inescapable is a dilemma. Either we despair, or we believe. There is no middle course, no razor-edge of non-committal on which to balance precariously. Only he who believes in God wins the victory over despair. Only the infinite mercy of the Eternal Love, incarnate, suffering, dying, rising from the dead, is big enough for the tragedy of human existence. The dilemma is inescapable. Either despair which is Hell, or faith in Him who giveth us the victory."

[47]Evangelicals recognize that phrases such as "outer darkness" (Matt. 8:12), "where their worm does not die" (Mark 9:46), and "lake of fire" are metaphorical. This is not to deny the reality of hell as a place of eternal retribution. CF. John Calvin, *A Harmony of the Gospels Matthew, Mark and Luke*, vol. 1, trans. A.W. Morrison (Grand Rapids: Eerdmans, 1972), 129; Harry Buis, *The Doctrine of Eternal Punishment* (Philadelphia: Presbyterian and Reformed, 1957), 128–31; Charles Hodge, *Systematic Theology*, 3 vols. (New York: Scribners, 1876; reprint ed., Grand Rapids: Eerdmans, 1975), 3:868. As Hodge noted, the lake of fire was designed for the devil and his angels and they have no material bodies that could be harmed by elemental fire. As C.S. Lewis observed (*The Problem of Pain*, 113), all of these descriptions agree that hell is "unspeakably horrible." I would add that there is probably a very close connection between the metaphor and the reality. After all, the old earth is going to be burned up in some kind of fire (CF. 2 Pet. 3:10, 12).

[48]Criswell, *Expository Sermons on Revelation*, 5:97–98.

[49]Commenting on Rev. 20:10, Clark Pinnock ("The Destruction of the Impenitent," 257) says, "John's point seems to be that everything which has rebelled against God will come to an absolute end." That, however, is *not* John's point, if language means anything. John's point is that the Devil, the Beast, and the false prophet "will be tormented day and night forever and ever." CF. Alan W. Gomes, "Evangelicals and the Annihilation of Hell, part 2," *Christian Research Journal* (Summer, 1991), 12.

[50]Lewis, *The Problem of Pain*, 106–16; CF. Stott, "Response," 316–19; Packer, "Evangelicals and the Way of Salvation," 124–26.

[51]Lewis (*The Problem of Pain*, 115) argues that this was the chance that God took in creating beings with free will.

[52]Lewis, *The Problem of Pain*, 115.

[53]Lewis, *The Problem of Pain*, 116.

[54]Packer, "Evangelicals and the Way of Salvation," 126.

[55]Cynthia M. Stone, "Is Hell Necessary?" *Alliance Life* (July 31, 1991): 7, 9.

[56]Annihilationists argue that the term *eternal* (αἰώνιος) in Matthew 25:46 refers to eternal results and not eternal existence. Cf. Edward William Fudge, *The Fire That Consumes* (rev. ed., Carlisle: Paternoster, 1994), 18–19. The claim is unsubstantiated. Three observations concerning Matt. 25:41, 46 are in order: (1) Jesus clearly said that hell was created for the devil and his angels and that all the wicked share the same fate as the devil and his host. (2) Annihilation and the extinction of consciousness do not fit the context. As Shedd wrote long ago, "The extinction of consciousness is not of the nature of punishment. The essence of punishment is suffering, and suffering [requires] consciousness." (3) Αἰώνιος must therefore, in this context, refer to future, conscious, unceasing existence. Shedd wrote, "In all the instances in which αἰώνιος refers to future duration [including Matt. 25:46], it denotes endless duration. Cf. William G. T. Shedd, *The Doctrine of Endless Punishment* (New York: Scribner's, 1886; reprint ed., Minneapolis: Klock & Klock, 1980), 88, 92. As Gomes has written ("Annihilation, part 2," 11), the adjective αἰώνιος ("eternal, unceasing, everlasting") here describes the punishment itself, not merely the result of the punishment. Cf. *Exegetical Dictionary of the New Testament*, see "αἰώνιος," 1:47; Robert A. Peterson, "Does the Bible Teach Annihilationism?" *Bibliotheca Sacra* (Jan. 1999), 13–27.

[57]Whale, *Christian Doctrine*, 177.

[58]Whale, *Christian Doctrine*, 176.

[59]Morris, *The Biblical Doctrine of Judgment*, 72.

[60]Morris, *The Biblical Doctrine of Judgment*, 72.

[61]David Jeremiah, *Escape the Coming Night* (Dallas: Word, 1990), 217.

[62]Morris, *The Biblical Doctrine of Judgment*, 71; CF. P.T. Forsyth, *The Justification of God* (2ND. ed., London: Independent Press, 1948), 189–90.

[63]Lewis, *The Problem of Pain*, 108.

[64]James Montgomery Boice, *The Last and Future World* (Grand Rapids: Zondervan, 1974), 122–23.

THE SEVENTH LAST THING:

The New Heaven And The New Earth
Revelation 21:1-8

❦

Several years ago a reporter for a Chicago radio station took a survey at O'Hare Field, Chicago's busy airport. He stopped about 30 people in one of the terminals and asked them, "Do you know for sure that you are going to heaven when you leave this world?" The response from all 30 was a unanimous "No!" A few were indignant that he would ask such a question. Several said, "Why, of course, nobody could know such a thing as that." Human destiny! What an awesome thought to cross the mind. After someone has lived out his mortal life, what then?[1] According to a poll taken by Newsweek magazine, 77-percent of Americans believe in heaven.[2] Yet many do not want to talk about it.

This modern response to the Biblical doctrine of heaven demonstrates the great gulf between the Christian faith and the modern world. Does it make a difference? It makes the difference between hope and despair in the end, between two totally different views of life.[3] One view says there is no meaning in the dizzy course of events called life. It says that people must make up their own meaning, whether it be family or working or altruism or boating or jogging or chasing women or bar-hopping or getting high on other things. The ultimate issue, of course, is death, but modern man has scientific medicine and allied disciplines, so he tells himself that death is inevitable, a normal event of organic nature. But the truth is that death scares him. Life, then, is an insoluble riddle.

The other view—the Christian view—says that the ultimate questions—the meaning of life and the threat of death—are things about which the believer can have great assurance. For the believer the things said in Holy Scripture about the meaning of life and human destiny are his sure foundation.[4] Everything does not go down the drain at the end; rather, all the loose threads are finally tied together into a gloriously perfect tapestry. The tangled pathway of life does not lead over the cliff into an abyss; it leads to the golden castle. Death is not a hole in the ground; it is a door to everlasting joy and happiness.[5]

The Christian is a person who can live his life with hope. The world beyond this world is what makes the difference. This earth is heaven's womb, heaven's nursery, heaven's dress rehearsal. Heaven gives meaning to this earth. The Christian knows that he is his heavenly Father's child. This world has meaning because, in spite of its rebellion and sin, it is his heavenly Father's world. He faces death with hope because of his assurance that heaven is his ultimate home and his Savior has promised to take him there when he dies. This confidence toward death gives the believer confidence toward life, because life's road leads somewhere, it leads to heaven. The heavenly mansion at the end of life's pilgrimage makes a tremendous difference on the pilgrimage itself.[6]

Revelation 21:1–8 is all about heaven and the future life of the people of God. With this text John has arrived at "the last of the Last Things and the end of the visionary drama"[7] of the Book of Revelation. Here, he sees God create a new heaven and a new earth, after which a new Jerusalem will descend from heaven. God will dwell in this new city, and there will never again be tears, nor sorrow, nor pain.

This, in fact, is the "big idea" of the text: the glory and blessedness of life in heaven consists of the presence of God and communion with Him, the satisfaction of every yearning of the soul, and the absence of death, sorrow, and sin.[8]

THE VISION OF A NEW HEAVEN AND A NEW EARTH (VERSES 1–4)

THE APPEARANCE OF A NEW CREATION (VERSE 1)

The phrase "and I saw" introduces the seventh of the "last things" in John's survey of the events of the end time. In the eighth century before Christ, God promised the prophet Isaiah that He would "create new heavens and a new earth" (Isa. 65:17).[9] Jewish writers of the intertestamental and New Testament periods picked up the idea,[10] but it is Isaiah and his own vision from the Lord that are the sources of John's exposition. When John says "new"[11] it is probable that he means a completely new universe made of new materials[12] and not merely the renovation of the old heaven and earth.[13] He says, "the first heaven and the first earth passed away."[14]

The "first heaven" passes away, and a new atmosphere will surround the new world. There will be no more violent storms, deadly smog, or menacing blackness.[15] John also sees a "new earth." Nothing is said of the configuration, size, and appearance of the new earth,[16] but there is something quite different about it: namely, "there is no longer any sea."[17]

At first glance ocean lovers and fishermen might be taken aback at this statement. But consider for a moment why the ocean exists. Over 70-percent of the surface of our earth is covered with salt water, and the average depth of the ocean is 2.3 miles. Why does our planet need such a massive covering of salt water? The answer is to cleanse the earth and make life possible. The sea might be described as a big sewer system or, better, God's great antiseptic solution, composed of about 96% water, 3.5% salt, and about 0.5% trace elements—chlorine, magnesium, calcium, and the like. The salty brine of the sea purges, cleanses, and preserves our planet, making it fit to live in.

Many of the pollutants and waste that humans produce get washed out of the soil and into streams and rivers; others we deliberately dump there. The rivers wash these materials into the sea, and the antiseptic salinity of the sea absorbs, scrubs, and breaks down these pollutants and wastes. The sun heats the sea, causing only pure, clean water vapor to float up into the sky, forming clouds which bring refreshing rain back to the land—a continuous cycle of cleansing and renewal. But in the new earth there will be no more pollution, no more decay, no more need for cleansing, and thus no more need for a salty sea.[18]

The disappearance of the sea is a reminder of the transience of the present created order. There is something timeless about the sea. The same waves that carried the Pilgrim fathers to America still crash upon the coastline. People are tempted to think that this life is eternal, but it isn't—only God is eternal and self-sufficient. This present order of things is going to come to an end, and there is nothing that more powerfully communicates the idea than the assertion that "there is no longer any sea."

There's one other thing that should be mentioned: In the book of Revelation, as elsewhere in the Scriptures, the sea is associated with evil.[19] For example, Antichrist is described as a beast that comes up out of the sea (13:1; Isa. 57:20). The sea represents the disorder, violence, and unrest that marks the old creation (Isa. 57:20; Ps. 107:25–28; Ezek. 28:8), and is viewed by the writers of Scripture as hostile to mankind. For example, it was the sea that stood guard over John when he was imprisoned on Patmos, keeping him from his beloved churches in Asia.[20] As Morris notes, the sea is the first of seven evils that John says will no longer exist on the new earth, the other six being death, mourning, weeping, pain (21:4), the curse (22:3), and night (21:25; 22:5).[21]

THE DESCENT OF THE NEW JERUSALEM (VERSE 2)

John then sees "the holy city, new Jerusalem, coming down out of heaven from God."[22] This is the metropolis or capital of the new earth. The city is "out of heaven," its place of origin,[23] and it is "from God," its divine originator.[24] The city is described as "a bride adorned for her husband."

In chapter 19 the church as a people is described as the Lamb's bride or "wife." In this verse the term "bride" is used of her place of abode.[25] It no doubt describes the center of existence of redeemed humanity upon the new earth.[26]

Over the years I have performed a number of weddings, and I find it to be a rather nerve-wracking responsibility. I shouldn't worry, however, because no one is there to see me, nor are they there to see the poor young fellow next to me in the rented tux. They are there to see the bride. The highlight of every wedding is the moment when the bride makes her appearance. Heads turn, everyone stands, and there is a collective gasp. "Isn't she lovely! Isn't she beautiful!" And it is always true. The well-known Bible teacher, J. Vernon

McGee, said that in all the hundreds of weddings he had performed he had never seen an ugly bride.[27] On that day every young woman is radiant and beautiful.

This beautiful picture is used to describe the eternal abode of God's people. The pictures suggest the purity of Christ's redeemed and glorified people, the intimacy they shall enjoy with Him, and the community they shall have with one another—they shall live together in peace and joy.[28]

The name of the city, "Jerusalem," demonstrates that the blessings of eternity are grounded in the great events that took place in and around old Jerusalem—salvation was accomplished there.[29] When the New Jerusalem descends to the earth the distinction between heaven and earth seems to be forgotten. In a very real sense heaven will then be on earth.[30]

Many people are startled by what they read in verses 1–8. They have the idea—a Greek idea, not a Biblical one—that they are going to spend their lives in the sky. The Bible teaches, however, that man's ultimate destiny is an earthly destiny. As can be seen from this text, believers will spend eternity on the new earth, not in a heavenly realm removed from earthly existence.[31]

THE BENEFITS OF THE NEW ORDER (VERSES 3-4)

What will this heaven-on-earth existence be like? The Bible doesn't tell us a great deal. Unfortunately, people have a number of erroneous ideas about heaven and hell. There is an amusing anecdote about Billy Nicholson, the famous Irish evangelist who traveled extensively throughout Ireland, Scotland, and North America. He often used to answer questions from his audiences during his evangelistic meetings, and he became very experienced at handling hecklers. In one of his meetings he was preaching about heaven and a young man asked loudly, "Mr. Nicholson, in heaven how am I going to get my shirt on over my wings?" The preacher ignored him. A little later he again hollered out, "Mr. Nicholson, in heaven how am I going to get my shirt on over my wings?" The evangelist went on with his message. A third time the young scoffer cried out, "Mr. Nicholson, in heaven how am I going to get my shirt on over my wings?" Finally Billy Nicholson paused and looked at the young man. He then said to the congregation, "This fellow here is worried about getting his shirt on over his wings. He ought to be worried about getting his tail into his trousers!"[32]

There was a television producer for the British Broadcasting Corporation who was producing a documentary about Christianity in England. In the course of his research, he sent a memo to a clergyman who served as an adviser to the BBC on church affairs. The memo read, "How might I ascertain the official church view of heaven and hell?" The clergyman replied with a memo consisting of only one word: "Die!"[33] We do not have to die to discover God's truth about heaven and hell. We have already learned much about hell in chapters 19 and 20. Now in chapters 21–22 John relates God's revelation about heaven. There are many things we do not know about heaven-on-earth, but verses 3 and 4 do set forth a few of the important facts.

The Presence of God Upon the Earth (verse 3)

According to verse 3, John hears "a loud voice from the throne," probably one of the four living creatures or cherubs that make up God's throne (Rev. 4:6).[34] The voice from the throne says, "the tabernacle of God is among men, and He shall dwell among them." The translation "tabernacle" is not a good one; "dwelling" (NIV) is much better. The tabernacle was God's temporary abode in the wilderness, and John does not intend to say that God will live only temporarily among His people. From this point on God remains with His people throughout eternity.[35]

The Hebrew word for tabernacle is related to a verb meaning "to dwell." Later Jewish writers used the related word *Shekinah*, meaning the presence of God. In the Targums or Aramaic paraphrases of the Old Testament the Jews would use certain terms instead of the sacred name of God. They used *Shekinta* ("Presence"), *Memra* ("word"), and *Yeqara* ("glory"). These were "reverential insulators"— they kept the pious Jew from using God's name. Instead of saying that God spoke to man the Targums would say that the *Memra* ("word") spoke. Instead of saying that God appeared, it said that the *Yeqara* ("glory") appeared. Instead of saying that God met with praying men, it said that His *Shekinah* ("presence") was there.

It is very significant that the apostle John (John 1:14) used all three of the Targumic insulators in one sentence: "The Word (*Memra*) became flesh and dwelt (*Shekinta*) among us, and we beheld His glory (*Yeqara*)."[36] It is also significant that the very same Greek root word used in John 1:14 is used here for "dwelling" or "tabernacle;" that is, "He tabernacled among us, He dwelt among us." On the new earth God will dwell with His people, and "they shall see His face" (22:4).

How will believers see God? The answer is the same as that found in John 1:18 where it says of Jesus Christ that "He has explained Him" (NASB), "has made him known" (NIV). It is the function of God the Son to reveal God. Jesus Christ is the only God believers shall ever see! This is brought out in the Greek text (v. 3c) more clearly than in the NASB or the NIV. The leading Greek manuscript on Revelation (A, Alexandrinus) reads: "And He—God with them—shall be their God."[37]

The great prophetic name, *Immanuel* (Isa. 7:14) was given to Christ at His birth (Matt. 1:23). It means "God with us." Now at last, in the eternal city, Jesus Christ, the Son of God and God the Son, will dwell forever with His people.[38] The Greek text actually reads "peoples" and not "people."[39] In the old Jerusalem there was one elect nation, Israel. In the New Jerusalem, however, many different peoples, nations, and races make up redeemed humanity and will dwell with God in glory (Rev. 5:9).[40]

How, then, shall heaven or heaven-on-earth be described? First and foremost, heaven is heaven because Christ is there. Dwight L. Moody (1837–99) told the story of a young mother who became gravely ill. In order to let her rest her little girl was taken to a neighbor's home, where she continually asked to be taken to see her mother. The young woman did not improve, however, and she soon died. When at last the child was brought home she ran to her mother's sitting room, calling "Mother!" Then she ran to the master bedroom and then to various other rooms, all the time crying, "Mother." Her father took her and told her that her mother had died. She then looked at the neighbor and said, "Take me back. I don't want to stay here if I cannot be with Mother." Mr. Moody then said, "It wasn't the home that made it so sweet to the child. It was the presence of her mother. And so it is not heaven alone that is attractive to us; it is the knowledge that Jesus, our leader, our brother, our Lord is there."[41]

The Absence of Evil From the Earth (verse 4)

Mr. Moody's story illustrates something else about heaven-on-earth: there will be no sadness there. In verse 4 the reader is told several things that will *not* be there, though he is not told a lot about what *will* be there. John elsewhere writes, "It has not appeared as yet what we shall be" (1 John 3:2). Trying to tell us, in our present state, what heaven is like, said Ray Stedman, is like trying to explain the concepts of relativity and quantum physics to a two year old.[42]

A number of years ago I found an article in an old Christian magazine entitled, "One Thousand Things NOT in Heaven;" John lists five of them in verse 4.[43] First, he says, there will be no tears. This will not happen automatically. It is God the Son, the gracious Comforter, who wipes away the tears.[44] "Human hands are poor at drying tears,"[45] and there are all kinds: tears of persecution, tears of misfortune, tears of sympathy, tears of regret, tears of disappointment, tears of bereavement. God will dry them all.[46] In March, 1991 a small four year old boy fell to his death from a 53RD floor apartment. His father, guitarist Eric Clapton, wrote a song to express his grief and longing,

> Time can bring you down.
> Time can bend your knees.
> Time can break your heart,
> Have you beggin' please.

Beyond the door,
There's peace, I'm sure.
And I know,
There'll be no more tears
In heaven.[47]

I do not know the nature of Eric Clapton's relationship to Christ, but I do know that Clapton's lyrics are true, for inspired Scripture says, "And He shall wipe away every tear from their eyes."

Scottish businessman, evangelist, and Bible teacher Alex Ross told the story of an elderly Christian lady who lay dying as her husband sat by her bedside. As they held hands together both knew that the end was near. As she died, a tear trickled down the cheek of the dear old woman. Her husband took his handkerchief and very tenderly wiped the tear away, and then with a trembling voice said, "Thank God, Mary, that will be the last tear."[48]

All of the debilitating effects of sin will be gone. "There shall no longer be any death." Vernon McGee was talking a number of years ago to an engineer who had worked on the great interstate highway system that was built in the 1950s and 60s. "What is the biggest problem in highway design, going over mountains, going down valleys, or crossing over rivers?" The man answered without hesitation, "The biggest problem is missing the cemeteries." The earth is one big cemetery today, but there will be no cemeteries on the new earth.[49]

John sums up by saying, "The first things have passed away"—life as we know it with its sorrow, tragedy, and evil will be gone. Few commentaries bring out the meaning of this text like the final paragraphs of C.S. Lewis' classic novel *The Last Battle*. The young heroes and their family have been killed and find themselves in the Shadow-Lands, dead. Aslan, who represents Christ, tells them, "The term is over: the holidays have begun. The dream is ended: this is the morning." Lewis concludes, "The things that began to happen after that were so great and beautiful that I cannot write them. And for us this is the end of all the stories and we can most truly say that they all lived happily ever after. But for them it was only the beginning of the real story. All their life in this world and all their adventures in Narnia had only been the cover and the title page: now at last they were beginning Chapter One of the Great Story, which no one on earth has read: which goes on for ever: in which every chapter is better than the one before."[50]

THE CERTAINTY OF A NEW HEAVEN AND A NEW EARTH (VERSES 5–8)

THE PROMISE OF GOD (VERSE 5A)

Now, in verse 5, probably for the first time in the book of Revelation, God the Father speaks.[51] Almighty God tells

John to bring this message[52] to the struggling churches of Asia Minor and to all churches everywhere. They are words of reassurance: the new creation that believers see happening in their own personal lives (CF. 2 Cor. 5:17, "if any man is in Christ, he is a new creature") is going to take place one day on a cosmic scale.

THE GUARANTEE OF THE PROMISE (VERSES 5B–6A)

The Character of God

Write down the promise of a new heaven and a new earth, God says, "because these words are faithful and true." The words John has heard "are as true as they are tremendous."[53] They are trustworthy and true. As astonishing as it may seem, God is here vouching for the truth of what He has said. He is reminding His people that these promises rest on a secure basis, the promise of God Himself. The very character of God is in back of the promise of heaven. This is the God, it is elsewhere affirmed, who "cannot lie" (Tit. 1:2; CF. Heb. 6:18).

The Nature of God

Not only is the promise guaranteed by the faithfulness of God, it is guaranteed by His omnipotence. He says, "I am the Alpha and the Omega, the beginning and the end." Alpha and omega are the first and last letters of the Greek alphabet. The Lord God Almighty is the initiator of creation, the source and origin of all things, and He is the end of all things, the goal or aim of all things.[54]

God should not be thought of as the God of the Deists, who creates things like a watchmaker and lets them run without intervention. No, God creates everything, and He guides the whole process along to its desired conclusion.[55] "It is done," He says—literally, "They are done;" that is, His words have come to pass.[56] The verb here is a past (perfect) tense. The renewal of all things and the future blessing of God's people, resting as they do on the solemn assurance of Almighty God Himself, are spoken of as if they had already come to pass.[57]

AN INVITATION TO THE THIRSTY (VERSE 6B)

In the middle of His promises to His people God demonstrates that He is an evangelistic God to the end (CF. 22:17).[58] The invitation is taken from Isaiah 55:1, "Ho! Every one who thirsts, come to the waters; and you who have no money come, buy and eat. Come, buy wine and milk without money and without cost." The Lord Jesus offered the woman at the well (John 4:10–14) a drink that would satisfy all her spiritual yearnings. The forgiveness of sins, the cleansing, the life that all men and women yearn for is to be found in Christ. And it is free ("without cost") for the asking.

Philosopher Peter Kreeft says that our deepest need to-day is for reality. He calls this "the ontological thirst," the thirst for being. In every desire, for truth and goodness and beauty, we desire that the object be real. He says that our age is one of "self generated fantasies." Our spirits are starving; they are thirsty. Eventually, if only at death, everyone must meet reality face to face. Heaven is that ultimate reality, and we had better be prepared to enter. The only way to be prepared is to come to the One who can cleanse our sins and give us life.[59]

THE INHERITANCE OF THE OVERCOMER (VERSE 7)

In verse 7 John reminds his readers that it is the "overcomer" who is to inherit heaven-on-earth. The term "overcomer" relates to the doctrine of the perseverance of the saints, the doctrine that a true Christian remains steadfast until the end.[60] Every professing Christian is warned to remain faithful until the end, yet every true Christian is promised that God will keep him from stumbling (Jude 24). To the true believer God now makes the greatest promise of all: "I will be His God and he will be My son."

This promise was made to three men in the Old Testament. It was made to Abraham when God made a covenant with Him (Gen. 17:7). It was made to David's son in the Davidic covenant (2 Sam. 7:14). It was made to Messiah in a psalm that looks toward the millennial kingdom

(Ps. 89:27). And now this promise, that was made to Abraham, Solomon, and Messiah Himself, is made to the overcomers, the true believers who read the book of Revelation. They, along with all of God's "peoples" (v. 3), are united together in the great covenantal program of God.

Every week Christians gather together in various places around the world to celebrate the Lord's Supper. This is a covenantal meal that celebrates the "bond in blood,"[61] the "new covenant" (Luke 22:20) between Christ and His people that was established at the Cross of Calvary. It is a celebration that focuses on what Christ has done to incorporate believers into God's covenant program.

There is no greater honor in all the universe than is bestowed upon the person who is true to the Lord.[62] During the terrible Chicago fire of 1871, Dwight L. Moody's house burned down. As he surveyed the ruins a friend said, "I hear you lost everything." "Well," said Moody, "you understand wrong. I have a good deal more left than I lost." "What do you mean?" asked his friend. "You are not a rich man." Mr. Moody then opened his Bible and read to him Revelation 21:7, "He who overcomes shall inherit these things, and I will be His God."[63]

This tremendous passage about heaven-on-earth concludes with a warning for those who reject the "water of life." "Even on the threshold of unimaginable joy John cannot forbear a parting glance over his shoulder into the abyss."[64] Even here, in a sense, John continues to describe the heavenly city, but in a negative way. He speaks of the kind of people and practices that will not be found on the new earth. Those who reject Christ will go to the lake of fire. This is contrary to everything our world believes, but it is what God says. If all mankind were to ignore the Word of God, hell would still be real. As the apostle Paul says in another passage, "Let God be found true, though every man be found a liar" (Rom. 3:4).

Amazingly the creation of a new heaven and a new earth will not affect the status of the lake of fire and of the lost. They will still exist in eternity.[65] Hell—like heaven—is part of John's vision. The height of the mountain is appreciated from the depth of the valley. For salvation to be "good news" there must be "bad news" to be saved from. If all of life's roads lead to the same place, it makes no ultimate difference which road we choose. But if they lead to opposite places, to infinite bliss or infinite misery, then life is a life-or-death affair, a razor's edge, and our choice of roads is infinitely important.[66]

John singles out certain sinners for warning:

"The cowardly." John does not say "the timid" or "the shy." Rather, he is speaking of those who fear the threats of the Beast more than they trust the love of Christ. In

the spiritual warfare God values highly the virtue of courage. John speaks here of those who once professed to be Christians but who lacked genuine commitment.[67] They are those who side with the Beast during persecution of believers, and they shall go to hell.

The "unbelieving." This term might better be translated "faithless." It does not refer to people who lack faith but to those who renounce the faith. Nevertheless, the term may also be applied to all who refuse the gospel.

"Abominable" persons. [68] This expression is connected to the worship of the Beast in the end times (Rev. 17:4–5) and includes the impurities associated with pagan religions and cults, including unnatural vice. One of the extra-biblical books (2 Enoch 10:4–5, ADI–50) says, "This place is prepared for…those who on earth practice sin against nature, which is child corruption after the Sodomitic fashion, magic-making, enchantments, and devilish witchcraft… lies…fornication, murder."[69]

"Murderers." This speaks, especially in the context of the Revelation (Rev. 13:15), of the Beast's agents in killing the martyrs. As a class of criminal, murderers are greatly on the increase in our modern world. God will send them to hell.

"Immoral persons." Strictly speaking, this term refers to male prostitutes, but it probably includes all sexual sin.[70] Then, as now, it was impossible to avoid a sex-saturated society (CF. I Cor. 5:10). Our society flaunts sex, but our text says that the sexually immoral will be consigned by God to hell.

"Sorcerers." A sorcerer is a mixer of potions. The Greek term for "sorcerer" is the source of our English words *pharmacy* and *pharmaceutical.* With his magical potions or mind-altering drugs he claims to be able to communicate with spirits.[71] In Old Testament times communicating with evil spirits—and every spirit that a human being can conjure up is an evil spirit—was a capital offense (Exod. 22:18; Lev. 19:26, 31; 20:6; Deut. 18:9–11). The lake of fire is God's appointed doom for all who practice witchcraft, spiritualism—in contemporary parlance, channeling to spirits—devil worship, and other forms of sorcery. Our age smirks at this great sin; those who practice it will go to hell.[72]

"Idolaters." All worshippers of other gods—the countless millions of heathen in the past, present, and future—are given over to eternal judgment. Many in our culture do not have literal images yet they are idolaters. They worship the gods of materialism and pleasure. Whatever takes the place of God is an idol. This text, with apostolic authority, says that idolaters will go to hell.

"All liars." God is characterized by truth, and Satan is "the father of lies" (John 8:44). Lying is contrary to God's nature, and everything contrary to His character will be consigned to the lake of fire. Lying is commonplace in

our day. People sit and watch a political figure being interviewed on TV, and they chuckle at his evasions and cunning deceit. They know he is lying; the interviewer knows he is lying, and yet he lets the falsehood pass. People do not get very troubled by this. They think, "So what, they have always lied."

On a flight to Florida I sat next to a retired New York City policeman and I asked him if he had ever testified in court. He answered that he had testified over five hundred times. He then sat forward in his seat and emphatically added, "You know, in court, everybody lies!" Almighty God does not view these things with nonchalance. Among the seven things that God "hates," that are "an abomination to Him," in Proverbs 6:16–17 is "a lying tongue" (CF. Ps. 119:163).

John says that this dreadful place "burns," its fires are never exhausted. It is an agony of a terrible character.

CONCLUSION

The apostle leaves us with several lessons in his survey of "the last things." First, John clearly believes that God is sovereign and intends to fulfill His purposes in creation. The purpose of God in Scripture is "not a summons to human effort but a declaration of God's intentions."[73] All that John has set forth in his end-time chronology of "the Last Things" God will bring to pass.

The second lesson is that this present life on earth is conditional and probationary, it is a time of testing. God's purposes for His creatures are not fulfilled in this life. This life is not "all there is." Life is not what Macbeth called it, a "brief candle"[74] that, once snuffed out, ends all conscious existence.

"I didn't ask to be born," little Lucy shouts at her mother in the kitchen, in the comic strip *Peanuts*. Very true, we did not ask to be born. God asked it—He willed it—and God intends to prepare us for our eternal destiny. Here the gap between the Bible and modern thought is great. Modern man thinks that death ends everything. That is not true; on earth people are just passing through. Modern man says, "Make the best of it; get what kicks we can; when the end comes curse our fate." About 20 years ago a KLM jumbo jet crashed in the Canary Islands. The pilot's last words on the tape in the "black box" were, "God damn." A fitting exit for a modern man.[75]

The third lesson is that the Christian gospel is based on the premise that each person's destiny is based on the choices he or she makes on earth. People hold in their hands, under the sovereignty of God, the power to determine their everlasting futures. They are responsible to confess Christ as their Savior, trust His promise of forgiveness, drink of the free water that He offers. The alternatives are indescribable bliss or banishment forever from the presence of the Lord. A glorious future is certain for those who make the right choice in this life. There is a heaven, and a blessed residence there is promised to all who embrace Jesus Christ as Savior.[76]

It is a sobering fact that the choices of time are binding in eternity. There are many illustrations of this in life. A fatal decision on a battlefield can never be replayed. A climactic quarrel, a car accident, a murder—the moving finger writes and moves on. A hunter kills the last of a dying species of fowl; the bird will never be seen again. An author writes a pornographic book that destroys the character of a hundred children; that damage can never be recalled.

If heaven is certain for those who make the right choice in this life, hell is equally certain for those who choose some other way. Scripture tells us that Christ is the Way, the Truth, and the Life (John 14:6). If one bypasses Him for some other way, he or she will face judgment. This passage of Scripture again sets before us the question, *Quo Vadis?* Which way are you going?[77]

✿❦✿

NOTES

[1]Sherwood Eliot Wirt, "Destination Heaven," *Christianity Today* (August 12, 1977): 10. I am indebted to Wirt's essay for a number of the ideas expressed in this introduction.

[2]Kenneth L. Woodward, "Heaven," *Newsweek* (March 27, 1989): 52–53.

[3]Peter Kreeft, *Everything You Ever Wanted to Know About Heaven...But Never Dreamed of Asking* (San Francisco: Ignatius, 1990), 17.

[4]Wirt, "Destination Heaven," 10.

[5]Kreeft, *Everything You Ever Wanted to Know About Heaven...But Never Dreamed of Asking*, 17. Kreeft's book is the source of these and many other metaphors about heaven.

[6]Kreeft, *Everything You Ever Wanted to Know About Heaven...But Never Dreamed of Asking*, 17–18.

[7]Austin Farrer, *The Revelation of St. John the Divine* (London: Oxford University Press, 1964), 211.

[8]Isbon T. Beckwith, *The Apocalypse of John* (New York: Macmillan, 1919; reprint ed., Grand Rapids: Baker, 1979), 750.

[9]Beasley-Murray says that Isaiah's description of the new heavens and the new earth (chapter 65) is "almost wholly in terms of the present order of things." He errs, I believe, in that he fails to see that Isaiah discusses both millennial conditions (E.G., begetting of children, 65:20, 23) as well as the eternal state. Cf. G.R. Beasley-Murray, *The Book of Revelation, New Century Bible* (London: Oliphants, 1974), 306; Farrer, Revelation, 2.

[10]1 Enoch 45:4; 72:1; 91:16; Jubilees 1:29; 2 Baruch 32:6; 44:12; 57:2; 4 Ezra 7:75. Cf. R.H. Charles, *The Revelation of St. John*, 2 vols., International Critical Commentary (Edinburgh: T. & T. Clark, 1920), 2:203.

[11]The new heaven and new earth are described not as new in time (νέος), but as new in quality (καινός). Cf. Charles, The Revelation of St. John, 1:146. The problem of whether John is describing a renovated earth or a completely new earth is probably not to be completely solved by an analysis of the synonyms.

[12]The decisive factor, says Thomas, in favor of an entirely new creation is "the language of 20:11 which depicts an entire dissolving of the old, a vanishing into nothingness followed by a new creation in 21:1 without any sea" (Robert L. Thomas, *Revelation 8–22: An Exegetical Commentary* [Chicago: Moody, 1995], 440). Cf. Robert Govett, *The Apocalypse: Expounded by Scripture* (London,

1861; reprint ed., Miami Springs: Conley & Schoettle, 1981), 4:326; Charles, *The Revelation of St. John*, 2:193; John F. Walvoord, *The Revelation of Jesus Christ* (Chicago: Moody, 1966), 311. Dumbrell writes, "Isaiah has in mind the complete renewal, not merely the alteration of, the existing order (note the use of 'to create' Heb. בָּרָא; in Isa. 65:17)." Cf. William J. Dumbrell, *The End of the Beginning: Revelation 21–22 and the Old Testament* (Homebush West and Grand Rapids: Lancer and Baker, 1985), 167.

[13]The majority of scholars argue that John is describing the renovation of the old creation. The impressive list of writers who disagree with the view taken here makes me hold it with caution. Their arguments are five in number: (1) The exegetical argument. They argue that a proper exegesis of v. 5 (as well as Matt. 19:28; Acts 3:21; Rom. 8:19–22; and 2 Peter 3:10) suggests a renewal and refining of existing materials. In Matthew Jesus speaks of the "regeneration;" in Acts Peter speaks of "the restoration of all things;" and in Romans Paul speaks of the renewal of the old creation. (2) The theological argument. The view that the old universe is to be utterly destroyed and replaced suggests that the divine purposes will be frustrated by sin. (3) The Christological argument. It is hard to believe that the earth that was sanctified by the presence and works of the incarnate Son of God is to be destroyed. (4) The soteriological or anthropological argument. There is an analogy between redeemed man and the redeemed earth. Just as there is continuity between the earthly body and the resurrection body, so there is to be continuity between the old earth and the new earth. (5) The scientific argument. The intense heat of the final conflagration will not destroy matter but only give it a new form. See Irenaeus, *Against Heresies* 5.36.1, in *The Ante-Nicene Fathers*, vol. 1, eds. Alexander Roberts and James Donaldson (1885; reprint ed., Grand Rapids: Eerdmans, 1967), 566; William Kelly, *Lectures on the Book of Revelation* (London: G. Morrish, 1874), 465–66; J.A. Seiss, *Lectures on the Apocalypse* (9th ed., New York: Charles C. Cook, 1906), 3:367–77; Henry Barclay Swete, *The Apocalypse of St. John* (London: Macmillan, 1906), 271–72; R.C.H. Lenski, *The Interpretation of St. John's Revelation* (Minneapolis: Augsburg, 1943), 615; G.B. Caird, *The Revelation of St. John the Divine*, Harper New Testament Commentary (New York: Harper & Row, 1966), 265–66; John Sweet, *Revelation*, Trinity Press International New Testament Commentaries (London: SCM, 1979), 297; Henry M. Morris, *The Revelation Record* (Wheaton: Tyndale, 1983), 436; Wilbur M. Smith, *The Biblical Doctrine of Heaven* (Chicago: Moody, 1968), 223–36; Idem., *The Atomic Age and the Word of God* (Boston: W.A. Wilde, 1948), 126–63; Erich Sauer, *The Triumph of the Crucified* (Grand Rapids: Eerdmans, 1951), 179.

¹⁴Beasley-Murray (*The Book of Revelation*, 307) writes, "John's *language*, therefore, seems to demand the recognition that he viewed the new heavens and earth as newly created, in the strictest sense of the term, and that they replace a creation which has ceased to exist." He then goes on to reject this interpretation. It must be asked, however, by what criteria an author is to be exegeted if not by his language.

¹⁵Seiss, *Lectures on the Apocalypse*, 3:378; Govett, *The Apocalypse: Expounded by Scripture*, 4:325. It has been suggested that by "heaven" John means the abode of God. It is argued that the first heaven is destroyed not because of its imperfections but because of the symbols of remoteness (temple [15:8; 16:17], altar of incense [8:3]) and sin (altar of burnt offering [8:5]). Sin has now been vanquished and God dwells with man. Cf. Martin Kiddle, *The Revelation of St. John*, Moffatt New Testament Commentary (New York: Harper, 1940), 411–12. Smith (*The Biblical Doctrine of Heaven*, 235), on the other hand, asserts, "I cannot help but believe firmly that the abode of God…is not referred to here."

¹⁶Walter Scott, *Exposition of the Revelation of Jesus Christ* (4th ed., London: Pickering & Inglis, n.d.), 419.

¹⁷There are at least three other explanations of this clause offered in the commentaries: (1) There will be a sea on the new earth. (Friedrich Dusterdieck, *Critical and Exegetical Handbook to the Revelation of John*, Meyer's Commentary on the New Testament (6th ed., New York: Funk & Wagnalls, 1884; reprint ed., Winona Lake: Alpha, 1980), 476; Seiss, *Lectures on the Apocalypse*, 3:380–83; cf. Augustine, City of God 20.16, in *A Select Library of the Nicene and Post-Nicene Fathers of the Christian Church*, vol. 2, ed. Philip Schaff (1886; reprint ed., Grand Rapids: Eerdmans, 1956), 435–36). The clause is taken as parallel with the preceding clause (ὁ γὰρ πρῶτος οὐρανὸς καὶ ἡ πρώτη γῆ ἀπῆλθαν), with the οὐκ ἔστιν ἔτι repeating the ἀπῆλθαν (thus meaning "the first sea passed away" with the first heaven and earth). However, if this view were correct there would be an ἦν instead of ἔστιν and a repetition of πρώτη as with γῆ (Beckwith, *The Apocalypse of John*, 750). (2) John is unconsciously indebted to Babylonian creation myths, in which the sea is the water monster Tiamat, the special opponent of the Creator (Charles, *The Revelation of St. John*, 2:205). There is nothing in the context, however, to suggest any indebtedness to pagan mythologies. (3) John is expressing the dread of the sea felt by the ancient world, whose means of coping with its dangers were inferior (Beckwith, *The Apocalypse of John*, 751). However, one need only read John's de-

scription of Babylon's sea-borne luxury trade (18:17) to realize that John was not a fearful landlubber (Caird, *The Revelation of St. John the Divine*, 262). "Until the appearance of railways and steamboats it may be doubted whether there was any age in history in which traveling was easier or more general.... The seas [were] alive with merchantmen" (Samuel Dill, *Roman Society From Nero to Marcus Aurelius* (1904; reprint ed., New York: Meridian, 1956), 205).

[18]Ray C. Stedman, *God's Final Word: Understanding Revelation* (Grand Rapids: Discovery House, 1991), 336. Were one to object to Stedman's view on the ground that it is too "scientific," it should be noted that John wrote under divine inspiration. He need not have understood the vision to have recorded it. Henry Morris (*The Revelation Record*, 437) speculates that there will be no animals on the new earth and that the human population living in glorified bodies will no longer need water. The sea, which today serves as a basic reservoir for the maintenance of the hydrologic cycle and the water-based ecology and physiology of the animal and human inhabitants of the earth, will no longer be required. It seems to me that these speculative remarks, as interesting as they are, go beyond the data of Scripture. John does speak of "a river of the water of life" (22:1) on the new earth. Thomas writes, "These [I.E., 'the river of the water of life'] are literal waters that are of such a nature and quality as to answer to the new Jerusalem to which they belong. CF. Thomas, *Revelation 8–22*, 482.

[19]Swete, *The Apocalypse of St. John*, 272; CF. Beasley-Murray, *The Book of Revelation*, 307; Robert H. Mounce, *The Book of Revelation*, New International Commentary on the New Testament (rev. ed., Grand Rapids: Eerdmans, 1998), 381; Gale Z. Heide, "What is New About the New Heaven and the New Earth? A Theology of Creation from Revelation 21 and 2 Peter 3," *Journal of the Evangelical Theological Society 40* (March, 1997), 44–45.

[20]Thomas, *Revelation 8–22*, 440.

[21]Leon Morris, *The Revelation of St. John*, Tyndale New Testament Commentaries (Grand Rapids: Eerdmans, 1969), 243.

[22]Barclay argues that the background of the picture is Platonic, that the New Jerusalem is the pre-existent reality in the heavens of which earthly Jerusalem was a copy. However, it is more accurate to say that the earthly Jerusalem was a type of a future reality. John's perspective is not philosophical but eschatologi-

cal. CF. William Barclay, *The Revelation of John*, 2 vols. (rev. ed., Philadelphia: Westminster, 1976), 2:199.

[23]Govett (*The Apocalypse: Expounded by Scripture*, 4:167) and Scott (*Exposition of the Revelation of Jesus Christ*, 420, 430) assert that the new Jerusalem overhangs the earth during the millennium. Walvoord (*The Revelation of Jesus Christ*, 312–13) entertains this view but only as a possibility. He suggests that this satellite city could be the residence of the translated saints during the millennium. Other futurists (E.G., Seiss, *Lectures on the Apocalypse*, 3:327–40, 383–84), however, suggest that the new Jerusalem will be in heaven until the eternal state and that the translated saints will dwell on the earth as Christ's priest-regents during the millennium.

[24]Beckwith, *The Apocalypse of John*, 751.

[25]Scott (*Exposition of the Revelation of Jesus Christ*, 419) argues that cities are connected with time and not eternity. The New Jerusalem, he asserts, is not an actual city but is a metaphor for the church. CF. also Hanns Lilje, *The Last Book of the Bible*, trans. Olive Wyon (Philadelphia: Muhlenberg, 1957), 259.

[26]As Walvoord (*The Revelation of Jesus Christ*, 313) notes the marriage figure is used in Scripture for the saints of both the old and new covenants. He concludes that it is likely that the new Jerusalem will be the abode of the saints of all ages. CF. F.W. Grant, *The Revelation of Jesus Christ* (New York: Loizeaux, N.D.), 231; F.C. Jennings, *Studies in Revelation* (New York: Our Hope, 1937), 566–67.

[27]J. Vernon McGee, *Thru the Bible*, 5 vols. (Nashville: Nelson, 1983), 5:1064.

[28]Stedman, *God's Final Word*, 337.

[29]L. Morris, *The Revelation of St. John*, 243–44.

[30]Caird, *The Revelation of St. John the Divine*, 263; CF. L. Morris, *The Revelation of St. John*, 244.

[31]George Eldon Ladd, *A Commentary on the Revelation of John* (Grand Rapids: Eerdmans, 1972), 275. During the present age those who die go to heaven (2 Cor. 5:8). In eternity future, however, believers will live on the new earth. The

"heavenly Jerusalem" (Heb. 12:23) will then be on earth. Cf. also Thomas, *Revelation 8–22*, 443.

[32] As told by S. Lewis Johnson, Jr., "A New Heaven and a New Earth" (cassette tape, Dallas: Believers' Chapel, 1989–90).

[33] Stedman, *God's Final Word*, 333. According to Fadiman, the clergyman in question was Father Agnelius Andrew (b. 1908), a British Franciscan, and the BBC's adviser on Roman Catholic affairs. Cf. Clifton Fadiman, ed., *The Little, Brown Book of Anecdotes* (Boston: Little, Brown, 1985), 17.

[34] Charles, *The Revelation of St. John*, 2:205.

[35] Mounce, *The Book of Revelation*, 383.

[36] Caird, *The Revelation of St. John the Divine*, 264.

[37] Barbara Aland et al, *The Greek New Testament* (4TH ed., Stuttgart: United Bible Societies, 1993), 881. The UBS text gives the bracketed words a "c" rating.

[38] Cf. Swete, *The Apocalypse of St. John*, 274; Beasley-Murray, *The Book of Revelation*, 312.

[39] The UBS text gives λαοί a "B" rating. It is supported by a, A and twelve other minuscules. Cf. Bruce M. Metzger, *A Textual Commentary on the Greek New Testament* (London: United Bible Societies, 1971), 765.

[40] Swete, *The Apocalypse of St. John*, 274; Mounce, The Book of Revelation, 383.

[41] Dwight Lyman Moody, *New Sermons, Addresses, and Prayers* (New York: Henry S. Goodspeed, 1877), 80–81.

[42] Stedman, *God's Final Word*, 334.

[43] "One Thousand Things NOT in Heaven," *The Witness* (June, 1935), 129–31.

[44] Beasley-Murray, *The Book of Revelation*, 312.

[45]Seiss, *Lectures on the Apocalypse*, 3:384.

[46]Walvoord (*The Revelation of Jesus Christ*, 315) asserts that there is no ground for believing that John thinks of tears of remorse. "The emphasis here is on the comfort of God not on the remorse of the saints." That is like saying, "The emphasis here is on the comfort of God not on the sorrow (or bereavement, or persecution, etc.) of the saints." Surely John includes all kinds of tears.

[47]Eric Clapton, "Tears in Heaven," quoted by Terry Mattingly, "God, The Grammys, and Pop Religion," *Moody Magazine* (June, 1993), 34.

[48]Alex Ross, *"Fifty Years" in Christ* (Aberdeen: Alex. Ross, 1972), 227–28.

[49]McGee, *Thru the Bible*, 5:1066.

[50]C.S. Lewis, *The Last Battle* (New York: Macmillan, 1956), 173–74.

[51]Swete, *The Apocalypse of St. John*, 275. Charles (*The Revelation of St. John*, 2: 202) and Mounce (*The Book of Revelation*, 384, N. 23), however, say that God speaks in 1:8 and 16:1 and 17.

[52]A number of commentators take the phrase, "And he said" (καὶ λέγει, literally "he says," present tense) as another speaker other than God, such as an angel. This interpretation is based on the verb change from καὶ εἶπεν το καὶ λέγει and then back to καὶ εἶπεν (v. 5, 6). Cf. Swete, *The Apocalypse of St. John*, 275. However, the verb change is stylistic, and God is the speaker throughout. Cf. Mounce, *The Book of Revelation*, 385.

[53]Swete, *The Apocalypse of St. John*, 275.

[54]Mounce, *The Book of Revelation*, 385.

[55]Beasley-Murray, *The Book of Revelation*, 312; Caird, *The Revelation of St. John the Divine*, 266.

[56]Beckwith, *The Apocalypse of John*, 752.

[57]Beckwith, *The Apocalypse of John*, 752.

[58]Beasley-Murray (*The Book of Revelation*, 313) says the primary application of the invitation is to the believer. Swete (*The Apocalypse of St. John*, 277) says that the water is offered to the church and the world.

[59]Cf. Kreeft, *Everything You Ever Wanted to Know About Heaven...But Never Dreamed of Asking*, 23.

[60]Cf. James E. Rosscup, "The Overcomer of the Apocalypse," *Grace Theological Journal 3* (1982), 261–86.

[61]Cf. O. Palmer Robertson, *The Christ of the Covenants* (Grand Rapids: Baker, 1980), 7.

[62]Barclay, *The Revelation of John*, 2:206.

[63]As told by Warren Wiersbe, *The Bible Exposition Commentary*, 2 vols. (Wheaton: Victor, 1989), 2:622.

[64]Caird, *The Revelation of St. John the Divine*, 267. Caird, of course, is not using "abyss" in the technical sense of the intermediate abode of fallen angels. He is speaking, rather, of the lake of fire.

[65]McGee, *Thru the Bible*, 5:1067.

[66]I follow Kreeft (*Everything You Ever Wanted to Know About Heaven...But Never Dreamed of Asking*, 20) in the thoughts expressed here.

[67]Cf. Beasley-Murray, *The Book of Revelation*, 314; Caird, *The Revelation of St. John the Divine*, 267; Mounce, *The Book of Revelation*, 386.

[68]John's list widens from faithless professing Christians to include all, pagans included. Cf. Charles, *The Revelation of St. John*, 2:217.

[69]*Apocrypha and Pseudipigrapha of the Old Testament*, 2 vols., vol. 2: *Pseudipigrapha*, ed. R.H. Charles (Oxford: Oxford University Press, 1913), 435. Cf. Charles, *The Revelation of St. John*, 2:216.

[70]L. Morris, *The Revelation of St. John*, 247.

[71]*New International Dictionary of New Testament Theology*, see "Magic," by J. Stafford Wright, 2:558.

[72]Scott, *Exposition of the Revelation of Jesus Christ*, 427.

[73]For these concluding lessons I am indebted to Wirt, "Destination Heaven," 10–12.

[74]William Shakespeare, *The Tragedy of Macbeth* 5.5.23, The Yale Shakespeare (rev. ed., New Haven: Yale University Press, 1954), 95.

[75]Wirt, "Destination Heaven."

[76]Wirt, "Destination Heaven."

[77]Wirt, "Destination Heaven."